FINANCIALIZATION

FINANCIALIZATION

Economic and Social Impacts

MALCOLM SAWYER

agenda
publishing

First published in 2022 by Agenda Publishing

Agenda Publishing Limited
The Core
Bath Lane
Newcastle Helix
Newcastle upon Tyne
NE4 5TF
www.agendapub.com

ISBN 978-1-78821-230-4

British Library Cataloguing-in-Publication Data
A catalogue record for this book is available from the British Library

Typeset by Newgen Publishing UK
Printed and bound in the UK by Short Run Press Ltd

CONTENTS

ACKNOWLEDGEMENTS

Most of the analysis and lines of arguments pursued in this book arose from research associated with the research project on Financialisation Economy Society and Sustainable Development (FESSUD). I was the principal investigator of this European Union-funded research project, which ran for five years from December 2011 to November 2016 and was in preparation for two years prior to the start. This project was funded at €8 million by the EU and involved partners from 14 academic institutions and one non-governmental organization (NGO). I acknowledge, with thanks, the EU funding, which enabled many scholars to pursue wide-ranging research on financialization and its widespread impacts on the economy, society and the environment. The enthusiasm, commitment and scholarship of those involved in the FESSUD project were always a great support and have contributed to the research ideas in this book. I, though, take responsibility for the ideas expressed here.

I am grateful to Alison Howson for enthusiastic support for this book, her comments and her patience while it took so long to complete.

My greatest support has come, as it has for over half a century, from my wife Jan, for which I express my love and great thanks.

Malcolm Sawyer

LIST OF FIGURES AND TABLES

Figures

Tables

1

INTRODUCTION

The financial system, the financing and funding of production and investment in business through banks, financial institutions and stock markets have long been essential features of capitalist economies. The role of the financial sector has often been viewed in terms of supporting what may be termed the real economy, funding the establishment and expansion of firms, the provision of liquidity and the payments system. There have always been debates over the nature of the relationship between the financial system and the real economy, and how well the financial system serves the real economy.

The global financial crises of 2007–09 (hereafter GFC) followed three decades of intense financialization, which will be referred to below as the present era of financialization.[1] The plural "crises" is used here to indicate that there were major banking and financial crises in Iceland, Ireland, the UK and USA, which occurred around the same time and reached their height in the autumn of 2008. Although there were similar causes for these national financial crises there were also differences, and there were interactions and overlaps between them. The effects of these crises were exacerbated and spread through contagion – notably through effects of possession of "toxic assets" on banks' balance sheets and through recessionary impacts on international trade.

The initial signs of financial difficulties came in August 2007 with problems in the inter-bank market and then the financial difficulties at Northern Rock in the UK. The collapse of Bear Stearns was a further sign of crisis, which intensified in September/October with the failure of Lehman Brothers followed by many other financial institutions being bailed by governments. In Iceland, three major banks collapsed in October 2008 and control was taken by the Financial Supervisory Authority. In Ireland, one major bank (Anglo Irish) was nationalised in January 2009 and two (Allied Irish Bank, Bank of Ireland) were bailed out by the government in February 2009. In the UK, there were major bailouts of Royal Bank of Scotland (RBS), HBOS and Lloyds TSB in October 2008, with the UK government acquiring initially a 43 per cent stake

---

1. Although the term "global financial crises" is used, as Jessop (2013) has argued, it is more appropriately called a North Atlantic financial crisis given its epicentres were the UK and USA, along with Iceland and Ireland.

in Lloyds Banking Group and 82 per cent in RBS. There was also a banking crisis in Belgium, with its two largest banks, Fortis and Dexia, facing severe problems.

The collapse of Lehman Brothers in September 2008 triggered a broader run on the global financial system and signalled a systemic crisis (although difficulties in the financial system had been emerging during the previous 12 months). The then head of the World Bank, Christine Lagarde (2018), writing on the tenth anniversary of the collapse of Lehman Brothers, indicated that there had been a banking crisis in 24 countries and economic activity was still below trend in most countries.

The GFC of 2007–08 provided stark evidence of the global nature of the financial system and the interconnections between national financial systems. It threw into sharp relief the instabilities of the financial system, although the GFC was the latest in a series of financial crises in this era of financialization. Previous substantial ones include the Mexico crisis of 1994, East Asian crisis of 1997 and the Russian crisis of 1998. Indeed, the era of financialization since 1980 has been characterized by recurrent financial crises, with over 450 recorded since 1970, of which 151 were banking crises and the others currency and sovereign debt crises (Laeven & Valencia 2012, 2013, 2020). The ways in which the processes of financialization have caused or at least contributed to the financial crises has become a central question, which is considered below in Chapter 6.

The GFC drew to public attention that the rapid expansion of the financial sector had involved credit booms, the development of risky financial assets through securitization and property price booms, all of which were unsustainable and ended in a bursting of the boom. This book seeks to focus on the processes within the economy and the world of finance that underlie that incident and are still prevalent today long after the shock that brought the actions of the often mysterious world of the dark arts of finance into sharp relief.

Financialization, meaning the expansion of finance and financial institutions, has been a set of ongoing processes in industrialized capitalism for the past 200 years. Despite the crises, bubbles and boom-and-bust cycles of economic growth, a cursory look at the world shows the continuing economic, social and political power and influence of finance and the financial sector. At the personal level, our own involvement with finance and financial institutions, as compared with that of our parents' or our grandparents' generations, illustrates the level of change. Only a few decades ago, individuals would largely use cash to make their purchases, would shun debt and would own few financial assets. Since the 1960s, there has been the rapid growth of the use of credit cards, of payments by cheque and now debit card (rather than cash), the growth of various forms of consumer debt and, more generally, household engagement with financial assets and liabilities. At the global level, the expansion of finance and financial institutions has, in the past two or three decades, been experienced in almost every country of the world. The flows of finance and funds between countries and the operations of global financial markets are yet another dimension of the processes of financialization.

It is not only the economic importance of the financial sector that has grown, but also the social and political power of finance and the financial system. Financial institutions are notable contributors to political campaigns, particularly in the USA, and consequently strongly influence and indeed constrain the political agenda. Finance has increasingly penetrated our social life; as individuals we are connected into the financial system in real-time. Most of us can now bank using our phones, we access credit at the checkout to buy groceries, we take out loans for houses and education and we save for pensions. Our parents and grandparents, only 50 or 100 years ago, would have been paid in cash, with little if any access to formal banking, few owned their own home and hire purchase and credit cards were non-existent.

This growth in the economic, social and political importance of finance and the financial sector is the central feature of financialization. This book documents the growing scale and importance of financial institutions and markets, how the financial sector has evolved and changed since the 1970s, and which forces have generated that growth. Financialization has consequences for the global and national economy and society, and these are examined, particularly with reference to economic performance, growth and inequality. The aim here is to understand and expose the processes, the effects and impacts of financialization on the real economy, on individuals and corporations, society and on the polity over the past three decades.

Finance and money are central to the functioning of capitalism. Production has to be financed. Exchange and trade in goods and services has to be facilitated by money and credit. Investment and the accumulation of capital have to be funded. The financial sector provides a payments technology – the provision and transfer of money from one to another – to finance exchange. The government and central bank have key roles in setting what is regarded as the unit of account and in the supervision of the banking sector through which money is created and transferred between people.

The financial sector provides facilities for savings – people may, for example, accumulate deposits in banks. The financial sector provides loans to companies for the funding of investment expenditure. In doing so it evaluates the demands for loans and monitors their use. This role as facilitator casts the financial sector in a favourable light as it enables trade and encourages saving and investment. Yet, it occupies a position of very considerable power – it decides who receives loans and credit and on what terms they are determined. Groups can and have been excluded (or at least limited) from loans and credit, for example, based on gender or ethnicity.

The banking sector is often precarious, prone to credit booms that are followed by banking crises and often spiral into a general economic recession and increased unemployment. The financial sector expands through the innovation and introduction of complex financial products and the trading in those assets. Frequently, such trading involves speculation on future prices and asset price bubbles, which eventually burst. The tulip mania of 1636–37 in Holland, which lasted three months, and the South Sea Bubble of 1720 provide early examples of price bubbles followed by collapse (see, e.g., Baddeley & McCombie 2001 for discussion of these two episodes and relationship with theories of price bubbles). The dot-com bubble, which effectively burst in March 2000, provides a more recent example during which the Nasdaq Composite stock market index rose 400 per cent (1995 to 2000) followed by fall of 78 per cent by October 2002.

Financialization of the present era began to intensify from the late 1970s and has several characteristics that it shares with earlier episodes of financialization (notably the rapid growth of the financial sector). It represents major shifts in capitalism and in the relations between the financial sector and the non-financial sector, also known as the "real economy" of production, manufacturing and services. Financialization in the present era has occurred concurrently with other major shifts, which are broadly coincident in time, starting from the late 1970s and early 1980s. There are the shifts towards neoliberalism, privatization and deregulation, often associated with the tenures of Prime Minister Margaret Thatcher in the UK and President Ronald Reagan in the USA (although signs of such polices pre-date them). Globalization, including the growth of international trade and of foreign direct investment, the reduction of barriers to trade and of capital controls, has also been taking place. Neoliberalism and globalization have close interacting relationships with financialization.

The major themes

This book has the three major themes: the nature of financialization, the impact of financialization and the possible future of the financialization process.

On the first theme, the term "financialization" was coined relatively recently and, in the main, applies to terms such as "finance-led capitalism", which have been deployed in similar circumstances. It is a term that has become widely used within social sciences, including heterodox economics and political economy, although it has not generally been incorporated into mainstream economics. It is also a term that has been used in a range of different ways. Although the term "financialization" has a short history, the growth of the financial sector has a long one as an integral element of capitalism.

The exploration of the nature of financialization involves two strands: the first is to consider how financialization has been conceptualized and what is in practice meant by the term "financialization". It will become apparent that the term has been given different meanings and financialization has many dimensions. The second is to map out of the contours of financialization over the past four decades or so. This starts from a consideration of how the financial sector has grown, the pace of growth and its changing structure, for example the relative importance of banks, other financial institutions and of financial markets, and the development of complex derivative and securities. In this mapping the focus is on industrialized economies of Europe (particularly western Europe), North

America and Japan. Financialization has, however, in recent decades been a near-global phenomenon, with almost all countries seeing financial institutions and markets grow substantially. Further, economies are increasingly internationally linked and the financial sector plays a key role in those developments.

It is also relevant to discuss how the interaction between the financial sector and the real sector has changed: this ranges from the basis on which funds are provided to the real sector, the ways in which the ownership of equity by financial corporations impacts on the behaviour of non-financial corporations and the degree to which non-financial corporations themselves engage in financial operations.

The second theme of this book is the impact of financialization over the past three to four decades on economic and social performance. This ranges over issues such as how financialization has affected investment, including into research and development, savings and economic growth. I will be looking at the ways financialization has affected our everyday lives and what the consequences of financialization for environmentally sustainable development are. The growth of finance (often referred to as "financial deepening" and "financial development") has often been portrayed as something that promotes growth and efficiency. Later in the book, I will address whether that is still the case and whether it has ever been the case.

A final theme is to consider the future of financialization. Are there forces that will propel our economies and societies towards further financialization? If so, would further financialization be socially beneficial? Alternatively, is the financial sector now, in some sense, too big and absorbing too many resources so that many of its activities have become detrimental for the real economy (for example, actually contributing to lower growth and being one of the key causes of financial crises)? Are there policies of regulation, taxation and restructuring of the financial sector that would constitute definancialization and change the financial sector to better serve the economy, society and the environment?

What is financialization?

The general approach to financialization adopted here starts from the widely quoted definition provided by Epstein (2005: 3): "financialization means the increasing role of financial motives, financial markets, financial actors and financial institutions in the operation of the domestic and international economies". That definition can be extended to include the increasing role of finance in the workings of societies and polities.

Starting from that definition, the forms that those increasing roles have taken, how the financial sector has evolved and the consequences can be investigated. Within this broad idea of financialization, many different perspectives of financialization that have been advanced can be identified, drawing on a range of disciplines and analytical frameworks.

Van der Zwan (2014), in her survey of the financialization literature, identifies three broad approaches, which provides a convenient way of summarizing the range of perspectives on financialization.[2]

The first is "financialization as a regime of accumulation": this is the notion that financialization represents a distinct stage of capitalism. Authors such as Vercelli (2013) have elaborated on earlier eras of financialization (and specifically Vercelli identifies the period 1880 to 1929 as the first era of financialization), and this is elaborated on in Chapter 2. Eras of financialization share the broad characteristic of growth of the financial sector but differ in the forms that growth takes. In Chapters 4 and 5, I outline the significant ways in which the financial sector has evolved and grown over the past four decades. The relationships between the financial sector and the rest of the economy can also differ in the eras of financialization, including the ways in which the routes through which funds are provided by the financial institutions lead to different relationships between those institutions and the corporations and businesses.

The second idea is that of the "financialization of the modern corporation". This has strong links with the "pursuit of shareholder value", with financial institutions becoming highly significant owners of equity. The "pursuit of shareholder value" places focus on short-term profits at the expense of longer-term thinking and of the interests of other stakeholders, including employees and customers. "Shareholder value is not a neutral concept, but an ideological construct that legitimates a far-reaching redistribution of wealth and power among shareholders, managers and workers" (Van der Zwan 2014: 102).

The third is the "financialization of the everyday life" and is reflected in numerous ways, ranging from the greater engagement of people with the financial sector – notably in respect of credit and debt – through to the incursion of financial institutions into pension provisions. "By participating in financial markets, individuals are encouraged to internalize new norms of risk-taking and develop new subjectivities as investors or owners of financial assets" (*ibid.*).

Financialization, neoliberalism and globalization

The period since circa 1980 has often been viewed in terms of neoliberalism and of globalization as well as of financialization. Neoliberal ideas of the free market, free trade and the reduction of government control and influence came to dominate the approach to national economies and the Keynesian model of government intervention was sidelined.

Globalization has involved the rapid growth of international trade and of foreign direct investment. It has required the financing of international trade and the funding

---

2. We shall see in Chapter 2 that authors have used terms such as finance capitalism and finance-led capitalism with similar meanings to financialization, particularly the first two streams, which Van der Zwan (2014) identifies.

of foreign direct investment and portfolio investment, all of which involved the growth of financial activities. The gross flows of capital across national borders have rapidly increased and current and capital account imbalances have grown. Banks and financial institutions have themselves opened up branches and offices in foreign territories and markets.

Neoliberalism emphasizes the economic and social benefits of the extension of market mechanisms, the spread of market transactions into areas previously excluded and on "freeing up" markets through deregulation. Deregulation of the financial sector, often under the labels of financial liberalization and the lifting of "financial repression", played a significant role in stimulating the growth of the financial sector and, as will be seen in later chapters, feeding into credit booms that were followed by busts.

The expansion of the financial systems has gone alongside the expansion of the market system. The expansion of capitalist markets into areas previously outside the scope of such markets has entailed the corresponding growth of the financial systems and, indeed, such expansion requires financing and funding by the financial system. The growth of international trade and cross-border investments has similarly involved and required the growth of the financial systems. In recent decades, financial systems have expanded into domains where they had previously played a very limited role, such as in private pension arrangements.

The scale of the financial sector has grown considerably since circa 1980 in most countries. Most of this has come from the growth of financial markets rather than in increasing numbers of banks and from the fusion between financial markets and banks. Securitization, derivatives and the extensive and high-frequency trading in financial assets have all been developed since the 1980s. There has been a proliferation of financial instruments and increased complexity in the nature of those financial instruments.

The structures of the national financial sectors have also changed in important ways, although at different speeds and dependent on the "initial conditions" under which the sector started. The changes have generally included a rising concentration of the financial sector, moves from regional to national-based banking systems, the decline of mutual and public ownership in the financial sector (such as building societies in the UK), the rapid growth of "shadow banks" and financial institutions such as private equity.

Financialization has been a near-universal and global phenomenon over the past few decades. However, it has proceeded at a different pace and taken various forms so that we might call it a process of "variegated financialization". In Chapter 4, there is an overview of the ways in which the financial sector and its operations have grown and changed in the industrialized countries. The quantitative changes for the G7 countries (Canada, France, Germany, Italy, Japan, UK and USA) are documented. In Chapter 5, I briefly document the extent of financial sector growth in the regions of the world, which illustrates the near-universal nature of the growth of the financial sector and also the varying levels and growth rates of financialization.

The doctrines of neoliberalism emphasize the benefits of competition and what would be termed free markets. Banks and other financial institutions have generally been highly regulated in terms of licensing of banks as deposit takers and control over interest rates to be charged and loans to be granted, and with a close relationship with the central bank.

Financialization in the present era has been closely linked with liberalization and deregulation, as the interests of the financial sector press for removal of limitations on their activities, and the lifting of such limitations has spurred the sector's growth. Economists and policymakers were often critical of what was termed "financial repression" as holding back savings and investment, and thereby economic growth. Lifting financial repression through liberalization and more generally de-regulating the financial sector was argued to lead to higher growth.

This liberalization can in itself generate crises, particularly when credit expansion is rapid. There has been a general history of financial liberalization leading to financial crisis, not least as evidenced by the financial crises of 2007–09, which has been particularly linked to deregulation.

The pursuit of shareholder value

The pursuit of shareholder value has been closely associated with financialization. Financial institutions have increasingly become shareholders in non-financial corporations, whether on their own behalf or through investing on behalf of private individuals (for example, pension funds). The general notion of the pursuit of shareholder value is to boost share prices through dividend payments, which are often viewed to lead to pay-out of profits at the expense of investment. As the financial institutions are often the shareholders, the pursuit of shareholder value comes in the interests of the financial institutions. The arguments are examined of how such a pursuit by financial institutions impacts on the decisions of non-financial corporations in respect of investment, research and development, etc. The empirical evidence is examined of these possible effects of financialization on investment and capital accumulation, and thereby growth is also examined, with the general perspective that there has been a dampening effect on investment.

A driver of inequality or enabler?

The period of financialization has accompanied a marked rise in social inequalities (in contrast with the experiences of industrialized societies in the pre-1980 period). Inequality refers to the inequalities in the distribution of income and of wealth between people. The nature and rate of inequality has proceeded at a different pace in different countries and the nature of the rising inequality is briefly summarized and contrasted with the earlier postwar period. I explore the connections between financialization and rising inequality from a theoretical and an empirical perspective. It has been argued that financialization has contributed to rising inequality as earnings within the financial sector are particularly unequal and that inequality has grown notably because of the contentious inflated bankers' bonuses, for example. Financialization also contributes to the elevation of incentives and inequality.

The interaction between rising inequality and the growth of household debt in the generation of the 2007–09 financial crises will be explored in the following chapters in more detail. It is evident, however, that inequality played a significant role in the generation of the USA's financial crisis but not in general in the financial crises of the UK, Ireland, etc., nor in the transmission of the financial crisis globally.

In the lead-up to the financial crises, there was a substantial growth of the incomes (wages, profits) of the financial sector relative to the rest of the economy. How should those shifts of income be regarded? Defenders of the financial sector would attribute those shifts to the productive endeavours and efficiency of the financial sector. Alternatively, they could be regarded as a result of the economic and political power of the financial sector and that the rewards of managers and others in the sector are akin to capture of economic rents rather than reflecting their levels of productivity. I will argue (based on empirical evidence) that the shift represents the capture of economic rents by the financial sector and not increased productivity; indeed, it is my view that the financial sector has served as a drag on the economy.

Financialization of everyday life

Financialization has involved the spread of finance, financial motivations and calculations into everyday life. What are the benefits and costs of the financialization of the everyday? "Financial inclusion" involves more people being drawn into the financial system rather than being "financially excluded", in particular from access to credit. But that is not without consequences. The growth of household debt has been a pronounced feature of financialization in industrialized economies and it has proceeded at different speeds in different countries. This rising debt has become a driver of growth but has tendencies to be precarious and to contribute to economic instability.

To understand what is going on, there is a need to answer two questions: first, why has there been such a growth of household debt? The focus is often placed on households' desire for debt; here the focus is on the role of financial institutions in promoting household debt in the face of an overall level of savings in excess of the investment needs of companies. Second, while household debt and liabilities have risen so have household financial assets. The distributional aspects of that need to be examined; for example, is this the rich getting richer (more financial assets) and poor getting poorer (more financial liabilities)?

The third element of the financialization of the everyday is the increased involvement of the financial sector in activities that had previously been the preserve of the state and/or mutual sectors. The provision of mortgages for house purchase has often been provided by mutual organizations (such as building societies in the UK) and state-backed institutions (such as Fannie Mae and Freddie Mac in the USA), and these have often been displaced by profit-based financial institutions. Private pension provision (whether on an individual or collective basis) has been encouraged to supplement or replace state provision. Private pension arrangements provide a major growth area for financial institutions and a major source of profits.

Has the financial sector become dysfunctional?

Using terms such as financial deepening and financial development, there has been an extensive literature that found a positive relationship between financial deepening and economic growth. However, many recent studies have found that, for industrialized countries with large financial sector, the relationship appears to no longer hold as far as industrialized countries are concerned. One of the key purposes of the financial sector has been viewed in terms of facilitating savings, linking savings and investment, and monitoring the use of funds provided, which are viewed as enabling economic growth. If resources are being used in the financial sector and yet it appears to be no longer fulfilling one of its key purposes, questions arise about the benefits of the financial sector.

This leads to a consideration of why the relationship between the size of the financial sector and economic growth may have changed. Two particular features stand out. The first is that much of the growth of the financial sector has been in the extensive trading of financial assets, with the growth of securitization and derivatives, which do not themselves facilitate savings and investment. The second relates to the growth of household debt and its provision by financial institutions, which does not contribute to investment and its funding.

The period of financialization has also been a period of financial crises. Particularly, banking crises have imposed substantial costs on the economy in terms of lost output and increased unemployment. The argument that recession after financial crisis is the counterpart of rapid, credit-fuelled expansion is examined and found wanting. While economic growth eventually resumes after a financial crisis, it does so from a lower base, and the losses during the recession are often not regained (see Chapter 6).

The financial sector uses resources of labour, often highly skilled labour. Yet, as this chapter has argued, it now does not contribute to enhancing economic performance.

The chapter concludes by asking whether the financial sector has become "too big" and too powerful.

If it has become "too big" and if the ways in which it has grown over the past three decades have not been net beneficial for the rest of the economy and society, is it feasible for financialization to be allowed to continue? The weight of the financial sector on the real economy, particularly on its growth potential and profitability, might lead to pressures from the real sector for it to change. This is unlikely. Policies to shift the financial sector towards serving society better through the development of alternative stakeholder banking and financial institutions are outlined. A significant part of the policy programme is to ensure that the financial sector is not only less unstable but also that sufficient funds flow into "green investment". The chapter concludes with the political obstacles to definancialization.

2
THE TERRAIN OF FINANCIALIZATION

The term "financialization" has come into usage relatively recently, although many of the processes of financialization itself are long-standing phenomena of capitalism that were recognized and discussed well before the term itself was coined. Other terms such as "finance-led capitalism" and "finance capitalism" express similar ideas to financialization as a "regime of accumulation" (see below). The term "financialization" has been used in many ways that appear mutually inconsistent (Vercelli 2013: 20). This chapter explores the meanings attached to the term and indicates how financialization is approached in this book. It sets out the key elements that have been associated with financialization, particularly since 1980. These elements are not always mutually consistent, nor do they apply in all experiences of financialization.

Financialization involves large and increasing scales of financial institutions and financial markets, the greater roles of financial motives in the operations of domestic and international economies and their impacts on polities, social life and the environment (following Epstein 2005: 3 as quoted previously). Financialization is not just a matter of there being a large financial sector (however that is judged), but one of a financial sector whose scale and impacts on the economy, society and public life are increasing. When the size of the financial sector is measured (as will be done in Chapter 4), it is seen to be generally increasing relative to the size of the economy (as measured, for example, by gross domestic product [GDP]).

One dimension of financialization involves the growth in the scale of operations of banks and other financial institutions, including but not limited to the volumes of deposits taken and of loans provided. Financial markets include stock and equity markets, foreign exchange markets, securities markets and so on, and their growth can be viewed in terms of the capitalization of the financial assets, which are traded in the relevant markets, and in terms of turnover of the assets. The role of these financial markets could also be judged by the extent to which funds are raised through the new issue of equity shares (less the retirement of assets), although in recent times in many countries stock markets have not been the net source of funds to corporations as the issue of new shares has been more than offset by buy-backs of shares and purchase of shares of one company by another in the process of acquisition.

However, it is not just that the scale of financial institutions and markets have increased but also that the nature of these financial institutions have shifted. There has been, for example, a decline in mutual and state-owned institutions relative to privately owned ones. It will also be seen that there has been a general tendency for the scale of financial markets (as measured, for example, by stock market capitalization) to grow relative to financial institutions (which could be measured by the level of bank deposits). There has also been a blurring of the distinction between the role of financial institutions and that of financial markets, as banks have become more engaged in financial market transactions. The nature and structure of financial institutions (one group of financial actors) have evolved and, in turn, the scale and range of their activities have tended to grow often quite rapidly. Hardie *et al.* (2013) speak of "market-based banking", where banks become more involved in the development of and trading in financial assets in financial markets, which has been a notable trend.

Households and individuals have been increasingly drawn into involvement with finance and financial transactions. For centuries, many transactions have been monetized with payment for goods and services in notes and coins. For individuals in most (if not all) countries it is a relatively recent phenomenon (of the past 50 years) that the majority of households have had bank accounts but now payment by cheque has been superseded by debit cards and then electronic transfer and the extensive use of credit cards. Involvement of individuals within the financial sector extends much further into loans and debt, use of savings accounts and acquisition of financial assets, including through pension funds. These increased involvements by individuals with financial institutions is another aspect of financialization and an element in what can be termed "the financialization of the everyday". Financial calculations and decisions play a much more important role in our lives than ever before.

Defining financialization

The use of the term "financialization" and the literature analysing it has boomed in the past three decades or so. Correa, Vidal and Marshall (2012: 258) cite numerous authors who "have been considering the implications of the notable increase in financial activity and the greater influence of banks, investment funds, hedge funds, and other financial intermediaries on the economy and the management of large firms", and the earliest one mentioned is De Bernis (1988). Foster (2007) writes that "the current usage of the term 'financialization' owes much to the work of Kevin Phillips, who employed it in [Phillips, 1993] and a year later devoted a key chapter of his *Arrogant Capital* [Phillips 1994] to the

'Financialization of America,' defining financialization as 'a *prolonged* split between the divergent real and financial economies'".

Foster (2007), along with others, has argued that the origins of the term "financialization" are obscure, although he states that it began to appear with increasing frequency in the early 1990s. Engelen (2008: 112) places "the earliest publications with 'financiali(z/s) ation' in their title" from 2000. Since then 23 papers and books on financialization have been added, with a rapid increase in 2007 when no less than six titles were included. Gary Dymski reports,[1] from a Web of Science search on topic words used in papers, no mention of "financializ(s)ation" prior to 2000 in journals that he classified as heterodox economics and regional studies and geography, with small mentions thereafter (averaging less than two annually in each case), and then a rapid acceleration after the GFCs with an average in double figures after 2012. Van der Zwan (2019: 454) notes the scope of publications on financialization, with "more than 460 academic journal articles with 'financialization' or 'financialisation' in the title have been published, and many hundreds more take financialization as their topic". The term financialization did not receive a mention in mainstream journals until 2015, although the growth of the financial sector under headings such as financial deepening had been much discussed.

The studies and analyses that attract the term "financialization" can be contrasted with the studies and analyses that go under the headings of finance and financial economics. Van der Zwan (2019: 454) notes that financialization scholarship has been undertaken across many social science disciplines, including political economy, heterodox economics, social accounting studies, sociology and geography. In contrast, the analysis of finance and financial markets from a mainstream economics perspective is heavily based on optimizing behaviour under conditions of risk, often with heavy use of mathematical modelling. Financialization scholarship deploys a wide range of methodological and epistemological approaches. The mainstream economics approaches to finance have generally viewed financial markets as operating efficiently, whereas financialization studies have taken a much more sceptical view, as will be apparent in later discussions.

Krippner (2005: 181) noted that "numerous researchers have used the term [financialization] in exploring various aspects of rise of finance, but the literature on financialization is at present a bit of a free-for-all, lacking a cohesive view of what is to be explained". Van der Zwan (2014: 111), in a similar vein, notes that "despite the usage of a common terminology, financialization covers a host of empirical phenomena at different levels of analysis". Michell and Toporowski (2014) express concerns about how the term and concept of financialization is being used. They note that economists have often separated the "real" economic variables from the money and credit variables, exemplified in the so-called classical dichotomy that separates monetary and financial factors from real factors, with the former having no long-term impact on the latter. But "credit systems

---

1. Personal communication.

have always been more complex than the 'real' economic transaction with which they are associated". They then argue that "such economists are therefore prone to appeal to nebulous processes of financialization to explain the more complex financial operations that they find in the real world. The use of the term in different contexts and with different meanings makes it of dubious analytical value" (*ibid.*: 69).

Sweezy (1994: 2) wrote of "the triumph of financial capital" where "once cut loose from its original role as a modest helper of a real economy of production to meet human needs, [it] inevitably becomes speculative capital geared solely to its own self-expansion". In his view, in the first half of the twentieth century, capital accumulation processes continued to be focused on industrial capital, with financiers playing a greater role as partners of industrial capitalists. After the so-called "golden age" of capitalism (late 1940s to mid-1970s; Marglin & Schor 1992), there was a tendency for stagnation to take over and sources of demand stimulation were required. He saw this as arising over the preceding two decades (early 1970s to early 1990s), coming from financiers who were seeking new business. Sweezy writes of the development of a relatively independent "financial superstructure sitting on top of the world economy and most of its national units". He indicates that financial expansion had been considered to accompany an expansion of the real economy and then asks "is it really possible that this is no longer true, that now in the late twentieth century the opposite is the more nearly the case: in other words, that now financial expansion feeds not on a healthy real economy but on a stagnant one?" Sweezy thought that it was possible and was happening and that an inverted relation between the financial sector and the real sectors was the key to understanding the new global trends in the economy. He also observed that rather than investing in productive assets, non-financial corporations were placing their funds in financial assets – a theme that is followed up in Chapter 7.

The features of "financial capital" that Sweezy (1994) discussed have continued to be seen by many as important dimensions of financialization, but there are many more. It is helpful to identify broad themes and analytical approaches within the financialization literature. In general, many of the themes identified refer to features and characteristics of what Vercelli (2013) labelled the "second financialization" and what is referred to in this book as "financialization of the present era", which dates from the late 1970s through to the present, although within that period there have been variations in the pace and effects of financialization. The first general characteristic of financialization is that of the increasing economic and political roles of the financial sector.

Krippner (2005) identified four broad themes within the literatures on financialization, which I draw on, although reordered. Two of them are to some degree quantitative in nature, which relate to "the growing dominance of the capital markets over systems of bank-based finance" (*ibid.*: 181) and the rapid growth of trading in financial assets alongside a proliferation of new financial instruments.[2] In Chapters 4 and 5, the quantitative

---

2. For a critique of the bank-based, market-based financial system, see Sawyer (2014a).

evidence is presented, broadly confirming the growth of capital markets and of financial institutions, with the former often growing faster than the latter.

Banks accept deposits from the public and provide loans to firms and households.[3] As such, banks link together savings (placed into deposits) and investment (funded by loans). Banks provide other services – traditionally much of the payments system, and now increasingly other functions often including insurance (see, e.g., Ertürk & Solari 2007). An important feature of banks is that some of their liabilities count as money – that is deposits (the liabilities of the banks) in current or chequing accounts that can be readily transferred between individuals and accepted in payment, serving the function of money as a means of payment.[4] Banks then, through provision of loans, create bank deposits and money. A higher provision of loans enables expenditure to expand, possibly creating boom conditions and unsustainable expansion.

Financial institutions, including banks, have increasingly engaged in financial market operations. Stock markets can also be viewed in terms of raising funds for corporations through new issues and, similar to banks, serve to link together savers and investors. However, most activities of stock markets and other capital markets involve the sale of existing financial assets, and their expansion in past decades has involved the development of a wide range of financial assets (through securitization) and high volumes of trading.

The other two themes identified by Krippner (2005) are more qualitative. She identifies a broad theme as the rise of shareholder value. This has often become expressed in the phrase "the pursuit of shareholder value". The primacy of shareholder interests over those of other stakeholders (workers, consumers, managers) has become a central theme in the financialization literature. The "pursuit of shareholder value" can be viewed in terms of impacts on economic and social performance. This is further discussed below and is the focus of attention in Chapter 7.

Another broad theme identified by Krippner (2005) is the increasing political and economic power of a *rentier* class. Rentier income is based on the passive ownership of financial and real assets. As such it would cover income based on interest, dividends, capital gains and rent of property. In Chapter 4 the developments of rentier income are mapped out. The notion of a "rentier class" conjures ideas of the wealthy capital-owning class able to live off their rentier income.

The position is now more complex in two respects. The first is that interest, dividends, capital gains and rent paid by non-financial corporations (and also financial

---

3. This should not be read to mean that deposits received by banks constrain the volume of loans that can be made. For clearing banks, whose liabilities (deposits) are regarded as money, loans create money and deposits, and can be created ahead of deposits. In making a loan, the bank expands its balance sheet with assets (loans) and liabilities (deposits) growing. Savings and investment banks, in contrast, do not create money (their liabilities not counting as money) and deposits, which then does constrain their ability to lend.

4. These remarks apply to what are often termed clearing banks or commercial banks but not to savings banks or investment banks.

corporations) often accrue to financial institutions, including pension funds, unit trusts and others. Those financial institutions may own assets in their own right but also manage assets on behalf of individuals. Pension funds, for example, manage assets that have been funded by pension contributions, for which they extract substantial fees and pay out pensions derived from the rentier income received. The second is, as this example suggests, that the beneficiaries of rentier income now include retirees as well as the wealthy.

New financial instruments would include derivatives, collateralized debt obligations (CDOs) – and so-called synthetic CDOs or CDO-squared – asset-backed securities and mortgage-backed securities. Asset-backed securities pay returns to investors based on cash flow, which is in turn collected from the pool of assets that it owns. The complexity of many of these financial instruments and their role in increasing systemic risk rather than reducing it are discussed in Chapter 9, along with their contribution to the generation of the GFCs, with its location in sub-prime lending, mortgage-based securities and toxic assets.

Krippner follows Arrighi (1994) "in defining financialization as a pattern of accumulation in which profit-making occurs increasingly through financial channels rather than through trade and commodity production" (Krippner 2005: 181). "Financial" here refers to activities relating to the provision (or transfer) of liquid capital in expectation of future interest, dividends or capital gains. In her paper, Krippner uses two measures to gauge financialization. One of the measures is the source of revenue of non-financial firms from financial assets (labelled portfolio income coming from interest payments, dividends and capital gains) relative to corporate cash flow. For the USA, there is an upward movement in portfolio income largely accounted for by increases in the interest component, rising to around 10 per cent in $c.$1970 tending to rise to around 40 per cent by the late 1980s, with some fluctuating rises thereafter (statistics taken from Krippner 2005, Figure 5). The other measure compares profits in the financial and the non-financial sectors of the economy. From a figure of around 10 per cent in 1950 the ratio of profits in the financial sector to profits in the non-financial sector rises (with some fluctuations) to reach around 50 per cent by 2001 (the end of the period).

Hein, Dodig and Budyldina (2015c: 1) speak of financialization and "finance dominated capitalism" since the early 1980s "starting in the USA and the UK and spreading over the developed and, subsequently also the developing capitalist world". They continue that "this stage of development has been characterised by the expansion of financial markets, the introduction of new financial instruments, and the increasing dominance of financial motives in economic activity. Over the last 30 or so years, finance has come to dominate industry, and non-financial corporations have increasingly engaged in financial as opposed to productive activities. Alignment of management with shareholder interests reflected the shifting focus towards pursuing short-term 'shareholder value' maximization instead of the long-run growth objectives of the firm" (*ibid.*: 1–2).

Van der Zwan (2014), in her survey on financialization, identifies three broad approaches to the study of financialization, which have some overlap with those given by Krippner (2005) but with one major addition. The three approaches identified are "financialization as a regime of accumulation", "the financialization of the modern corporation" and "the financialization of the everyday". It is appropriate to consider each of these in turn.

Regimes of accumulation and stages of capitalism

In speaking of financialization in terms of a regime of accumulation or as a stage of capitalism is to be thinking of financialization of the past four decades or so. It locates financialization as a central feature of capitalist development in recent decades. There are then features of present capitalism, which are different from those of earlier capitalisms, although the essential features of capitalism as an economic and social system based on private property ownership and the drive for profitable accumulation continue.

The term "regime of accumulation" is generally associated with the French school of regulation theory, as "a historically specific but relatively long-lived means by which capital accumulation is ensured".[5] It defines "(i) a dominant ensemble of industries whose production methods and intended markers share similar characteristics; (ii) a set of national government measures designed to support these industries; and (iii) a complex set of rules, norms, and institutions designed to ensure stable and positive relations between firms, the state, and wage workers" (Castree, Kitchin & Rogers 2013).

Writing from a regulationist perspective, Boyer (2000: 112) postulates "a financialized growth regime as the latest candidate for replacing Fordism", in which "the hierarchy among institutional forms … is drastically shifted: the financial regime plays the central role that used to be attributed to the wage-labour nexus under Fordism". He presents a theoretical (and steady-state) model of such a financialized growth model. This could be viewed as something of an ideal type (in the sense of Weber) and Boyer focuses attention on the USA for such a regime, and indeed Boyer (2013) indicates that finance-led growth may apply in the USA and UK but not elsewhere.

Boyer (2000: table 1) portrays the finance-led growth regime in the following terms. The wage-labour nexus is characterized in terms of employment flexibility, profit-sharing and pension funds (see Chapter 9), with the form of competition described as mainly on financial markets but with trends towards oligopoly. The monetary regime is viewed in terms of the prevention of the emergence of financial bubbles, although there has not been a great deal of success in that respect. The state/society relations are "under scrutiny of financial markets" and "search for credibility". The international regime is

---

5. Hein, Dodig and Budyldina (2015) have a detailed discussion of the French regulation and the social structures of accumulation approaches, as well as the post-Keynesian approach.

characterized in terms of "trends towards global finance". And the risk of systemic financial instability threatens the "coherence and dynamic of the growth regime".

Boyer (2000) envisages the UK and the USA as typical cases and the discussions in later chapters consider how far this regime applies to other countries. In his Table 1, Boyer compares this finance-led growth regime with a range of "alternative emerging growth regimes and redesign of institutional forms". These are "Toyotism" (a word derived from the perceived nature of the production processes of Toyota car company) of which Boyer takes Japan pre-1990 as a typical case; service-led economy (a typical example is the USA in the 1980s); information/communication technologies-led (a typical case is Silicon Valley since the mid-1980s); knowledge-based economy (the USA in the 1990s); competition-led (most Organisation for Economic Co-operation and Development [OECD] countries since 1985); and export-led (newly industrialized countries of East Asia before 1997).

The major characteristic of the finance-led growth regime comes from the central role played by finance and the financial sector and the alliances between shareholders (often the financial sector) and management, which compares with the labour-capital compromise that was a dominant feature of the Fordist regime, which preceded the finance-led regime.

Aglietta and Breton (2001) view the growth of financial markets, alongside information technology development, as "one of the pillars of the new economy". They develop a model of a finance-led economy in which there is an active market for control of corporation that pushes corporations to boost their share price to limit the threat of being taken over. Boosting share prices means distributing more dividends or buying back shares. Retained profits are reduced and as a consequence there is lower investment, which would have been funded by retained profits. The more active the market for corporate control the lower the investment, the rate of capital accumulation and thereby the lower the growth potential. This dimension of financialization comes from the "pursuit of shareholder value", which has potentially important implications if the conclusion of that growth would be lower.

Writers within the social structure of accumulation (SSA) tradition have also analysed a different stage of capitalism that involves a dominant role of the financial sector. The neoliberal SSA involves capital's domination of labour in contrast to the capital-labour compromise of the "regulated capitalist SSA" (namely the postwar SSA of the Fordist era). The neoliberal SSA also involves the retreat of government and regulation, unrestrained competition, separation of the financial from the non-financial sector and neoliberal ideology of unrestrained markets. The contrast is again with the "regulated capitalist SSA" of interventionist government, restrained competition among corporations, the financial sector serving the non-financial sector and a mixed economy.[6] Kotz (2008) argues that within the neoliberal SSA the changing roles and scale of finance in the economy

---

6. This paragraph draws heavily on Hein, Dodig and Budyldina (2015: table 1.3), which summarizes Kotz (2008).

are not best captured by the idea of the dominance of the financial sector but what he terms "financialization" as the expanding role for finance in economic activity. He argues that "the immediate cause of the financialization process of recent decades is found in neoliberal restructuring, rather than financialization explaining the rise of neoliberalism. However, financialization also has deeper roots that are unrelated to neoliberalism" (Kotz 2008: 2).

Dumenil and Levy (2005: 17) argue that all features of capitalism "point to the crucial position of finance at the centre of the new neoliberal setting". For these authors, "it is finance that dictates the forms and contexts in the new stage of internationalization, it is not internationalization or globalization that creates the insuperable necessity for the present evolution of capitalism".

Lapavitas (2011) argues that financialization is a systemic transformation of capitalist economies with three fundamental elements. The first is significant changes in the relations between non-financial corporations and banks with corporations relying more on internal finance and on raising funds in financial markets. The second is that banks have turned toward households as source of profits through increased lending (on mortgages, consumer debt) and financial assets (pensions, insurance, etc.). This is the obverse side of the "financialization of the everyday", and the third element mentioned by Lapavitas.

Financialization is a shift towards the financial sector, although Lapavitas notes that the capacity of the financial sector to generate employment is limited (as is documented in Chapter 4). It does, though, have implications for employment and work conditions, as will be considered in Chapter 6, particularly related to the effects of the "pursuit of shareholder value" associated with financialization.

Other writers have viewed financialization (or terms such as financialized capitalism) as a new era or stage of capitalism. For example, within the *Monthly Review* monopoly capitalism school, Foster argues that "Changes in capitalism over the last three decades have been commonly characterized using a trio of terms: neoliberalism, globalization, and financialization. … [F]inancialization is now increasingly seen as the dominant force in this triad. The financialization of capitalism – the shift in gravity of economic activity from production (and even from much of the growing service sector) to finance – is thus one of the key issues of our time." He argued that this did not mean that capitalism had entered a new stage, as the basic problem of accumulation within production remained unchanged. It was rather that "financialization has resulted in a new hybrid phase of the monopoly stage of capitalism that might be termed 'monopoly-finance capital'" (Foster 2007: 1). The relationships between financialization, globalization and neoliberalism are further explored in the next chapter.

There are different ways of viewing stages, eras and periods of history. In economic and social terms, that used by French regulationists and the SSA is one such method. Minsky (1988, 1993) identified four stages of capitalism, which can be relevant for finance and financialization. Minsky was analysing American capitalism, and the question always arises as to whether they can be generalized to other capitalist economies. Minsky's four stages were commercial capitalism, financial capitalism, managerial capitalism and money-manager capitalism. In each stage the relationship between finance and the real economy differs in significant ways.

Under commercial capitalism, the financial institutions are largely concerned with the financing of trade, whether at a local level or trade at a distance. Finance capitalism became dominant in the 100 years ending with the First World War. Minsky portrayed that period as "characterized by the emergence of financial organizations that could mobilize vast resources for projects such as railroads, utilities, mills and mines. The financing either took place within banks – the German universal banking structures – or through markets – the British and American structures which led to the emergence of independent bankers. In both cases the banking structures became the centers of economic power" (Minsky 1988: 29).

Managerial capitalism, which Minsky identifies as emerging from the interwar depressions and the Second World War, featured a much larger role for government, including the welfare state and an initially robust financial structure. A particularly relevant element is that the managers of corporations operated more independently of the banking communities than before. "As long as the flow of dividends was sustained corporate management was largely independent of stockholder control. In this structure, corporate management, legally an agent of stockholders, was the dominant actor. Corporate managements, controlling large cash flows, had freedom to pursue alternative even inconsistent goals" (*ibid.*: 31).

In the postwar era, "money-manager capitalism" emerged from managerial capitalism. Pension funds, mutual funds, bank trust funds and endowments of private institutions grew and became owners of a large portion of equity of corporations. These institutional shareholders actively manage funds with frequent buying and selling of stocks, pursuing the objective of maximizing total portfolio returns over each short period of time. Minsky argued that takeovers and financial restructuring, such as leveraged buyouts, were facilitated by institutional funds seeking high returns. The financial independence of corporate management is diminished under money-manager capitalism. Minsky also regarded money managers as a large part of the market for securitized financial instruments.

Whalen (2012) argues that Minsky had been concerned that money-manager capitalism would be accompanied by a fragile financial structure (by comparison with the regulated managerial capitalism) making it more susceptible to economic and financial crisis. This can be seen to be borne out by the much greater incidence of financial crisis in the past four decades as compared with the preceding decades. Minsky had also doubted that this money-manager capitalism would enhance capital development of the USA economy. Whalen (2012) notes the considerable overlap between Minsky's money-manager capitalism and the literature on financialization. There are the similarities with the "pursuit of shareholder value" and its consequences for investment and employment (further discussed in Chapter 6). Whalen (2012: 257) indicates how Minsky's "discussion of each stage centred on three questions: What is being financed? What is the pivotal source of financing? What is the balance of economic power between business and banking?".

Many have postulated that there were shifts in the capitalisms of North America and western Europe in the late 1970s and early 1980s due to globalization and neoliberalism, and the coming into power of Thatcher in the UK, shortly followed by Reagan in the USA, are seen as signalling a different era of privatization, deregulation and a shift from the Keynesian welfare state of the postwar era. Financialization is viewed as another major aspect of the shifts.

In this section the purpose has been to highlight the work of a range of authors who have viewed financialization of the present era as changing the structures of capitalism and the relationships between finance and the non-financial sector. The brief summary here cannot, though, do justice to the rich literature on financialization and stages of capitalist development. It has, though, to be emphasized (again) that the particular forms of financialization and its effects on the economy, society and polity differ between countries and regions. As is emphasized in Chapter 4, financialization is variegated as capitalism is variegated.

Pursuit of shareholder value

The "pursuit of shareholder value" can be viewed as a statement of what corporations should do and/or a statement of what corporations actually do. The "pursuit of shareholder value" seeks to elevate policies of the corporation and correspondingly demotes the interests of other stakeholders. The idea that owners (capitalists) pursue some form of profit maximization is of long standing and many theories of the firm are centred on the assumption of the pursuit of profit maximization. The "pursuit of shareholder value" can be seen as a continuation of that tradition.

The advocacy of the pursuit of shareholder value and of profit maximization often comes from some notion that "economic efficiency" results. Such advocacy can be contrasted with ideas that corporations are managerially controlled and managers pursue their interests at the expense of the shareholders. It can also be contrasted with ideas that a corporation has numerous stakeholders and, as such, responsibilities towards the stakeholders – for example, employees, customers and, more generally, social responsibilities.

The pursuit of shareholder value can be seen in terms of a reassertion of the interests of shareholders against the notions that corporations had become managerial controlled.

Berle and Means (1932) provided one of the earliest expressions of the idea that in corporations with a large number of shareholders, the managers would pursue their own interests without significant control from the shareholders. Developments in the 1950s and 1960s included what became termed as managerial theories of the firm (such as Baumol 1959, Marris 1964) in which managerial interests were pursued to some degree in conflict with shareholder interests (e.g. sales revenue maximization versus profit maximization). It was recognized that shareholders had some residual power to constrain the activities of managers and, specifically through the operation of a takeover constraint, whereby a low valuation ratio (ratio of stock market value to capital of company) would trigger a takeover bid (Marris 1964).

The "market for corporate control" was used by authors such as Jensen and Meckling (1976), Jensen (1986) and others to express the idea that the stock market is the forum in which companies can in effect be bought and sold, and consequently exercises corporate control. This "market for corporate control" operates in such a way as to enforce some form of profit maximization and to discipline managers who do not pursue profits. Thus, the "market for corporate control" is a way in which maximization of shareholder return could be enforced and place tight constraints on managerial prerogatives. Whereas authors such as Meckling and Jensen would praise the pursuit of shareholder value and the role of the "market for corporate control" as enhancing efficiency, authors on financialization, particularly within the post-Keynesian tradition, have focused on the effects on investment and growth. Chapter 6 explores this idea in much more detail with an emphasis on the empirical work in the effects of financialization and the "pursuit of shareholder value" on investment and growth.

The "pursuit of shareholder value" is an application of the arguments of Friedman (1970) that the responsibility of a corporation and its managers is to make as much profit for the stockholders as possible and that the only social responsibility of business was to use its resources and engage in activities designed to increase its profits. But as Van der Zwan (2014: 102) notes "shareholder value is not a neutral concept, but an ideological construct that legitimates a far-reaching redistribution of wealth and power among shareholders, managers and workers". In later chapters (Chapters 7 and 8) the empirical investigations of the effects of financialization and the pursuit of shareholder value on income distribution and inequality and on employment conditions are reviewed.

Financialization of the everyday

Financialization of the everyday refers to the increasing involvement of individuals with the financial sector and that involvement can be indirect as well as direct. At its simplest, it encompasses the higher proportion of individuals who hold bank accounts and make payments by cheque and electronic transfer rather than using cash, coins and (central) bank notes. It includes the acquisition of financial assets, whether in the form of deposits with financial institutions or the purchase of equity and bonds. It has generally involved debt and borrowing, whether to fund house purchase (mortgages) or consumer expenditure.

The proponents of financialization might view this through the lens of "financial inclusion", which is enabling the participation in the financial system for payments and borrowing, in what some have called the "democratization of finance". Indeed, as will be discussed in Chapter 8, financialization as a process of involvement in the financial sector can be viewed as enabling for those previously excluded from formal financial arrangements, whether to enable house purchase or creation of small businesses. This "financial inclusion" for the previously excluded may well be a push for reducing inequality and alleviating poverty; the empirical investigations on this are reviewed in Chapter 9.

Another further aspect of the "financialization of the everyday" is the shift away from the welfare state's provision of social security towards private provision, where there are differences across countries depending on the "starting point". Pension provision is a major element of the social safety net but there is increasing reliance on the private sector, which involves growth of the financial sector and profits. Thus, the individual's pension becomes dependent on the expertise and honesty of pension fund managers and on the performance of the stock market prices, rather than on the state.

Periods of financialization

The term "financialization" has been used in several different ways and there are many different dimensions to financialization. It may also be evident that authors have investigated financialization from a range of disciplinary and inter-disciplinary perspectives and different analytical frameworks. Financialization has been a long-standing feature of capitalism for over one and half centuries in the sense of finance and financial motives tending to grow, although not in a uniform manner. The different episodes of financialization indicate that there are also periods of non-financialization, or definancialization, as the economic and political power of the financial sector retreats.

The forms that financialization takes differ from period to period (as in the work of Fasiano, Guevara and Pierros 2018, relating to the USA). Since 1980 the processes of financialization have been near global. Further, these processes have got underway at different times, with, in general, industrialized countries being at the forefront and emerging markets at later stages, with the growth of financialization in central and eastern European countries starting with the collapse the USSR in the 1990s.

The term "variegated financialization" can be used to indicate that the forms of financialization have differed across countries and take place in the context of "variegated capitalism". Variegated capitalism recognizes that there are diversities and variabilities between economies, which are dominated by profit-oriented, market-mediated relations.

In a similar vein "variegated financialization" is a recognition that the expansion of the size, power and influence of the financial sector has occurred in many economies, although taking different forms and starting from different places and in different institutional settings. In this context it has to be mentioned that much of the research on financialization, particularly early work, focused on the USA and the UK and the findings of the nature and impacts of financialization may not generalize to other countries, which have experienced financialization in different ways.

Within the broad scope provided by the extended Epstein definition, the aspects of financialization discussed above can be viewed as focusing on particular dimensions. These aspects may well have contradictory elements, and empirical and theoretical analyses of them may well reveal that these aspects do not "fit" in with the experiences in the world and that the aspects evolve over time and differ between economies.

Financialization since circa 1980 (which will be referred to as financialization in the present era) has proceeded alongside what may be termed globalization and neoliberalism. What is meant by those terms and the interdependences and interrelationships between globalization, neoliberalism and financialization are major topics in Chapter 3. It is also often observed that, at least for the industrialized countries of Europe and North America, inequality of personal income has tended to increase, which is documented in Chapter 8. The distribution of income between profits and wages has tended to move in the direction of profits, and profits (on limited information) from non-financial sector towards financial sector. The pursuit of shareholder value can be anticipated to push income towards profits, which is further discussed and evidence is presented in Chapter 7. That chapter also explores the relationships between financialization and inequality more generally.

Financialization involves the increasing roles of finance and of the financial sector. Finance is an inanimate flow of credit, loans and money. The financial sector controls the flows of finance – receiving deposits from the non-financial economy and providing loans and credit to the non-financial economy. The financial sector operates as a conduit for the flow of finance. However, it is not like a simple channel that facilitates the flow from one group (savers) to another (investors). It is rather that the direction of the flows of finance depend on decisions made by people working in the financial institutions (and now often by algorithms that determine who is deemed creditworthy and who is not). A major part of the power of the financial sector comes from its role as deciding who receives loans and who does not. This power may range from credit ratings for governments and other organizations through to "red lining" (taking its name from a red line being drawn around areas of towns or cities to exclude properties in such areas or people living there from mortgage provision, which was particularly prevalent in the USA) (see, e.g. Dymski, Hernandez & Mohanty 2013, which is further discussed in Chapter 9).

The power of the financial sector can be reflected in its profits and in the pay of executives of financial institutions. As will be seen in later chapters, many have seen financialization as reflected in a shift of profits towards the financial sector and in the growth of rewards of the executives representing rent rather than productivity.

It would not be possible to envisage capitalism without a substantial financial sector. Commercial banks and stock markets date back to before the nineteenth century and their growth gets underway during that century alongside industrialization. Indeed, "financialisation is hardly a new phenomenon in circuits of capital. What is perhaps relatively new is the extent to which finance has found its way into most, if not all, of the nooks and crannies of social life" (Lee *et al.* 2009: 727–8).

Bortz and Kaltenbrunner (2018) place the start of international finance at the time of the Crusades (the first of which was in the late eleventh century) and ask whether the financialization process is simply a matter of volume. They argue that there have been distinct domestic financialization processes alongside changes in international financial markets and the ways in which economic agents relate to those markets. "These changes have gone beyond a mere increase in international capital flows, and have entailed important changes in the type of actors, instruments and market dominant in international financial relations ... [t]here change have been shaped by, and have themselves exacerbated the subordinated position of DEE [developing and emerging economies] in the international economic and financial system and hence have contributed to uneven international development" (*ibid.*: 376).

Financialization, particularly in terms of the increasing role of financial institutions and markets, has been an ongoing process throughout capitalism. Vercelli (2013: 22) envisages that "the secular tendency towards a progressive financialization of the economy has developed very slowly because it has been often constrained – if not repressed – for religious, ethical, and political reasons", and points to usury laws as one example. In recent decades, what was termed "financial repression" involved control over level of interest rates (particularly on deposits) and over level of credit. Indeed, "the driving force of financialization as evolutionary process is rooted in a fairly continuous flow of financial innovation, some of which are epoch making, meant to remove existing obstacles to the flexibility of exchanges" (*ibid.*: 21).

In the growth of the financial system through innovation, Vercelli (2013: 23) emphasizes the double-edged nature of financial innovation. On the one hand, at the microeconomic level, "financial innovations increase the current and intertemporal flexibility of choices". On the other hand, "flexibility-enhancing innovations very often produce negative externalities at the macro level. In particular, a micro increase of efficiency produced by enhanced flexibility is often accompanied by more systemic instability that may jeopardize systemic efficiency". Innovation (in banking practices, in types of financial institutions, in financial products, etc.) and financial liberalization have been hallmarks of financialization in the present era.

Vercelli (2013) identifies two periods of rapid financialization. The first is dated from the second half of the nineteenth century through to the start of the Great Depression around 1929. In this first period of financialization, much attention is placed on the financial sectors of the USA and a range of European countries (notably the UK and Germany), although there were some global aspects in that portfolio investments were made by those industrialized countries in other countries. But the financial sectors of those other countries were not on the scale of the industrialized countries. In the first financialization, capitalism expanded, supported by the state, into new geographical areas through imperialism and colonialism. Vercelli views the first financialization as "bank-based financialization", whereas the second financialization is viewed more in terms of "market-based financialization".

Tomveronachi (2020) speaks in terms of "ages of financial stability" since the late nineteenth century. The first period, running through to 1929, was characterized by "the increasing relevance of monetary and financial factors in expanding the breadth of economic fluctuations". The post-1929 period through to the end of the Second World War is viewed in terms of the assertive role of nation states in war and in the emerging welfare state. He analyses two accomplishments of this period – the Glass-Steagall Act regulating the US financial system and the Bretton Woods agreement with a negotiated monetary order intended to govern monetary relations among independent states within a fixed exchange framework. However, "their weaknesses, due in part to a limited vision of the functioning of the financial system and to the pressure by financial vested interests, were responsible for their later demise." (*ibid.*: 171).

The immediate postwar Bretton Woods period, lasting until the effective collapse of Bretton Woods fixed exchange rate regime in August 1971, meant that "low exposure to private global finance and domestic constraints on banks' operations may be at least in part responsible for its limited number and depth of financial crises". The period since the collapse of Bretton Woods, broadly the present era of financialization, shows that "the increasing domination of vested interests helped by the theoretical laissez-faire approach produces the reversal of state protagonism, a heavy qualitative and quantitative evolution of finance, and related changes in financial regulation and supervision" (*ibid.*). The resulting financial fragility leads into the many financial crises. Hence, two periods of financial instability connected with financial globalization, with the first culminating with the 1929 crisis, while the second characterizes the more recent experience starting from the 1970s.

Statistics on loans can be used to illustrate one of the features of earlier periods of financialization, and there would be comparable rises in bank deposits as loans are one side of banks' balance sheets and deposits on the other. The picture in Figure 2.1a for the period 1870 to 1929 relates to seven major countries (which now make up the membership of the G7) and is of general rising loans to GDP ratio. In the case of Germany, the general rise took the loans to GDP ratio from 24 per cent in 1870 to 104 per cent in 1914, to be followed during the First World War and the postwar recession a fall to 5 per cent in 1924, and then gradual rise.

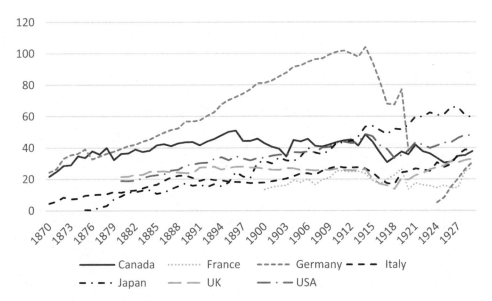

Figure 2.1a Bank loans to GDP 1870 to 1929 (per cent)

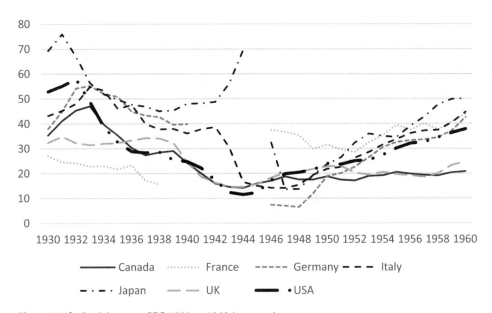

Figure 2.1b Bank loans to GDP 1930 to 1960 (per cent)

The notion that the period 1930 to 1960, encompassing the depressions of the inter-war period, the Second World War and the postwar recovery, was one from which financialization was largely absent, is illustrated in Figure 2.1b. The loans to GDP ratio tended to decline during the 1930s and to rise during the 1950s, with the ratio being significantly lower in 1960 as compared with 1930 (France being the only exception).

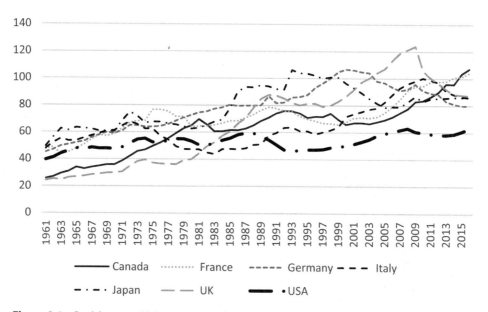

Figure 2.1c Bank loans to GDP 1960 to 2016 (per cent)
Source: calculated from statistics from Jorda-Schularick-Taylor, Macrohistory Database www.macrohistory.net/data/ (downloaded November 2020)

Treating the loans to GDP as one element of financial deepening and financialization, these data fit with the pattern of financialization in the period from 1870 (when the data start) to 1929, followed by a period of definancialization.

The 1950s and 1960s for the industrialized countries can be seen as a recovery from the definancialization of the interwar period. Vercelli (2013) portrays the second period of financialization emerging from the collapse of the Bretton Woods system in the early 1970s. In this second period, financialization has become a near-universal phenomenon and closely associated with neoliberalism and globalization, which are to be viewed as three mutually reinforcing phenomena.

Over the period 1960 to 2016, all the G7 countries show a very substantial increase in the loans to GDP ratio as may be seen from Figure 2.1c. The loans to GDP ratio in 2016 was on average well over double the ratio in 1960, with substantial increases for all the countries included.

Figure 2.2 reports the ratio of M3/GDP for the period 1870–2015, recalling that M3 is a measure of the stock of money, including bank deposits in chequing and time deposits (as well as notes and coins in circulation). This can again be considered a measure of financial deepening. These figures for M3 show similar trends to those for loans, albeit in general at a slower pace of increase.

These simple statistics serve as an illustration of the long-standing growth at varying paces of the financial sector. As indicated above, financialization in the present era is more than the growth of financial institutions. The periodization from Minsky mentioned above is a reflection of that. A further illustration comes from the work of Fasianos,

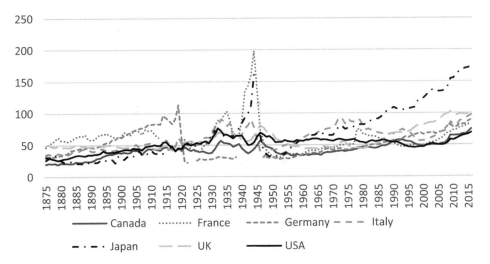

Figure 2.2 Broad money/GDP (per cent), 1875–2015
Source: calculated from statistics from Jorda-Schularick-Taylor, Macrohistory Database www.macrohistory.net/data/ (downloaded November 2020)

Guevara and Pierros (2018: 35). With specific reference to the USA during the twentieth century (plus the first decade of the twenty-first) they identify "four distinct regimes, marked by structural breaks in the institutional setting of the economy, which affected the functioning of the financial sector". A first period lasts from the beginning of the twentieth century until 1933 and the ensuing regulation of the financial sector, notably the Glass-Steagall Act. The second is the remaining years of the 1930s, while the third covers the years of the "golden age of capitalist development" through to 1973. The fourth period encompasses 1974 to 2010, a period of "financialized capitalism".

In the first period (1900–33) the authors find for the USA that there was dominance of the financial sector with the income share of the financial sector moderately high. There was shareholder orientation with moderate intensity of financial innovation. Household indebtedness was considered moderately high and income inequality high. Free capital mobility prevailed and there was inclination to financial crises.

In the next two periods (1934–40 and 1945–73) the authors find there was not financial sector dominance with the income share of the financial sector low. Financial regulation, low-income inequality, absence of free capital mobility and low inclination to financial crises were other common features of the two periods. The authors considered that in the 1934–40 period, intensity of financial innovation was moderate, switching to high in the 1945–73 period. Household indebtedness moved from low in the earlier period to moderate in the later period.

The final period (1974–2010) was judged to be rather similar to the first period. The differences, which indicate a more intense financialization in the recent period, put the income share of the financial sector as high (rather than moderately high), and a high intensity of financial innovation and high household indebtedness.

Conclusions

The terrain of study of financialization is viewed in terms of the increasing role of financial motives, financial markets, financial actors and financial institutions in the operation of the domestic and international economies, societies and social life, polities and political debates and the ecosystem. The focus is on financialization in western industrialized economies since circa 1980. It is recognized that this is only a partial view in that financialization has been a near-global phenomenon, particularly since 1990.[7]

Financialization in the present era has proceeded alongside globalization and the application of neoliberal doctrines, and in Chapter 3 some of their interrelationships with financialization are explored. In Chapter 4 the focus is on the changing nature and scope of the financial sector over the past four decades or so. The general perspective can be summarized in the term "variegated financialization", which is a general phenomenon of growing financial sector and finance with many variations between countries and over time. Within that chapter, the statistics used extend through to mid-2010s where possible, and the discussion is split into the pre-GFCs of 2007–09 and the post-GFCs as a prelude to considering how far the trends of financialization have continued and whether there is evidence of a definancialization (as occurred after 1930).

Financialization is a global phenomenon and, in Chapter 5, features of financialization in DEEs are considered. In subsequent chapters, the dimensions of financialization – financial liberalization, "pursuit of shareholder power" and "financialization of the everyday" are examined in detail. Financialization has gone alongside higher inequality and the relationship is also examined. These chapters discuss how these dimensions of financialization have developed (and indeed whether the claims made with respect to these dimensions have actually occurred) and explore the consequences of these dimensions for economic and social performance. Consideration of those consequences is brought together in Chapter 11, when the question is asked as to whether the financial sector and finance have become dysfunctional. The final chapter is a forward look at definancialization.

---

7. In part, 1990 or thereabouts is significant as marking the collapse of the Soviet Union and the COMECON (a byname for the Council for Mutual Economic Assistance) system.

3
FINANCIALIZATION, NEOLIBERALISM AND GLOBALIZATION

Although my focus is on the financialization of the past four decades, there have been earlier periods of financialization. The processes involved in financialization during the past 40 years have taken many forms, and although these waves of financialization, as in earlier financializations, have taken shape in the western industrialized countries, they have subsequently spread to most countries around the globe. For western industrialized countries, the quarter of a century ending in 1973 has often been portrayed as the "golden age of capitalism" (Marglin & Schor 1992), with relatively high rates of economic growth and low unemployment, and a Keynesian welfare state policy framework. The period since circa 1980 has generally been one of intense financialization and of globalization. It is also often described as a neoliberal era in social, political and economic terms.

There is a great deal of debate about the scope and definition of each of the three terms – financialization, globalization and neoliberalism. They were by no means new phenomena and each has a long history. There have been intensifications of financialization and globalization in the decades after 1980, although as considered below, with some slowing down or even reversal since the GFCs. Agendas of deregulation, privatization and marketization, which are closely associated with doctrines of neoliberalism, have been replacing the social democratic Keynesian agendas of the earlier postwar years. Epstein (2005: 3), for example, argued that, since circa 1980, "the economies of the world have undergone profound transformations. Some of the dimensions of this altered reality are clear: the role of government has diminished while that of markets has increased: economic transactions between countries have substantially risen; domestic and international financial transactions have grown by leaps and bounds. ... In short, this changing landscape has been characterized by the rise of neoliberalism, globalization and financialization".

Financialization has been a near-global phenomenon over the past four decades or so. Its dimensions in the industrialized economies of western Europe and North America are elaborated on in Chapter 4, and the features of financialization in emerging markets and developing economies are outlined in Chapter 5. The purpose there is to indicate the trends of financialization and how they compare with those of the industrialized countries.

This chapter begins by considering finance as a facilitator of the processes of globalization and the degree to which finance has been involved with the growth of international trade (in financial services) and with foreign direct investment. This chapter also considers the links between neoliberalism and financialization, and financialization and the state.

Globalization and financialization

Globalization has involved the growth of trade between nations, the internationalization of production organized across national borders and supply chains, the expansion of foreign direct investment and portfolio investments. It has often involved a regionalization in the sense that the growth of trade occurs within a region of countries and is fostered by free trade and customs unions between neighbouring countries (e.g. NAFTA, the free-trade area of Canada, Mexico and the USA – now the US–Mexico–Canada Agreement (USMCA) and the European Union, which involves more social and political integration than being simply an economic customs union). Globalization has involved increased flows of capital across national borders and also the migration of people. It involves the development of rules governing international transactions and of international organizations such as the World Trade Organization (WTO). The focus here is on the trade and capital flow features of globalization.

The period 1870–1914 can be described as the first "golden age" of globalization with world trade relative to GDP moving from 9 per cent in 1870 to 16 per cent in 1914. A period of deglobalization followed with the trade to GDP ratio falling to 5.5 per cent, around one-third of the level in 1914. A period of reglobalization came after the Second World War with world trade approaching the pre-1914 levels in the late 1970s. In a fourth era of hyperglobalization, trade to GDP rose to 33 per cent in 2008. "Global FDI [Financial Development Index] as a share of world GDP, which hovered around 0.5 per cent through the 1970s and into the 1980s peaked at near to 4 per cent just before the global financial crises" (Subramanian & Kessler 2013: 5). During the 1990s, globalization continued apace, with FDI growing at an average annual rate of 15.3 per cent, international trade at 6.2 per cent and global GDP at 3.8 per cent (UNCTAD 2020: 123). The corresponding figures for the 2000s are 8 per cent, 9 per cent and 7 per cent. In the 2010s, FDI barely grew, with an average annual rate of 0.8 per cent, and international trade at 2.7 per cent annual rate growing slightly slower than global GDP at 3.1 per cent.

There has been much recognition of an era of globalization starting in the late nineteenth century and ending with the First World War. Hirst and Thompson (2019: 16) argue that the second half of the twentieth century was not remarkable when compared with the period 1850–1914, when "in that period flows of merchandise trade, capital investment and labour migration were all comparable to or greater than those of today". The interwar years, and particularly the 1930s, involved a contraction of globalization. Throughout the postwar period, there has been a strong revival of globalization. Palley (2018) argues that postwar globalization can be divided into two eras. He characterized a "Keynesian era second globalization", which like the first era of globalization was driven by "gains from trade" alongside rising real wages in the industrialized countries. The subsequent "neoliberal third globalization" has been driven by foreign direct investment and the development of international supply chains.

Vercelli (2013, 2016), among others, has noted the overlap of timing between financialization and globalization during the first era of financialization. "The process of financialization may thrive only to the extent that the spatial constraints on exchange are removed, while the process of globalization may be implemented to the extent that it is supported by internalized finance" (Vercelli 2013: 25). As Vercelli argues, the processes of financialization and of globalization need the cross-country flow of goods, services and capital as permissive factors in their growth. The interwar period saw the reversals of globalization under impacts of protectionism and depression, and the financial collapses that heralded the start of a definancialization (as noted in Chapter 2).

The postwar period has generally been one in which international trade has grown faster than global GDP. This expansion has been fostered by international and regional trade agreements, rounds of general tariff reductions and the emergence of regional free-trade blocs such as the European Union, ASEAN (Association of Southeast Asian Nations), NAFTA and Mercosur. International trade tended to grow rapidly, at least until 2009 when there was sharp fall in the immediate aftermath of the GFCs. International trade through to 2008 grew around twice as fast as world GDP, and Figure 3.1 shows the rise in merchandise trade from 17.5 per cent of global GDP in 1980 to a peak of 25 per cent in 2007, before falling back to 21.4 per cent in 2019. Trade in commercial services (data are only available from 1980) shows a doubling from 3.3 per cent of global GDP in 1980 to 6.9 per cent in 2019.

The growth rate of exports in goods (in real terms) shows a slowdown: from annual growth rate of 6 per cent in the 1990s to 4.9 per cent in the 2000s and to 3.8 per cent in the decade ending in 2019.

International trade requires financing, credit and insurance arrangements, and the growth of international trade then requires the growth of the financial sector in those respects. The exchange of currencies, and hence the development of foreign exchange markets, accompanies the growth of international trade. However, it is often observed that the growth of foreign exchange dealings far outstrips that required for the financing of international trade and, indeed, financing associated with foreign direct investment. The figures in Table 3.1 refer to daily averages. With trading on a five-day-a-week basis, the volume of currency trading in 2016 was equivalent to nearly 20 times global GDP.

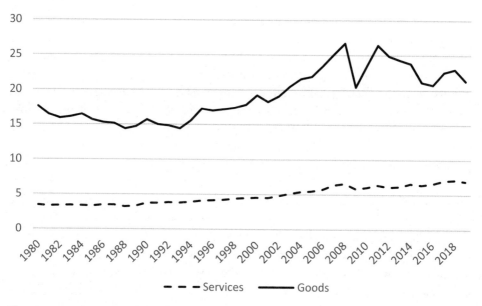

Figure 3.1 Trade/GDP ratio (per cent)
Source: calculated from WTO data (trade) and World Bank (GDP)

Table 3.1 Over-the-counter (OTC) foreign exchange turnover by country in April 1986–2019, "net-gross" basis

Daily averages, in billions of US dollars

1986	1989	1992	1995	1998	2001	2004	2007	2010	2013	2016	2019
206	744	1,115	1,633	2,099	1,705	2,608	4,281	5,045	6,686	6,514	8,301

Source: BIS data

The rapid growth of the trade in financial services in the 2000s is illustrated in Figure 3.2 (figures before 2005 are not available). The top line is the global exports in financial services, showing a rapid increase from 2005 to 2007 of around 60 per cent, with further growth after 2009 and over a 12-year period from 2005 a 111 per cent increase. Although the exports of financial services by the UK and USA continued to grow (in nominal terms), their market share declined and the USA overtook the UK. The dominance of the UK and the USA in respect of financial services is clearly evident.

The WTO's negotiations on financial services concluded successfully on 12 December 1997 after 70 WTO members reached a multilateral agreement to open their financial services sectors. The landmark agreement brings trade in this sector – worth trillions of dollars – under the WTO's multilateral rules on a permanent and full

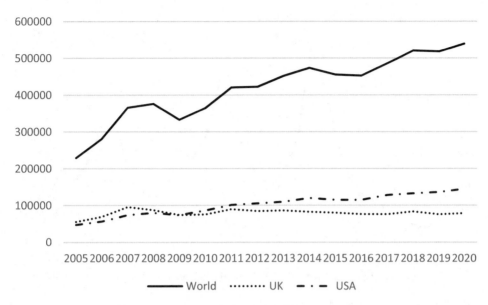

Figure 3.2 Exports of financial services (millions of US dollars)
Source: calculated from WTO data

most-favoured-nation basis. The agreement covers more than 95 per cent of trade in banking, insurance, securities and financial information.[1]

The operation of multinational corporations on an international basis has been long-standing of many centuries, although in the early days such companies were more akin to trading companies. In global terms, the flow of foreign direct investment rose from around 0.5 per cent of global GDP in the first half of the 1980s to peak at 4 per cent in 2000, and maintained a figure of around 2 per cent thereafter (Figure 3.3). The increase in scale is considerable, although it could be compared with gross investment to GDP ratios of the order of 20 per cent.

The stock of foreign direct investment (Figure 3.4) rose almost continuously from 1990 onwards with a significant drop around the time of the GFCs (likely to be related to issues of valuation) starting from just over 5 per cent of global GDP and reaching 35 per cent by 2016. The growth of foreign direct investment is not just a matter of investment across international boundaries but the coordination of production across borders through the operation of transnational corporations and the development of international supply networks.

The expansion of the financial system in the global setting is a dimension of financialization and has implications for the rest of the economy. Global financialization involves the growth of financial markets that operate on a global basis. The use of the term "market" brings connotations of a specific geographic location and with a very low

---

1. See WTO press release, "Successful conclusion of the WTO's financial services negotiations", www.wto. org/english/news_e/pres97_e/pr86_e.htm

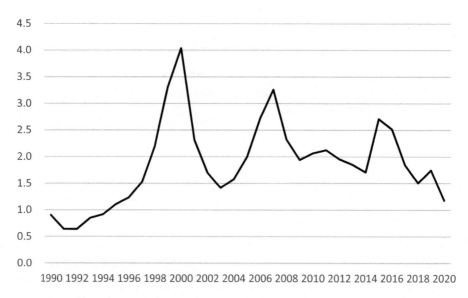

Figure 3.3 Inflows of FDI as percentage of GDP
Source: calculated from UNCTAD and World Bank data

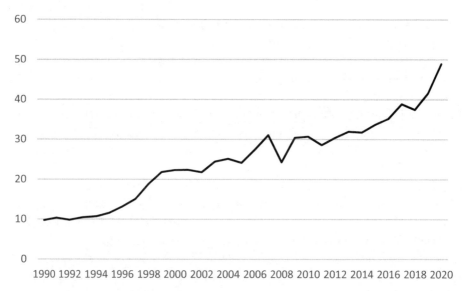

Figure 3.4 World stock of FDI as percentage of GDP
Source: calculated from UNCTAD and World Bank data

degree of price diversity within the market. In the digital age, the location of buyers and sellers in a market becomes of less significance. Financial markets in different locations are linked – if a commodity is traded in several different markets, arbitrage between the markets would likely lead to some uniformity of price; the feasibility of such trading is dependent on the absence of controls on movement between countries and trading taking place in the same currency such as the US dollar. Global financialization also involves higher flows of capital between countries and particularly gross flows of capital – that is capital flows from country A to country B and from B to A, and again fostered by lowering or removal of capital controls.[2]

The gross flows of capital across national borders have rapidly increased and current and capital account imbalances have grown. Global financial markets and linkages between national financial markets intensify. One measure of what is sometimes labelled "international financialization" is the ratio of foreign assets plus foreign liabilities to GDP of a country. The median value of that ratio for 24 industrialized countries since 1970 is shown in Figure 3.5 with a doubling of the ratio during the 1990s and a more than doubling between 2000 and the onset of the GFCs, and a flattening off after the GFCs.

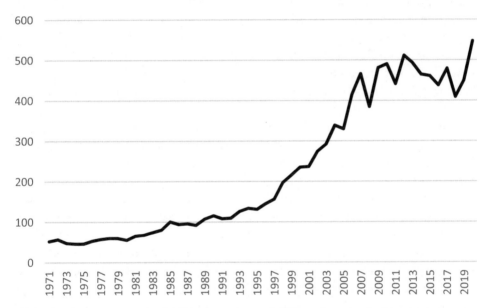

Figure 3.5 Foreign assets plus liabilities (percentage of GDP; median value for 24 countries)
Source: calculated from Lane, P. & G. Milesi-Ferretti, External Wealth of Nations database (based on Lane, P. % G. Milesi-Ferretti, 2018, "The external wealth of nations revisited: international financial integration in the aftermath of the global financial crisis", *IMF Economic Review* 66, 189–222.
Countries included: Australia, Austria, Belgium, Canada, Denmark, Finland, France, Germany, Greece, Hungary, Iceland, Ireland, Italy, Japan, Netherlands, New Zealand, Norway, Poland, Portugal, South Africa, Spain, Sweden, Switzerland, Turkey, United Kingdom, United States

---

2. The distinction may be drawn (e.g. Thompson 2019: 35) between an inter-nationalized [with a hyphen] economic structure and a globalized economic structure. "An *inter-nationalized economy* is an economy made up of a series of individual national economies that interact between themselves mainly via activities like trade interdependency, investment integration and migration. … [A] *globalized economy* would be an economy that existed as a single economic entity in its own right somewhat beyond the interacting individual national economies".

Although global financial markets are spoken about, it is still the case that financial markets trade in financial assets denominated in different currencies, and without a global currency aligned with a global central bank willing and able to act as a lender of last resort. But there are a few countries that can borrow in international markets in their own currency and benefit from being able to do so. The dominance of a few major currencies in the currency trading illustrated in Table 3.1 is related to the currency hierarchies. The ability of a country to borrow (whether from its own residents or from overseas) in its own currency provides protection against fluctuating value of liabilities and, for the government, the ability to tax and to issue money to enable payment of interest and principal of debt. A currency that is high up in the currency hierarchy has greater liquidity and a stable value of the currency and benefits from lower borrowing costs (Kaltenbrunner 2015).

Kaltenbrunner and Painceira (2018: 290) argue that the hierarchical international monetary system changes the financial behaviour of domestic economic agents and thereby the structure of the financial system (further discussed in Chapter 5). Two processes are at work. "The first process highlights the phenomenon of reserve accumulation and the changing behaviour of domestic banks. The second points to ECEs' [emerging capitalist economies] sustained external vulnerability".

Commodities are often traded on what may be regarded as closely interlinked markets, which could be considered global markets, often using the dollar as the unit of account. There has long been provision of hedging and forward contracts in such markets, which on the one hand seeks to transfer risk between the parties to the contracts and on the other facilitates speculation. One element of the processes of securitization and derivatives has been the growth of securities, which are based on primary commodities. As UNCTAD (2015: 21) wrote: "financialization of commodity markets refers to the observation that commodities have become an asset class for portfolio investors, just like equities and bonds". They add that there is "a significant body of analysis suggest[ing] that commodity price dynamics have changed substantially since the early 2000s, and that these changes have been associated with a sizeable increase in financial investors' positions on commodity markets, as well as with changes in the composition of these positions. ... [The evidence on financial positions on commodity markets (assets under management)] increased dramatically prior to the global financial crisis and during the period 2009–2011. They reached a peak of almost $450 billion in the first half of 2011 and declined from a level that was still over $420 billion in January 2013, to about $270 billion in May 2015. While this is a sizeable drop, the level ... is still close to its pre-crisis peak of mid-2008."

There has long been trading in assets that are linked with commodities (alongside trading in commodities themselves). The most notable example would be trading future contracts for commodities, which would enable, for example, a commodity producer to secure a price for future delivery. The rapid growth of commodity-related assets would suggest the scale of trading in these assets has gone way beyond that required for such hedging. The financialization of commodities is one dimension of the spread of finance into areas hitherto untouched. The crucial question is whether economic and social purpose results from the development of commodity-related financial assets. The development of and trading in such assets has resource costs. Are there matching benefits? Further, does the trading in such financial assets have effects, for good or ill, on the real economy?

Financialization and neoliberalism

Neoliberalism, like the terms financialization and globalization, is contested and conjures up a range of interpretations. The doctrines of neoliberalism celebrate the workings of competitive "free" markets spurred on by incentives and pursuit of profits and emphasize the extension of market mechanisms – the spread of market transactions into areas previously excluded – and on the deregulation of markets. Neoliberalism emphasizes the beneficial roles of markets and of competition, drawing heavily on Austrian and neoclassical economics. The neoclassical tradition leads to the view that perfectly competitive markets lead to outcomes that are deemed efficient and (Pareto) optimal. The assumptions that need to be made (such as absence of externalities and economies of scale) may be viewed as strong (implausible) but, nevertheless, used to underpin arguments for removal of restrictions and regulations, which are considered to hamper a competitive outcome.

The Austrian approach stresses the entrepreneurial discovery processes of competition. A case for a neoliberal policy agenda based on such theoretical analysis rests on that analysis providing a good guide to how a capitalist economy operates (see various chapters in Saad-Filho & Johnston 2005). Following Harvey (2005: 2), neoliberalism is in the first instance a theory of political economic practices that proposes that human well-being can best be advanced by liberating individual entrepreneurial freedoms and skills within an institutional framework characterized by strong private property rights, free markets and free trade. The role of the state is to create and preserve an institutional framework appropriate to such practices. The state has to guarantee, for example, the quality and integrity of money. It must also set up those military, defence, police and legal structures and functions required to secure private property rights and to guarantee, by force if need be, the proper functioning of markets. Furthermore, if markets do not exist (in areas such as land, water, education, health care, social security or environmental pollution), then they must be created, by state action if necessary. But beyond these tasks the state should not venture. State interventions in markets (once created) must be kept to a bare minimum because, according to the theory, the state cannot possibly possess enough information to second-guess market signals (prices) and because powerful interest groups will inevitably distort and bias state interventions (particularly in democracies) for their own benefit.

The policy agenda, which has close connections with what was described as Thatcherism and Reaganism and with many elements of the Washington Consensus, promotes liberalization and deregulation as moves towards "free" markets. It promotes the extension of markets into areas of economic and social activity that were organized and coordinated through cooperation and social rules and norms. It promotes "free" trade, private over public ownership and mutual cooperative ownership and, as such, privatization. In this context "free" is put in quotation marks as the notion of a free market is challenged – any market operates under some forms of contract law and social norms and often with the exercise of market.

The Washington Consensus (a term coined by Williamson 1990; see Rodrik 2006) had numerous dimensions that fostered globalization, neoliberalism and financialization. These include interest rates that are market determined and positive in real terms, trade liberalization, liberalization of inward foreign direct investment, privatization of state enterprises and deregulation. In Chapter 6, the ways in which the general financial liberalization agenda was promoted and the effects of financial liberalization on economic performance and the occurrence of financial crises are discussed further.

Many authors have linked financialization (at least in the present era) with neoliberalism. Vercelli (2013, 2016), for example, portrays it as a neoliberal financialization. The argument here is that financialization and, more generally, perceptions of the financial sector have strong elements of "neoliberalism in action".

In the promotion of markets and competition, and drawing on welfare propositions in neoclassical economics, there are strong notions that (perfect) competition promotes economic efficiency. In the financial literature, financial markets are often portrayed as in some sense efficient. The term efficiency has been used in a range of different ways but obviously conveys something desirable and identifies markets and financial institutions more broadly with being efficient. In the finance and in significant parts of the macroeconomics literature, the efficient-market hypothesis (EMH) postulates that, in a competitive market, asset prices fully reflect all available information.

Fama (1970: 383), who was awarded the Nobel prize in economics for his work on asset pricing, argued that "[t]he primary role of the capital market is allocation of ownership of the economy's capital stock" rather than the allocation of funds. However, he saw that "the ideal is a market in which prices provide accurate signals for resource allocation: that is, a market in which firms can make production-investment decisions, and investors can choose among the securities that represent ownership of firms' activities under the assumption that security prices at any time 'fully reflect' all available information. A market in which prices always 'fully reflect' available information is called 'efficient'".

There are three variants of the hypothesis: "weak", "semi-strong" and "strong" forms. The weak form of the EMH claims that prices on traded assets reflect all past, publicly available information; the semi-strong form claims that prices reflect all publicly available information and that prices instantly change to reflect new public information. The strong form of the EMH additionally claims that prices reflect all information, even that which is only available to some ("insiders"). The significance of the EMH is its predictions, specifically that market prices reflect relevant information. In a sense, financial assets, whether equity, bonds or currency exchange trade at a "fair value". Prices of assets follow a random walk insofar as information arrives in a "random fashion", and since the price incorporates relevant information, it would not be possible for an individual's financial returns to systematically outperform the market.

The growth of the financial sector has been fuelled by deregulation and has featured the growth of market mechanisms. The movements towards deregulation and liberalization of the financial sector are discussed in Chapter 5. The degree to which there has been privatization and demutualization of financial institutions is documented in Chapter 4.

Neoliberalism celebrates the role of markets and the extension of markets into areas of human life where they had not previously operated. Individuals become much more engaged with financial calculations than previously (as will be explored in Chapter 9). Functions and activities that had been undertaken within the family or by the state are increasingly undertaken by and through financial markets and institutions. A notable example is pension provision and the shifts from public (often pay-as-you) pension arrangements to occupational pensions and private/individual provision. The expansion of the financial sector is thereby enhanced (specifically pension funds in that example), and individuals become reliant on the financial sector and its performance for their pensions rather than on the state or the family. The pension fund accumulates pension contributions and becomes a substantial owner of bonds and equity and, as such, becomes one part of financial institutions and others pursuing shareholder value (see Chapter 7 on shareholder value and its consequences).

Financialization and the state

The state is closely entangled with the processes of financialization. Karwowski (2019) points to four ways in which financialization works in and through public institutions and is promoted by public policies. She labels these fours ways in terms of adoption of financial logics, advancing financial innovation (i.e. the promotion and creation of new financial instruments and markets), embracing financial accumulation strategies and directly financializing the lives of citizens. It has long been recognized that markets do not occur spontaneously, rather the state becomes closely involved through provision of money, contract law, property rights and the regulation of competition and monopoly. In a similar vein, financialization is fostered by the state.

The growth of the financial sector has been promoted over the past decades through deregulation and liberalization, and the ways in which this has operated and their effects are further examined in Chapter 6. The liberalization has generally fostered the promotion and creation of new financial instruments and markets and, in turn, financial innovation has made regulation difficult.

The state has for many centuries drawn on financial markets and banks for borrowing. Public investment is often perceived in terms of borrowing from the financial sector. The private sector, and specifically the financial sector, have become more closely involved through public-private partnerships (PPP) and private finance initiatives (PFI), which have the effects of more costly finance and the closer involvement of the financial sector (as discussed in Chapter 10). The "financialization of the everyday" is one of the major dimensions of financialization. The privatization of activities previously undertaken by the state has been a route through which the financialization of the everyday has evolved.

Davis and Walsh (2016: 669–70) consider the role played by the UK state in the rise of financialization in the UK, and the institutional mechanisms by which financialization was supported. The authors focus on the relationship between and policies promoted by the Treasury and the Department of Trade and Industry (which went through numerous name changes). "The departments covering trade and industry were generally directed by economic thinking which sought to manage and boost UK-based industries, at home and abroad. They were central to the tripartite politics and Keynesian economic consensus that had directed the UK state's policy framework from the late 1930s onwards." They note that the Department of Trade and Industry had close links with trade unions and business leaders. In contrast, the Treasury's main outside links were with City institutions and the Bank of England. "In terms of hard fiscal and regulatory measures, the Treasury made a series of changes that were designed to free up markets generally ... but often worked to benefit financial markets at the expense of UK industry." The Treasury and Department of Trade and Industry actively contributed to the financialization of British industry, including through the privatisation programme, which between 1979 and 1996 involves 59 major public sales of government-owned businesses worth £65 billion and 88 private sales worth £6.7 billion. Further, "the government entered into Public-Private Partnerships (PPP) agreements and began outsourcing many state services" (*ibid.*: 667) with, in 2007, 20 per cent of public expenditure on outsourced services.

The financial sector has proved adept at exercising power through lobbying. The approach to the regulation of the financial sector (Chapter 8) illustrates the ways in which the financial sector is able to set the policy agenda, exercise "regulatory capture" and generally frustrate reforms. The "revolving door" of senior public servants and financial executives moving back and forth between the public sector and the private sector employment contributes to "norms and discursive practices [being] shared across public authorities and financial institutions, forming an epistemic community" (Karowowski 2019: 1008).

Conclusions

Financialization, globalization and neoliberalism (and the expansion of capitalist markets) are three sides of the same triangle. The statistics in the next chapter will illustrate some dimensions of the processes of financialization since circa 1980. The intensities of financialization will be well illustrated, particularly during the 1990s and the 2000s, with a tendency for financialization to slow after the GFCs. Globalization in terms of the growth of international trade and foreign direct investment have to also tended to slow after the GFCs.

The expansion of the financial sector facilitates the growth of trade, foreign direct and portfolio investment, and trade and investment cannot grow without an accompanying growth of finance. However, the exchanges for financial assets have far exceeded that required for the financing of international trade. The expansion of the financial system in its size and scope is supported by academic theorizing on the efficiency of markets in general and financial markets in particular, which comes to the fore in Chapter 5 in respect of the promotion of deregulation and financial liberalization.

Financialization is, in several respects, neoliberalism in action, with the promotion of market activities and the spread of market activities into previously non-market arenas. Neoliberal policies to promote markets and competition and to reduce regulations have been promoted on the grounds that economic efficiency and performance would thereby be improved. The growth performance of industrialized economies alongside the general rises in income and wealth inequality cast questions such a proposition; in Chapter 6 doubts are cast on such a proposition as it relates to the financial sector and its reregulation. Chapter 8 examines the impacts on inequality and poverty of the triangle of financialization, globalization and neoliberalism with emphasis on the impacts of financialization.

4

THE CHARACTERISTICS OF (VARIEGATED) FINANCIALIZATION IN THE PRESENT ERA

In this chapter I set out the ways in which the financial sector has evolved and expanded over the past three to four decades and enquire into variations in the rate of expansion since the GFCs. In the discussion, it is evident that the developments in the financial sector conform to the working definition of financialization in terms of an increasing role for financial markets, financial actors and financial institutions. There has been a general substantial growth of the financial sector but the rates of growth vary widely across countries, which is perhaps not surprising in light of the differences in the scale of the financial sector at the beginning of the 1980s in different countries. In comparing the growth of the sector across a range of developed countries we can assess the extent to which there has been a convergence between the financial systems. The differences, which are revealed below, within the general processes of financialization are termed "variegated financialization".

The statistics in this chapter relate to what are termed by the International Monetary Fund (IMF) and others as advanced economies, with DEEs considered in the next chapter. The statistics are presented (where available) for each of the G7 countries. As far as the available data permit, the coverage of the data starts around 1980, although it will be seen that many of the data series (at least on a consistent basis) do not start until the mid-1990s.

In setting out the characteristics of financialization, this chapter is limited to quantitative measures relating to industrialized economies. Financial liberalization and deregulation of the financial sector, as part of the neoliberal agenda, has been a feature of the present era of financialization, at least through to the GFCs of 2007–09, and this is documented and discussed in Chapter 6.

Scale and structure of the financial sector

The features of financialization[1] include the rapid growth of financial institutions and their assets and liabilities, the growth of financial markets, including equity markets,

---

1. This listing follows that of Ashman and Fine (2013) and Fine (2011) with elaborations.

and a tendency for markets to grow faster than financial institutions. There is a proliferation of types of financial assets through derivatives and securitization, and the growth of futures markets in an extended range of items. In basic terms this is "the capitalization of almost everything" (Leyshon & Thrift 2007). In other words, it is the formation of financial assets, the value of which is based on a prospective stream of income where that future income can be based on interest payments on loans.

The shift from financial assets issued by financial institutions with a fixed rate of interest to financial assets based on a future income stream increases speculative activities; that is, speculating on price changes. The development of futures markets and derivatives involves trading in financial assets rather than trading in commodities. The increase in corporations engaging in financial investment rather than productive investment is another related aspect of financialization. The greater involvement of households with the financial sector is reflected in rising household debt (and some of the consequences of the rising debt will be examined in Chapter 9).

Banks have traditionally shared the common feature of holding deposits from individuals and from corporations and of making loans. The ability of an institution to accept deposits is generally subject to legal approval and regulation, and the general term bank is used for a deposit-accepting institution. In general, banks "borrow short and lend long" in the sense that bank deposits can generally be withdrawn at short notice, whereas loans are provided on a longer-term basis. This poses issues of illiquidity (if deposits are withdrawn) and insolvency (if the value of assets of banks falls and the prospect of loan defaults).

Clearing banks are those banks whose liabilities (deposits) are widely used as a means of payment and are readily transferable between people, and therefore count as money. Clearing banks generally have a close relationship with the central bank, holding reserves with the central bank, which operates as a "lender of last resort" to clearing banks. For such banks, it is the process of loan creation through which deposits and thereby money is created, and it can be said that "loans create deposits". The balance sheet of the bank expands with loans being assets for the bank and deposits being a liability for the bank; for the public, loans are liabilities and deposits assets.

For other types of banks, often labelled investment banks or savings banks, lending is constrained by the deposits they hold ("deposits create loans"). The expansion of economic activity relies on the existence of clearing banks, otherwise lending would be constrained by prior deposits; in turn, investment expenditure would be constrained by prior savings. Significant developments in the sector have involved market-based banks; that is, the merging together of banks as institutions and market operations (Hardie *et al.* 2013). The securitization of mortgages (in mortgage-backed securities) was a major contributing factor to the GFCs. Mortgage companies were able to bundle mortgages into asset-based securities with tranches; the securities were given high credit ratings even though the underlying mortgages were difficult to evaluate and the risks of default of mortgages were interrelated.

Stock and equity markets have long offered an alternative mode of investment funding. An element of financialization has come from the encouragement of the development of stock markets, consequent to the financial liberalization that followed deregulation efforts by governments (as discussed in Chapter 7). The growth of stock markets in terms of capitalization over the past few decades is illustrated below (Figures 4.4–4.6). However, in recent years and in many countries the stock market has not been a net source of funding. There have often been outflows of funds from the stock market through mergers and through corporations being taken back into private ownership, including by private equity companies, rather than inflows of funds to support new businesses. The rise in stock market capitalization can reflect that some profits are retained within a business and reinvested and the value of the company thereby grows.

Employment and output in the financial sector

The simplest measures of the scale of the financial sector relate to employment and output. I begin with the share of employment of the financial sector in the total, which is illustrated in Figure 4.1, covering the G7 countries (Canada omitted through lack of data) and EU15. There is a tendency for the employment share of the financial sector to decline – only the USA, in the period up to the GFCs, shows a small increase in the share. It is also notable how relatively small in employment terms the financial sector

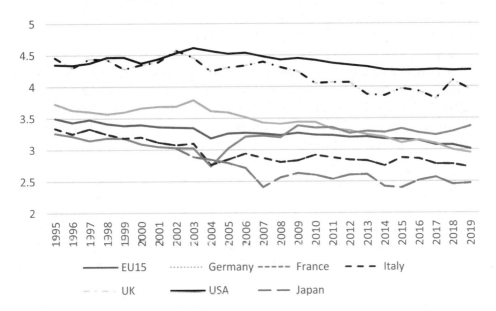

Figure 4.1 Employment shares of the financial sector
Source: Eurostat, Bureau of Labor Statistics

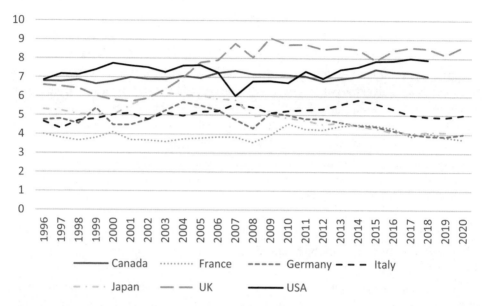

Figure 4.2 Value added of the financial sector as percentage of total
Source: calculated from OECD National Accounts

is – averaging around 4 per cent in the UK and the USA and around 3 per cent in the other countries. The financial sector is not a great generator of jobs and – as will be explored in Chapter 10 – may overall have a negative impact on jobs.[2] It is something of a paradox to start the discussion on financialization with a measure that indicates a relatively small scale of the financial sector and little by way of expansion.

The share of value added of the financial sector in total value added of the economy is illustrated in Figure 4.2. It is readily apparent that the value-added share is considerably larger than the employment share (averages in the range 1½ to 2¼ times higher), implying substantial higher labour productivity in the financial sector. There are issues over the measurement of output (value added) in the financial sector; see, for example, Christophers (2011), as discussed below in Chapter 10.

Financial deepening

Financial deepening refers to the increased provision of financial services. The simplest measures refer to the size of the banking system as measured by bank deposits (or similar) and the scale of the stock market. In studies on the relationship between the size of the

---

2. It should, though, be noted that finance is relatively narrowly defined and in the broader scope of the Finance Insurance and Real Estate (FIRE) employment is more buoyant (see, e.g. Brown, Spencer & Veronese Passarella 2017: fig. 1).

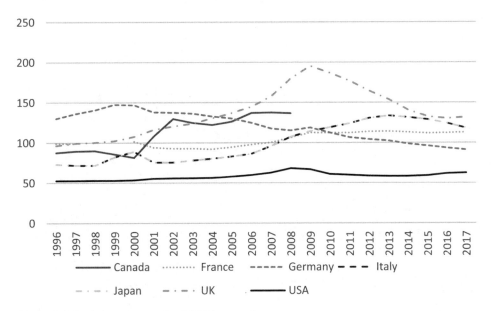

Figure 4.3 Bank deposits as ratio of GDP (per cent)
Source: based on data from Financial Development and Structure Dataset, compiled by Aslı Demirgüç-Kunt *et al.* (2019)

financial sector (sometimes referred as financial development) and the size or growth of the economy, measures such as the value of bank deposits to GDP and stock market valuation to GDP have been frequently used (see Chapter 10).

The growth of the banking sector (as measured by bank deposits relative to GDP) for the G7 countries is illustrated in Figure 4.3, which presents a mixed picture. Bank deposits (relative to GDP) rose in Japan from 72 per cent in 1996 through to over 130 per cent in 2013 with some decline thereafter. The ratio in Germany declines through the period, and the USA experiences little change. The UK has strong growth in the ratio to 2009 followed by decline.

The strong upward trends of stock market value (relative to GDP) in the period after 1975 are clearly evident in Figure 4.4. The starting point of 1975 comes after the stock market crashes of 1973–74. The exception to the strong upward trend is clearly Japan, where the stock market (and property) prices soared during the 1980s peaking in 1989, followed by a decline in the stock market value ratio to GDP of nearly 60 per cent by 1998, followed by a rising ratio. The period since the GFCs stands in some contrast with more of a flat picture in respect of the ratio of stock market value to GDP, although the USA (after 2010) and Japan (after 2012) have a substantial upward trend.

Alongside the growth of stock market capitalization, there has been a tendency for a greater volume of transactions in stock markets and increase in the average length of time for which a stock is held. Figure 4.5 illustrates the increase in the number of transactions, where the total value of shares transacted in a year relative to GDP is given for the G7 countries over the period 1996 through to 2017. It can be readily seen that there is a

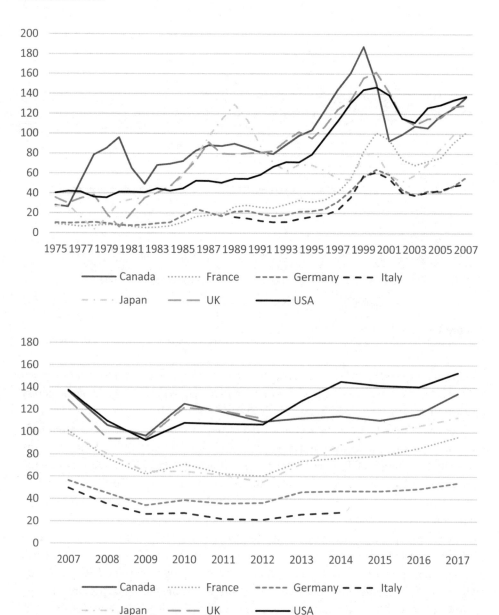

Figure 4.4 Stock market capitalization to GDP (per cent)
Source: based on data from Financial Development and Structure Dataset, compiled by Aslı Demirgüç-Kunt *et al.* (2019)

general upward trend through until the GFCs. A comparison between Figure 4.5 and Figure 4.4 suggests that the turnover of stocks within a year is of the same order of magnitude as the total value of stocks. In effect, stocks are held on average for a year, although there is enormous variation. Some holdings might only last for perhaps a second for

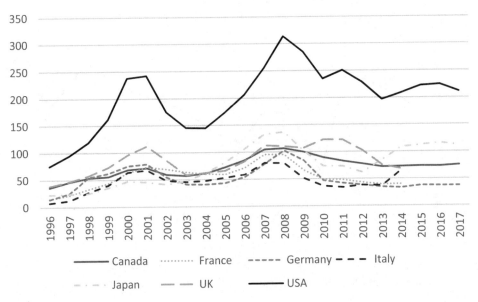

Figure 4.5 Value of traded shares as ratio of GDP (per cent)
Source: based on data from Financial Development and Structure Dataset, compiled by Aslı Demirgüç-Kunt *et al.* (2019)

those involved in high frequency trading (HFT), through to holding for many years as longer-term investment. There can be significant implications of the volume of turnover. Shareholders who are frequently buying and selling shares have little interest in corporate governance but do have interests in profiting from day-to-day movements in the share price (see Chapter 7).

The global scale of stock markets is illustrated in Figure 4.6, where it can be seen that global stock market capitalization has generally been around 80–100 per cent (as a ratio of global GDP). The sharp falls around the time of the GFCs are evident as is the general recovery since and regaining the pre-GFC peak. An indication of the relative scale of stock markets is given in Figure 4.7. The rapid growth of stock markets in emerging markets in the 2000s is evident, with a more than doubling in share of total capitalization, followed by a substantial decline. The stock markets of the European Union have declined in importance relative to the rest of the world.

These statistics on bank deposits and stock market capitalization clearly illustrate the growth in scale of the financial institutions and that they have grown significantly faster than GDP. These data are often used in empirical work as a key measure of finan cial development or financial deepening, particularly in debates over the relationships between financial development and economic growth (this is extensively discussed in Chapter 9). The observation can, however, be made that economic growth in western Europe, North America and Japan has tended to be somewhat lower over the past few

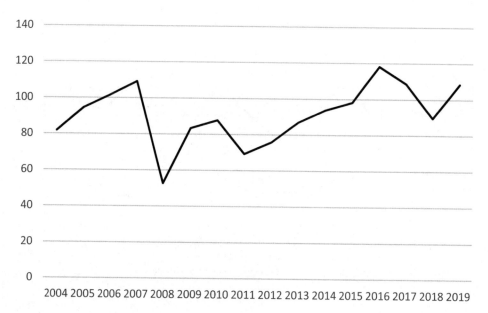

Figure 4.6 Global stock market capitalization to GDP (per cent)
Source: calculated from SIFMA Capital Markets Fact Book, 2020; IMF data on GDP

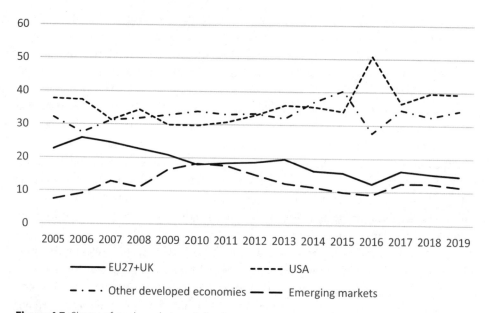

Figure 4.7 Shares of stock market capitalization
Source: calculated from SIFMA Capital Markets Fact Book, 2020

decades than hitherto and has been accompanied by rapid growth in the financial sector. These statistics also suggest that stock market capitalization grows relative to bank deposits, which many have indicated is an element of financialization.

Financial instruments, growth and complexity

Since the late 1970s, there has been an expansion and proliferation of financial instruments, including financial derivatives and securitization (including asset-based securities, CDOs).

Securitization represents a major shift in the relationship between financial institutions and borrowers. The pre-securitization model can be described as "originate and hold", whereby financial institutions and banks would originate a loan (mortgage) and then hold the loan on their balance sheet as an asset for the duration of the loan period. With securitization, this became "originate and distribute", whereby banks and financial institutions turn the mortgages into securities, which are then sold to financial institutions and others.

Securitization is the creation and issuance of debt securities (bonds) where the interest on the bonds/securities and the repayment of the principal comes from the cash flows generated by a separate pool of assets. Securitization is used by financial institutions and businesses to immediately realize the value of an asset, which is expected to yield a future cash stream. Securitized mortgages are known as mortgage-backed securities whereas asset-based securities are securitized assets based on other loans, such as car or student loans.

The late 1980s marked the beginning of a new era in derivatives trading, which has experienced rapid growth, both in the volume and types of derivatives traded, and has seen the emergence and use by market participants of a vast literature of valuation and risk management models. A key feature of these large and apparently liquid markets was the widespread use of mathematical valuation and risk management models by market participants (Lindo 2018). The complexity of the financial instruments has meant that the risk evaluation of them becomes virtually impossible.

The development and growth of financial derivatives and securitization (such as mortgage-backed securities) has been particularly significant in their consequences for risk and crisis. Kay (2015: 297–8) argues that "volumes of trading in financial markets have reached absurd levels   levels that have impeded rather than enhanced the quality of intermediation and increased rather than diversified the amount of risk to which the global economy is exposed. The capital resources needed to reconcile these trading volumes with stability have not been available; nor will they ever be". The complexity of financial products feeds into financial instability with resulting damage on the non-financial economy.

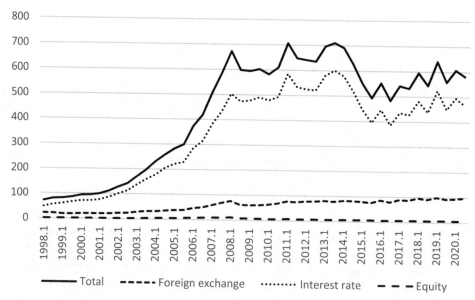

Figure 4.8 Derivatives: global totals (notional principal $ trillions)
Source: BIS data

The growth of derivatives is indicated in Figure 4.8, where the rapid growth over the decade from 1998 to 2007 is clearly visible, with a more than a ninefold increase. Since the GFCs, derivatives have not experienced further growth and indeed were lower in 2019 and 2020 than in 2007. The amount outstanding in 2020, at around $600 trillion, can be compared with a global GDP of around $80 trillion.

Growth of financial institutions

In Figures 4.9 and 4.10 the growth of financial institutions over the period 2002–19 is illustrated – in Figure 4.9 assets of financial institutions measured in trillions of dollars, and in Figure 4.10 scaled by GDP. The data refer to what is termed the 29-group[3], which comprise the major financial centres. Banks – deposit-taking financial corporations – remain the largest group of financial institutions. The rapid growth in the years prior to the GFCs is evident with their financial assets rising from $52 trillion in 2002 to $123.3 trillion in 2008. The increase in the size of banks slowed after the financial crises with a rise to $137.8 trillion in 2016, a pace significantly slower than the rise in world GDP.

---

3. Argentina, Australia, Belgium, Brazil, Canada, Cayman Islands, Chile, China, France, Germany, Hong Kong, India, Indonesia, Ireland, Italy, Japan, Korea, Luxembourg, Mexico, the Netherlands, Russia, Saudi Arabia, Singapore, South Africa, Spain, Switzerland, Turkey, the UK, the USA.

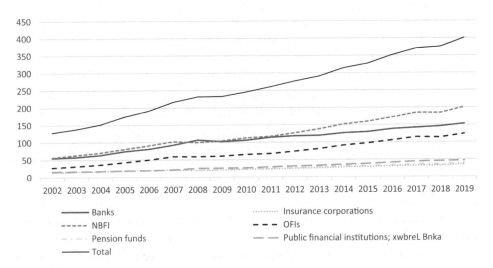

Figure 4.9 Assets of financial institutions: G29 trillions of US dollars
Source: 2020 Global Monitoring Report on Non-bank Financial Intermediation www.fsb.org/2020/12/global-monitoring-report-on-non-bank-financial-intermediation-2020/

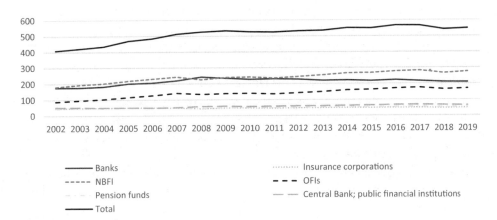

Figure 4.10 Assets of financial corporations as ratio to GDP (per cent)
NBFI: non-bank financial institutions; OFI other financial institutions; CB, PFI: central banks plus public financial institutions
Source: 2020 Global Monitoring Report on Non-bank Financial Intermediation www.fsb.org/2020/12/global-monitoring-report-on-non-bank-financial-intermediation-2020/

Central bank financial assets rose substantially in the 2010s, reflecting quantitative easing from $4.5 trillion in 2002 to $10.1 trillion in 2007 and then $26.2 trillion in 2016.

The assets of pension funds, however, nearly tripled between 2002 and 2016, which is an illustration of the financialization of the everyday in that it reflects greater involvement of individuals in private pension arrangements, an issue I return to in Chapter 9. The non-bank financial intermediaries (broadly speaking what has become termed "shadow banks") show substantial and continuing growth.

Although the operations of what are now termed shadow banks extend back many years, it was only in 2007 that the term "shadow bank" was coined by Paul McCulley in a 2007 speech at the annual financial symposium hosted by the Kansas City Federal Reserve Bank in Jackson Hole, Wyoming. In McCulley's talk, shadow banking referred mainly to non-bank financial institutions that engage in maturity transformation; deposits, normally short-term, are used to fund loans that are longer term. Shadow banks generally raise short-term funds in the money markets and use them to buy assets with longer-term maturities.

Shadow banks differ from commercial banks in several respects. Shadow banks are not money creators (as deposits with them are not transferable between individuals and are not treated as a means of payment) and do not have access to borrowing from central banks, which act as the "lender of last resort" to commercial banks. Commercial banks have often operated with deposits from the public where the deposits are to some degree covered by insurance, whereas shadow banks borrow from money markets. Commercial banks are subject to bank regulation in ways that shadow banks are not. The key aspects of intermediation are maturity transformation (borrowing short, lending long), liquidity transformation (using highly liquid liabilities to buy less-liquid assets), leverage (borrowing to buy assets in the hope that the costs of borrowing are lower than the benefits of the assets acquired) and credit risk transfer. The key elements of shadow banking are the lack of regulation, the lack of access to support by a central bank and their engagement in potentially risky activities. A further aspect comes from the interconnectedness within the financial system and specifically the interconnectedness between shadow banking and "regular banking" and the potential risks of contagion.

The Financial Stability Board (FSB) defines shadow banking as "credit intermediation involving entities and activities (fully or partly) outside of the regular banking system". Some authorities and market participants prefer to use other terms such as "market-based finance" instead of "shadow banking". The FSB has what it considers a "narrow measure of shadow banking", which includes "non-bank financial entity types that authorities have assessed as being involved in credit intermediation that may pose financial stability risks" (FSB 2018: 2). The FSB approaches shadow banks in terms of their economic functions. The five functions are listed in Table 4.1 along with the illustrations of the entity types that fulfil the relevant functions.

The recent growth of shadow banking and the different functions are given in Table 4.2., which shows the increase from 2003 to 2008 is 67 per cent and the increase continued after the GFCs at around 80 per cent between 2010 and 2018. The significance of these shifts is that the "shadow banking" sector is much more lightly regulated and supervised.

Table 4.1 Shadow bank classifications by function

EF	Definition	Typical entity types
EF1	Management of collective investment vehicles with features that make them susceptible to runs	Money market funds, fixed-income funds, mixed funds, credit hedge funds, real estate funds
EF2	Loan provision that is dependent on short-term funding	Finance companies, leasing/factoring companies, consumer credit companies
EF3	Intermediation of market activities that is dependent on short-term funding or on secured funding of client assets	Broker-dealers, securities finance companies
EF4	Facilitation of credit creation	Credit insurance companies, financial guarantors, monolines
EF5	Securitization-based credit intermediation and funding of financial entities	Securitization vehicles, structured finance vehicles, asset-backed securities.

Source: FSB (2018)

Table 4.2 Evolution of the narrow measure by economic function

	EF1	EF2	EF3	EF4	EF5	Unallocated	Total (rounded)
				USD trillion			
2003	7.3	2.7	4.6	0.1	3.0	0.4	18.0
2004	8.2	2.8	5.4	0.1	3.5	0.5	20.5
2005	9.8	2.8	6.0	0.1	4.5	0.5	23.6
2006	11.3	3.0	6.9	0.1	5.4	0.2	26.9
2007	14.1	3.5	7.8	0.1	6.3	0.2	32.0
2008	14.6	3.8	6.2	0.1	6.1	1.5	32.3
2009	15.5	3.5	5.6	0.1	6.5	0.8	32.1
2010	16.7	3.4	3.5	0.1	5.3	0.9	30.0
2011	18.6	3.4	3.6	0.2	4.8	0.6	31.2
2012	22.2	3.0	3.7	0.2	4.5	0.7	34.3
2013	25.4	3.1	3.8	0.2	4.4	0.6	37.4
2014	28.7	3.3	4.1	0.2	4.5	0.6	41.3
2015	31.9	3.3	4.0	0.2	4.4	0.8	44.6
2016	34.9	3.4	3.9	0.2	4.4	1.1	48.0
2017	38.2	3.6	4.1	0.2	4.8	1.1	52.0
2018	38.3	3.9	4.5	0.2	4.8	1.2	52.9
2019	43.5	4.1	4.7	0.2	4.9	1.4	58.0
2020	47.4	4.3	4.9	0.2	4.7	1.7	63.2

Source: Dataset accompanying Global Monitoring Report on Non-Bank Financial Intermediation 2019 from Financial Stability Board www.fsb.org/2020/01/global-monitoring-report-on-non-bank-financial-intermediation-2019/

Foreign exchange dealings

A further example of the growth of trading in financial assets as one dimension of financialization comes from the foreign exchange markets. International trade in a good market would generally require that the seller eventually receives payment in their own currency whether it is the buyer or seller who exchanges one currency for another. It is

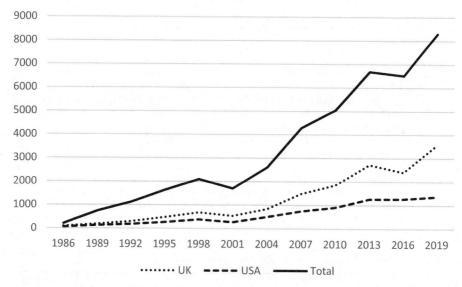

Figure 4.11 Foreign exchange turnover
OTC foreign exchange turnover by country in April 1986–2019, "net-gross" basis
All instruments
Daily averages, in billions of US dollars
Source: Bank of International Settlements, Triennial Central Bank Survey

well known that the volumes of buying and selling of currencies on the foreign exchange markets vastly exceeds that which would be required to provide for the volume of international trade to take place.

The data in Figure 4.11 show a dip in trading foreign exchange instruments between 1998 and 2001, perhaps related to the introduction of the euro (hence the currencies that entered the euro were no longer being exchanged for each other). Growth of 150 per cent between 2001 and 2007 was followed by continued but lower growth between 2007 and 2013 of 56 per cent, and then a slight decline through to 2016, followed by a substantial rise to 2019.

Household assets and liabilities

The rise of household debt has often been seen as an integral part of financialization and as part of the involvement of households with the financial sector. The expansion of household debt during the 2000s prior to the GFCs was a driving force for the expansion of demand but one involving instability and lack of sustainability. The pattern of household debt in Figure 4.12 illustrates the considerable differences between the G7 countries, reflecting national differences in attitudes towards debt and borrowing for house purchase. There is a generally sharp increase in household debt (relative to household disposable income) over the period 1995 to 2008 with changes of over 35 percentage

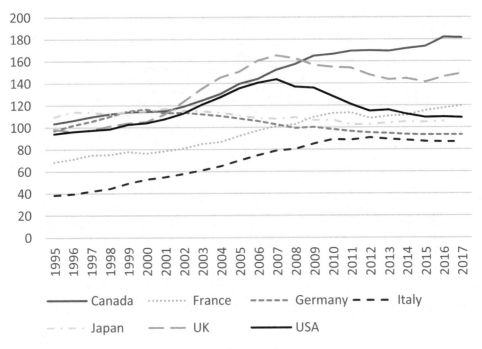

Figure 4.12 Household debt as percentage of disposable income
Source: calculated from OECD Dataset

points, although Japan and Germany are exceptions with virtually no change. After the GFCs, the picture is much more mixed with four of the countries in Figure 4.12 showing a decline, and others showing a much slower rise than pre-GFC.

The rise of household debt has taken place against a background of rising household wealth. For the seven countries in Figure 4.13, the wealth to income ratio rose from 601 per cent in 1995 to 752 per cent in 2007, dipped to 693 per cent in 2008, rising again to 795 per cent in 2015. The fluctuations in the wealth to income ratio are linked to fluctuations in house and equity prices, both of which are subject to considerable fluctuations.

The rise in financial assets (relative to wealth) illustrates the greater involvement of households with finance. Decisions have to be made with regard to which assets to acquire. The involvement may be direct or indirect, an example of rather indirect involvement comes through pension funds. Such involvements, whether through debt or through asset ownership, form part of the financialization of the everyday, to which I return in Chapter 9.

Rentier income

Financialization has been related by many to the rise of rentier income. As Epstein and Jayadev (2005: 48) note: "There is no commonly accepted definition of rentier, rentier

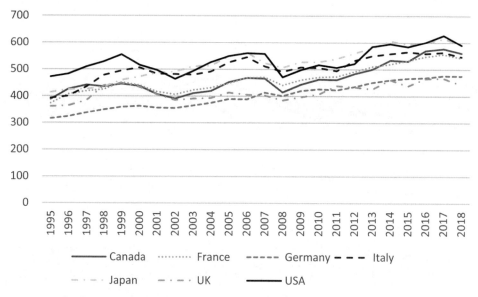

Figure 4.13 Net wealth of households as percentage of GDP
Source: calculated from data downloaded from OECD National Accounts

income or rentier class. Perhaps the most famous definition of rentier is the one offered by Keynes. In his *General Theory*, Keynes refers to the rentier as 'the functionless investor', who generates income via his ownership of capital, thus exploiting its 'scarcity-value' … the notion of the functionless investor is thus a popular and respectable way to define the term *rentier*. However, another definition and the one we will adopt, better reflects the notion of financialization as an active process and the rentier as an active agent. Our definition thus includes profits from financial market activity of the financial industry, including, of course, banks, stockbrokers and insurance companies."

Rentier income is envisaged in terms of receipt of income and passivity. Rentier income can be seen in terms of interest, dividends (without active participation in management) and rent. However, much of those forms of payments are made in the first instance to the financial sector, which then in effect retains some for its profits and management expenses and passes on some to households. Households may then receive rentier income directly from their ownership of assets and from pension and similar payments. Households themselves can be a source of rentier income in the sense that households in debt pay interest charges usually to financial institutions, who in turn make payments to households who hold deposits with the financial institutions concerned. Dünhaupt (2012) uses the approach of rentier income as received by households and compares that with the Epstein and Jayadev (2005) approach.

Rentier income can be viewed through the lens of the recipient; that is, in terms of income received in a passive manner based on supply of funds. But rentier income can be viewed in terms of payments made by corporations and others to the supplier of funds.

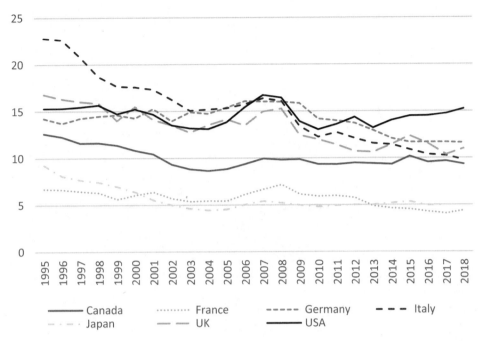

Figure 4.14 Property income as ratio of GDP (per cent)
Source: calculated from data downloaded from OECD National Accounts

In a world where there are no financial intermediaries, the payments out by corporations would be equal to receipt of income by households. However, in a world where there are financial intermediaries, much of the payment of rentier income goes in the first instance to financial institutions. In turn, they make charges for their services and make rentier income payments to households. Further, households themselves are paying interest on past borrowing and those interest payments are at least indirectly received by other households, although again would in general pass through financial institutions.

In Figure 4.14 statistics are given for rentier income as received by households (which differs from rentier income as paid out by corporations in ways that are indicated in the previous paragraph). It is measured in current prices and, as such, makes no allowance for inflation (so interest payments are in nominal terms rather than real terms) nor does it incorporate capital gains. The general picture is one of rentier income rising up to the financial crisis with some declines thereafter, arising from the low interest rate environment as illustrated in the second part of Figure 4.15.

Concentration in the banking industry

The structure of the banking sector in particular has tended to change in the direction of becoming more concentrated (although some, such as the UK, were already highly

63

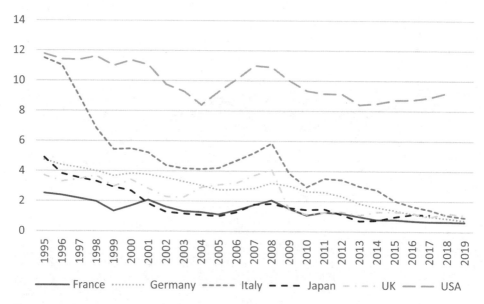

Figure 4.15 Interest receipts as ratio of GDP (per cent)
Source: calculated from data downloaded from OECD National Accounts

concentrated), less regionalised as regional banking gave way to national banking, and more internationalized. Detzer *et al.* (2013), drawing on European Central Bank (ECB) data, report a five-firm concentration ratio for Germany rising from 17 per cent in 1997 to 25 per cent in 2009; corresponding figures for France were 40 per cent to 47.2 per cent, Italy 25 per cent to 34 per cent, and the UK from 24 per cent to 40.8 per cent. The unweighted average for the euro area was 45 per cent in 1997 rising to 57 per cent in 2009. Relating to the period since 2003, ECB (2017: 47–8) reports:

> a gradual increase in market concentration. ... The level of concentration tends to be higher for smaller countries and lower for larger countries. In terms of changes over time, the banking sector has tended to become more concentrated mainly in countries undergoing deep banking sector restructuring processes, such as Greece and Spain. Some concentration can also be observed in Germany, Italy (although these two countries still have the lowest concentration levels in the euro area), Lithuania and Malta. The gradual increase in concentration in the euro area took place in a context where the (relative) size of the banking sector was shrinking (from 3.1 times to 2.7 times GDP between 2008 and 2015).

By 2020, the average five-firm concentration ratio for financial institutions among the 27 member countries of the European Union was 67.2 per cent. Only five countries recorded five-firm concentration below 50 per cent – two of these (France, Italy) had a ratio within

1 percentage point of 50 per cent; Austria, Germany and Luxembourg recorded a ratio in the 30–40 per cent range. The figure for the UK in 2019 (before departure from the EU) was 31.2 per cent.[4]

Mutual and cooperative ownership

Financial institutions have often been a mixture of privately owned, mutual and cooperative-owned and state-owned. Those owned by mutuals, cooperatives and the state can often be viewed as "double bottom line institutions" in that they have in general to at least break even and to pursue a range of social objectives, such as provision of funds for groups excluded on gender, ethnicity, for environmental projects and so on. A feature of the present era of financialization has often been some decline of mutual and cooperative ownership and particularly the role of state ownership.

State ownership of banks has been a relatively common feature of capitalist economies, although of generally little importance in the USA or UK. In the early 1980s, there was some expansion of state ownership of banks, notably in France and Greece. However, from then there has been a strong trend away from state-owned banks, albeit with some, often temporary, reversal with the nationalization of banks and other financial institutions after the GFCs.

The privatization of state-owned banks was a part of the general wave of privatizations, particularly during the 1990s and 2000s. Frangakis and Huffschmid (2009: 17) report that 13.8 per cent of privatization proceeds 1977–2006 in the EU15 were in finance and real estate. For the EU15 the authors report 113 cases of bank privatizations sold for $64 trillion over the period 1985 to 2007, largely during the 1990s. Italy ($17 trillion), France ($13.6 trillion) and Germany ($9.9 trillion) were the three largest in terms of assets sold. Over the period 1982–2000, their Table 12.1 reports 114 bank privatizations in 18 OECD countries in the sample, with a value of $80.9 billion, and 156 bank privatizations in 33 non-OECD countries included in the sample.

Boehmer, Nash and Netter (2005) report that in the period 1982 to 2004 in a sample of 101 countries, 51 countries privatized a state-owned bank, involving 270 transactions out of 2,137 privatizing transactions. The average size of transaction was $442.1 million (median $156.3 million), with the state often maintaining a majority stake (for banks on average 48 per cent [41 per cent median]) of enterprise sold.

Mutual financial organizations have a long history in the areas of housing finance and insurance, dating back to the nineteenth century and before. In the UK, building societies were founded on the principle of mutuality – demutualization became much easier by the passage of the Building Societies Act in 1986. A mutual organization builds up funds

---

4. Figures drawn from EU structural financial indicators prepared by the ECB.

over the years, which are collectively owned by its members; demutualization, in effect, converts the collective ownership into private ownership and each member receives a share of the accumulated funds.

Building societies had been local in origin and generally retained the name of the locality in which they had originated. In the UK, they had experienced consolidation and rationalization. From 819 societies in 1950, the number had declined to 273 by 1980, and 110 by 1989. The first major demutualization came in 1989 with the Abbey National. Over the next 20 years, many followed and six of the building societies converted to listed banks, all of which lost their independence (as with Abbey National taken over by and then rebranded as Santander) or went bankrupt. During the era of consolidation, building societies continued to expand in terms of number of branches, depositors and borrowers, peaking in 1988. They had been dominant in the provision of mortgages and had largely been limited in their activities to the provision of mortgage. However, building societies have lost their dominance as banks and other financial institutions have offered mortgages and building societies diversified their activities into loans and banking facilities as the legal restrictions on them were lifted.

In Germany, the number of banks declined significantly. Detzer *et al.* (2013) report a decline from 3,359 in 1980 to 1,988 by 2012. Private banks had tended to grow, with assets up from 23.5 per cent of the total in 1980 to 38.3 per cent in 2012. Within that it was the so-called big banks (in the end four in number) that held over a quarter of assets in 2012 from under a tenth in 1980.

The savings bank sector consists of Sparkassen (primary savings banks), owned by local city and county governments, the regional Landesbanken, generally owned jointly by regional associations of the Sparkassen and regional state governments, and the Deka Bank. The cooperative banking sector consists of primary cooperative banks; credit cooperatives owned by their members, though, also provide retail banking services to non-members.

With some consolidation (primary savings banks down from 599 in 1980 to 426 by 2012), the Landesbanken maintained their share of assets, while the primary savings banks fell from 22 per cent in 1980 to 13 per cent by 2012.

The cooperative sector also saw consolidation, with the regional institutions falling from ten to two, and the primary cooperative banks from 2,294 to 1,121, broadly maintaining their share of assets. Mortgage banks saw their share halve (from 13.6 per cent to 6.9 per cent), whereas foreign banks increased their market share.

Specialized banks, of which there are 17 in Germany, provide funding to promote investment in specific sectors. The largest is the publicly owned KfW (Kreditanstalt für Wiederaufbau), which issues bonds guaranteed by government to provide funds for investment in infrastructure.

Fonteyne (2007: table 1) reports the market shares of bank branches of cooperative banks in nine European countries over the period 1994 to 2003. This reveals considerable differences between countries, with the share varying from 2.4 per cent in Greece (in 2003), 11.3 per cent in Spain, through to 52.6 per cent in Austria and 59.7 per cent in France. The shares of cooperative banks were broadly constant over the period, with the exception of the Netherlands, where the share rose from 25.9 per cent in 1997 (no data for 1994) to over 40 per cent in the early 2000s.

Profits in finance

Christophers (2018: 7) argues that financialization, in terms of the increased importance of the financial sector, in the USA "is, in short, a profit – and *only* a profit – phenomenon". As the data in his Figure 4.2 and in my Figure 4.1 above indicate, employment and output of the financial sector did not experience a rapid increase in the decades after 1980 but profits did, with the financial and insurance sector's share of profits rising from below 15 per cent in the early 1980s to over 25 per cent in the 2010s. He argues that profit persistence and growth in the financial sector "is fundamentally concerned with competition. US banking, and indeed the US finance sector more generally, was already disproportionately profitable … at the beginning of the 1980s" (*ibid.*: 3).

There is a paucity of data to substantiate the trends in profits of the financial sector outside of the USA. For the USA, Figures 4.16 and 4.17 confirm an upward trend in the

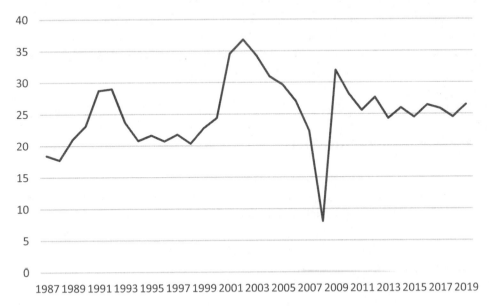

Figure 4.16 Profits of financial sector as percentage of total: USA
Source: calculated from Bureau of Economic Analysis Tables Table 1.1.5, 6.16A.16C, 6.16D

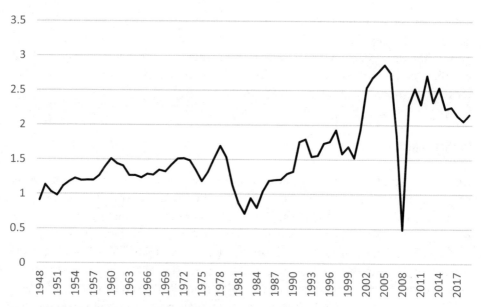

Figure 4.17 Profits of financial sector to GDP (per cent): USA
Source: calculated from Bureau of Economic Analysis Tables Table 1.1.5, 6.16A.16C, 6.16D

share of the financial sector in total profits, with a particularly sharp increase in the late 1990s/early 2000s (going alongside the dot.com bubble), and a sharp decline at the time of the financial crises, with rapid recovery. For the UK, the operating surplus of the financial sector (as a percentage of total) is shown in Figure 4.18 from 1970 onwards. The ratio rises during the 1970s, then slumps before rising sharply during the 1980s. After falling during the 1990s, it rises during the 2000s and maintains a level at around 15 per cent after the GFCs.

Post-financial crisis developments

The first era of financialization is generally viewed as coming to an abrupt end in the aftermath of the 1929–33 financial crises. The 1930s were characterized by protectionism and reversal of the previous globalization and recessions and depression. The question arises as to whether the financial crisis of 2007–08, although by no means the first financial crisis of the present era of financialization, has brought any similar slowing down or reversal of financialization. It is well known that there was a sharp recession following the financial crisis of 2007–08, followed by a weak recovery and signs that international trade has faltered in the decade since the financial crises (as further discussed in Chapter 11).

The GFC of 2007–08, like many others, had a pronounced and long-lasting effect on economic activity and output. Although there were many factors leading to the GFC, the

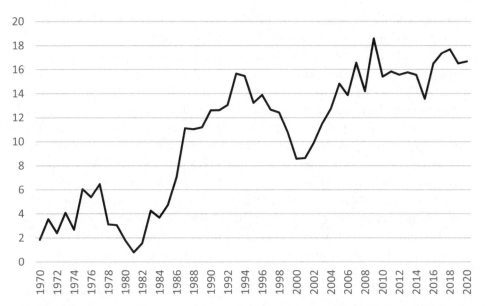

Figure 4.18 Gross operating surplus of UK financial corporations as percentage of total operating surplus
Source: derived from Office for National Statistics data

ways in which the regulatory environment had changed and had been implemented were seen as significant.[5] The changes notably included the Glass-Steagall Act in the USA, the growth of "shadow banking" outside of regulation and a relaxed attitude to implementation of regulation. In the aftermath of the GFC, perhaps the most dramatic shift with respect to the processes of financialization came with the general approaches to regulation of the financial sector.

Lapavitsas and Mendieta-Muñoz (2018: 494) examine for structural breaks in several statistical series measuring aspects of financialization. They find that "the period before the Great Recession was characterised mainly by rising financial profits, rising debt of the financial sector, and rising household and mortgage debt; in contrast, the period since the Great Recession has been characterised by stagnant financial profits, falling debt of the financial sector, and falling household and mortgage debt".

An overall summary of the statistics portrayed in the previous section could be that there are few cases of what may be termed absolute definancialization; that is, declines in the measure used. Stock market capitalization fell in the immediate aftermath of the crises but then recovered. Rentier income has tended to decline, which is a reflection of the ultra-low interest rates following central banks' reduction of policy interest rates and the effects of policies of quantitative easing. Derivatives and foreign exchange

---

5. See Arestis (2016) for discussion of the causes of the GFCs of 2007–09.

transactions display some ups and downs. For the other measures the general picture is one of slower or no expansion compared with the earlier periods.

The figures in this chapter readily portray the general expansion of the financial sector across a range of countries and therefore support the idea that financialization in the present era has been a very widespread phenomenon. It is also evident "by eye" that the starting point and the pace of change differ substantially across countries.

The growth of the financial sector in various dimensions has been near-universal and is evident in all the figures that are displayed here. The specific forms they take varies from country to country and the timing of these developments similarly varies. The term "variegated financialization" can be used to signify the pervasive but differentiated forms of financialization. The idea of variegated financialization can be viewed as an application of the general idea of "variegated capitalism" (Peck & Theodore 2007). "Variegated financialization captures two key things. One is the idea of financialization as a systemic process operating within and across nations. The other is the idea of financialization as a variegated process – how it unfolds within and impacts upon particular nations and regions is mediated by the institutions, politics and culture of those nations and regions" (Brown, Spencer and Veronese Passarella 2017: 67). Brown, Spencer and Veronese Passarella (2017) and Ferreiro and Gómez (2016) also provide evidence on the spread of the financial sector and the differences across countries, leading into notions of variegated financialization.

Karwowski, Shabani and Stockhammer (2020) identify seven financial hypotheses and investigate them in a cross-country analysis for 17 OECD countries in the two periods of 1997–2007 and 2008–17. The measures of financialization used are found to be only weakly correlated, which can indicate the existence of distinct processes of financialization. "There is strong evidence that financialization is linked to asset price inflation and correlated with a debt-driven demand regime. Financial deregulation encourages financialization." Overall, they suggest that "financialization should be understood as a variegated process, playing out differently across economic sectors and countries" (*ibid*.: 957).

Lapavitas and Powell (2013) argue that there are common underlying tendencies in the form and content taken by financialization in each country, which vary according to institutional, historical and political conditions. They use data from the USA, the UK, Japan, Germany and France to show some underlying tendencies that differ across countries in terms of the starting points and the pace of the trends. Non-financial corporation loans as a share of total liabilities has a cyclical aspect with a "gentle secular decline throughout the period signifying a weakening of the reliance of non-financial corporations on banks to fund assets" (*ibid*.: 365). There are two distinct levels, with Germany and Japan significantly higher than the USA and UK; the former two are usually seen as bank-based, whereas the USA and UK are market-based, with France moving from the former to the latter. There is a clear rise over time of total financial assets as a share of fixed assets.

They conclude that in all the five countries financialization of non-financial enterprises has taken place. There are indications that banks were moving away from "traditional" sources of funds (such as retail deposits) with the ratio of deposits to total bank liabilities showing a declining trend across the sample, except in the case of Japan after 1987. The ratio of household financial liabilities to gross disposable income "rises broadly across the sample until the end of the 1990s, with the possible exception of the UK where there is stagnation but at very high levels" (*ibid.*: 373). In the 2000s, however, the sample splits into two groups that follow distinct trends, with household debt tending to fall in Germany and Japan, and rise in the UK, USA and France. The rise in household debt comes from mortgages, and unsecured consumer debt is often not a rising part of household debt in the countries studied.

This type of summary finding, alongside the statistics set out in this chapter, reinforce the pervasive yet differentiated nature of financialization over the past four decades.

Conclusions

Many of the dimensions of financialization have been illustrated in this chapter. Although there are exceptions, the general pattern has been for substantial expansion of the financial sector in the past four decades. For some of the dimensions considered, there was a particularly rapid expansion during the 2000s up to the GFCs. There has often been a slackening of the pace of financialization since the GFCs and, in some instances, a levelling off. The experiences of the past four decades fit well with the ideas of variegated financialization; that is, a widespread financialization that has occurred at different paces and in different forms.

5

THE GLOBAL REACHES OF FINANCIALIZATION

A particularly remarkable feature of financialization since circa 1980 is that it has been a near-global phenomenon in that almost all countries in the world have been involved to a greater or lesser extent and starting from different scale and structures of the financial sector. As with the earlier era of financialization, the present one has occurred alongside and interacting with globalization.

The processes of financialization have been centred on and driven by the western industrialized countries. Most of the empirical analysis and evidence on financialization that is drawn on in other chapters largely relate to the western industrialized countries. In this chapter the coverage moves to other countries, many of which would be labelled "developing and emerging economies", using the terminology of the IMF.

The broad picture is of substantial financialization in a general sense, albeit with variations, taking different forms and at different speeds (as compared with the advanced industrialized countries). It is also a picture of later starts on financialization and, particularly and for obvious reasons, in the COMECON countries coming after the collapse of the Berlin Wall. It is important to not only explore the nature and speed of financialization in the developing and emerging market countries but also to relate the nature of that financialization to the positions of those economies in the global economy and the economic and social power relationships involved.

This chapter has two related aims. The first is to summarize the extent and nature of financialization around the globe and, in doing so, to reinforce that financialization has been a near-global phenomenon and that it has been a variegated process. The second is to consider how financialization proceeds and its effects in countries, which are not at the centre of capitalism but rather on the periphery.

I begin by making some comparisons between the scale of finance in a wide range of countries. The IMF has produced a set of FDIs that now cover nearly four decades. Svirydzenka (2016) sets how the indices are calculated, and these are available for a wide range of countries from 1980 onwards. For both financial institutions and financial markets, the three measures of depth, access and efficiency are taken, which are first combined into an index for financial institutions and financial markets, and then into an overall index for financial development.

For financial institutions, depth is based on private sector credit, pension fund assets, mutual fund assets and insurance premiums (expressed relative to GDP), access to bank branches and ATMs (per 100,000 adults) and efficiency on net interest margin, lending deposits spread, non-interest income to total income, overhead costs to total assets, return on assets and return on equity. For financial markets, depth is based on stock market capitalization, the stocks traded, international debt securities of government, total debt securities of financial corporations and total debt securities of non-financial corporations (all expressed relative to GDP). Access is the percentage of market capitalization outside the top ten largest companies and the total number of issuers of debt. Efficiency is measured by the ratio of stocks traded to capitalization (although why a higher rate of turnover should be regarded as increasing efficiency is not clear).

From the IMF's database on FDIs, I summarize the developments of these indices over the years 1980–2018. In Figure 5.1, the evolution of the overall FDI is plotted for those four decades for all countries, advanced countries, emerging markets and low-income countries. The statistics in Figure 5.1 illustrate that the advanced economies have much larger financial sectors than others. For each of the categories, there is a virtually continuous growth in financial development over the four decades, although the index for the advanced economies shows some decline after the GFCs. The path of financial

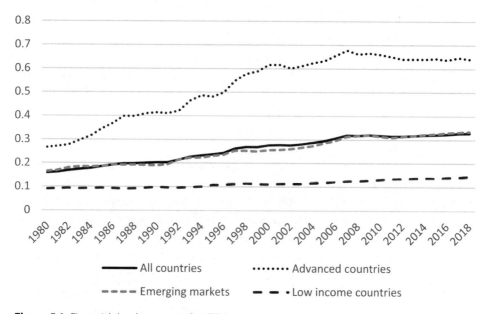

Figure 5.1 Financial development index (FDI)
Source: calculated from FDIndex database, IMF

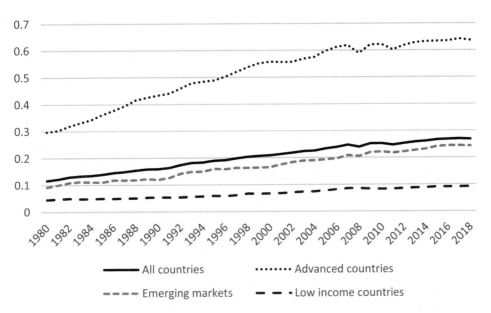

Figure 5.2 Financial institutions: depth (FID)
Source: calculated from FDIndex database, IMF

development provides a crude indicator of the pervasive nature of financialization in terms of the scope and reach of the financial sector.

Figure 5.2 refers to the index for depth of financial institutions. This can be broadly regarded as an indicator of the relative scale of financial institutions. The pattern here for depth of financial institutions is similar to that for overall financial development, although the depth for financial institutions continues to rise after the GFCs.

Figure 5.3 refers to the depth of financial markets and serves as an indicator of the scale of financial markets. Here there is a rapid increase in financial markets from the mid-1990s through to the GFCs, which helped generate financial instability. There is a noticeable decline in depth for advanced countries, which is not surprising given the falls in stock market prices that occurred at the time of the GFCs with some subsequent recovery.

The broad outline of differences between regions of the world is illustrated in Figure 5.4. The average FDI in Europe was around the same level as that for Latin and South America in 1980 but grew rapidly during the 1980s and 1990s (the latter particularly associated with the collapse of COMECON). The average FDI for Europe declines after the GFCs, although it largely continues to rise for the other regions. Africa maintains the lowest average FDI and the difference between Africa and the other continents tends to widen.

Karwowski and Stockhammer (2017) use six measures of dimensions of financialization developed for the openness of economies. The measures used relate

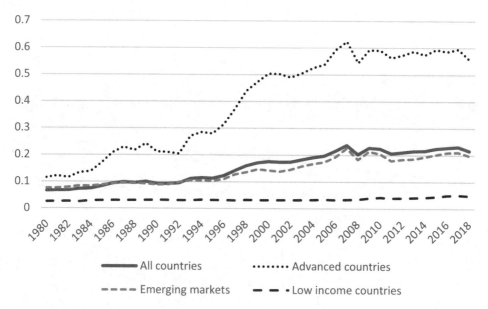

Figure 5.3 Financial markets: depth (FMD)
Source: calculated from FDIndex database, IMF

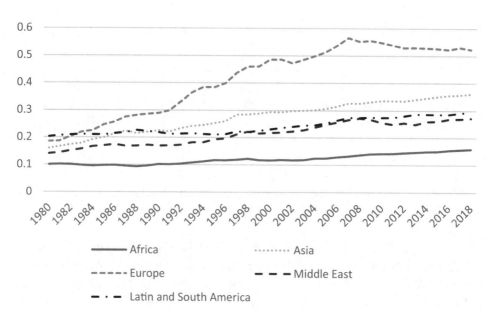

Figure 5.4 FDI by continent
Source: calculated from FDIndex database, IMF

to: (1) financial deregulation as measured by the IMF's financial reform index (used in Chapter 4); (2) foreign financial inflows as measured by stock of foreign liabilities (portfolio investment, FDI and other financial inflows), reflecting the financial engagement of economies; (3) asset price volatility (coefficient of variation of real house prices); (4) a shift towards market-based finance rather than bank-based finance, measured by the ratio of stock market value traded to bank credit; (5) the financialization of non-financial corporation financialization measured by debt of non-financial corporations as a percentage of GDP; and (6) household debt as a percentage of GDP, reflecting household financialization. They construct measures of these six dimensions for 17 emerging market economies covering Latin America, "emerging Europe", Africa and Asia.[1]

Table 5.1 Six financialization dimensions by quartile (1997–2015 averages or latest data)

Region	Economy	Financial deregulation	Foreign financial inflows	Asset price volatility	Market-based v. bank-based financial system	Non-financial corporation debt	Household debt
Latin America	Argentina	Mlow	Mhigh		Low	Low	Low
	Brazil	Low	Low	High	Mhigh	Mlow	Mlow
	Mexico	Mhigh	Low	Low	Mlow	Low	Mlow
Emerging Europe	Czech Republic	Mhigh	Mhigh	Low	Low	Mhigh	Mlow
	Hungary	High	High	Mlow	Mlow	High	Mhigh
	Poland	Mhigh	Mlow	Mlow	Low	Mlow	Mlow
	Russia	Mhigh	Mlow	High	Mhigh	Mlow	Low
	Turkey	Mlow	Mlow	Mlow	High	Low	Low
Africa	South Africa	Mhigh	Mlow	High	Mlow	Mlow	Mhigh
Asia	China	Low	Low	Low	Mhigh	High	Mhigh
	Hong Kong	High	High	High	High	High	High
	India	Low	Low	Mhigh	Mhigh	Mlow	Low
	Indonesia	Low	Mhigh	Mlow	Mlow	Low	Mlow
	Malaysia	Mlow	Mhigh	Mhigh	Low	Mhigh	High
	Singapore	High	High	Mhigh	High	Mhigh	Mhigh
	South Korea	Mlow	Mlow	Mlow	High	High	High
	Thailand	Mlow	mhigh	low	Mlow	Mhigh	Mhigh
Anglo-Saxon countries	UK	High	High	Mhigh	Mhigh	High	High
	USA	High	high	Mhigh	High	Mhigh	High

Source: Karwowski and Stockhammer (2017)

---

1. The countries included are Argentina, Brazil, Mexico, Czech Republic, Hungary, Poland, Russia, Turkey, South Africa. China, Hong Kong, India, Indonesia, Malaysia, Singapore, Thailand and South Korea.

The classification in Table 5.1 is by quartiles. This illustrates the variation not only across these countries but also across the different dimensions of financialization.

UNCTAD (2017) draws on IMF data for the value of assets of financial institutions relative to GDP as a measure of the size of the financial sector, the scale of external financial operations estimated by the values of cross-border assets and liabilities (relative to GDP) and financial concentration and power, for which the assets of the top five banks relative to GDP is used as a proxy. Although financialization is viewed as having started in the early 1980s in many developed countries, their statistics show "for all countries ... the dramatic acceleration of all indicators of financialization since the 1990s" (*ibid.*: 96) (and their data extends back to 1975).

The OECD countries included in the study show, as indicated elsewhere in this chapter, "a considerably greater degree of financialization on the three measures than developing countries" (*ibid.*).[2] Although the financial crisis of 2007–08 triggered some deceleration or even weakening of financialization in some OECD countries, it did not in the developing and transition economies.[3]

UNCTAD (2017) compares eight OECD countries over the period 1975–2015 and nine developing and transition economies for 1990–2015. They find that the pattern for the selected developing and transition economies differs only in degree compared with the OECD countries. The international investment positions of the developing and transition countries, as measured by total assets and liabilities combined, have been large, ranging from about 100 per cent of GDP for Brazil, China and Turkey, to 250 per cent of GDP for Chile and South Africa. The exception among them is India at around 65 per cent of GDP, although that represents a doubling over two decades. The rise in the foreign liability position has risen dramatically, which indicates a considerable rise in external vulnerability, especially when most of their external debts are not denominated in domestic currencies.

Karwowski, Shabani and Stockhammer (2020) distinguish between financialization of non-financial companies (measured by gross financial income and company debt, each as a percentage of total income), households (household debt as a percentage of disposable income) and the financial sector (financial sector value added and debt, each as a percentage of GDP). The scale of variation across countries can be illustrated by the averages the authors report for the period 1997–2007. Household debt as a percentage of disposable income varies from 46 per cent in Greece to 253 per cent in Denmark. For non-financial companies, the ratio of gross financial income to total income ranges from 5 per cent in Ireland to 41 per cent in Sweden, and ratio of debt to total income from 553 per cent in Austria to 1,370 per cent in the Netherlands. The value added of the financial sector as a percentage of GDP varies from 2.99 in France

---

2. France, Germany, Italy, Japan, Korea, Spain, UK and USA.
3. Brazil, Chile, China, India, Mexico, Russian Federation, South Africa, Thailand and Turkey.

to 8.24 in Austria, and debt of the sector from 151 per cent of GDP in Finland to 1,138 per cent in Ireland.

Their cross-country analysis is undertaken for 17 countries over the periods of 1997–2007 and 2008–17, so broadly pre- and post-financial crises. They find that the different financialization measures are only weakly correlated, which is indicative of a variegated processes of financialization. They find evidence linking financialization with asset price inflation and correlated with a debt-driven regime (i.e. a country where the rise in household debt has been a strong driver of economic activity). They find that financial deregulation encourages financialization. They report some limited evidence that market-based financial systems (rather than bank-based financial systems, see Chapter 3) are more financialized, despite the greater role of financial markets. Foreign financial inflows do not seem to be a main driver (noting that it is developed OECD countries that are in the sample). They also report no indication that an investment slowdown precedes financialization.

Bonizzi (2013: 89) reviews many studies on financialization in developing and emerging countries and groups their findings under numerous themes. He views as a key theme the implications of financialization for non-financial investment, with firms increasingly engaging in financial rather than productive investment. "The combined availability of high-return short-term financial investments and pressure from financial investors has led in many developing countries to a reduction in productive investments, which have fallen as a share of gross domestic product", which echoes findings for industrialized countries (see Chapter 7).

There is a transition to a more market-based financial system in many countries that had often relied on forms of directed credit through the banking system. The expansion of foreign banks into the domestic market is a common development and, in many countries, foreign banks have come to play important roles in the domestic economy. Bonizzi mentions in particular Brazil, Mexico, the Philippines, Eastern Europe, Mexico, South Korea and Turkey. He further finds that banks have been allocating an increasing proportion of credit to households, citing evidence relating to South Africa, Slovakia, South Korea, Brazil, Mexico, Poland and Turkey.

Dos Santos (2013) remarks on the dramatic rise in volume and significance of credit to households across a range of upper middle-income economies, with countries across Latin America, Central and Eastern Europe and South and East Asia experiencing credit to households growing into a major component of overall bank credit extension, often surpassing lending to productive enterprises.

Financial markets have long offered the ability for producers of commodities to sell their produce ahead of time and for users of commodities to buy ahead of time. The development of derivatives and securities based on commodity prices can be viewed in terms of the financialization of commodity markets. "Commodity prices have experienced a period of high volatility, starting to rise in the early 2000s and reaching unprecedented heights in 2008 and again in 2011. Since then, they have decreased considerably but remain highly volatile" (Ederer, Heumesser & Staaritz 2016: 462).

The effects of commodity price volatility have included food security and income volatility for countries dependent on the export of commodities. Commodities have often exhibited price volatility arising from fluctuations in supply arising from weather conditions or changes in demand, for example. The role of financial investors and their increasing presence on commodity derivative markets can add to price volatility. Ederer, Heumesser and Staaritz (2016), in reviewing empirical work, find that the majority of studies "cannot confirm a broadly consistent effect of Index Investors on commodity prices." Their own study uses prices of coffee, cotton, wheat and oil over the period from mid-2006 to mid-2012 using monthly data. Their results overall "suggest that the controversially discussed hypothesis of financialization of commodity derivatives markets can be supported. The increasing and often dominating presence of financial investors on commodity has affected price dynamics in these markets with important implications for physical commodity traders and the economic functions of these markets" (*ibid.*: 479–80).

I now provide some brief reviews of trends in aspects of financialization from a quantitative perspective across different regions of the world. In doing so, a picture emerges of the pervasive nature of financialization alongside the evidence of the differential paces of financialization.

Latin and South America

The index of financial development mentioned above is a composite index on the scale of the financial sector. The components of the FDI are portrayed in Figure 5.5 for Latin and South America. There is a general upward trend in FIA (financial institutions access), FID (financial institutions depth) and in FMD (financial market depth) around a low base; little trend in FMA (financial markets access) and FME (financial markets efficiency); and a significant fall in FIE (financial institutions efficiency) from the early 1980s to the mid-1990s, followed by general rise through to 2018.

The trends for bank deposits by major Latin and South America countries feature in Figure 5.6. Brazil stands out as experiencing the most rapid growth of bank deposits and ending the period with the highest ratio. Other countries show a mixture of little change in the trend over the two decades with small increases. The experience of those countries for which there are data is not included in the "big six", as indicated by the median, which shows a general upward trend with a near doubling of the ratio over the period.

The corresponding information for stock market capitalization is in Figure 5.7. There are massive differences between countries in respect of the scale of the stock market. Many countries have rather small stock markets and their figures are not included in Figure 5.7 where the stock market capitalization (relative to GDP) is less than 5 per cent.

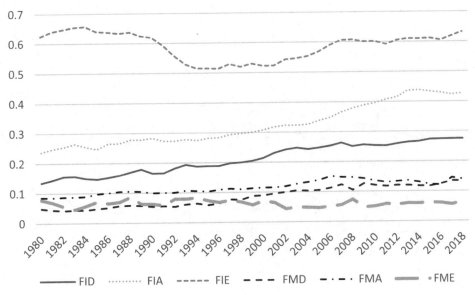

Figure 5.5 FDIs: Latin and South America
Source: calculated from FDIndex database, IMF
FID: financial institutions depth
FIA: financial institutions access
FIE: financial institutions efficiency
FMD: financial markets depth
FMA: financial markets access
FME: financial markets efficiency

There are countries where there appears to be little trend in the ratio of stock market capitalization to GDP. These include Argentina, Chile, Costa Rica, Ecuador, Paraguay and Uruguay (only Argentina shown). The other countries display a general upward trend at least until the GFCs. These include Brazil from 1996 to 2017, from 21 per cent in 1996 rising to 77 per cent in 2007 and to 43 per cent in 2017; and Columbia, rising from 17.5 in 1996 to 64 per cent in 2019 then to 37 per cent in 2017. The only downward trend appears in Venezuela (not shown) from 8.4 per cent in 1996, 12.5 per cent in 1997 to 3.7 per cent in 2012.

The impacts of financialization are illustrated by the experience of Mexico. Levy Orlik (2012: 253) views that "the principal effect of financialization has taken place in the production sector and in foreign trade, led by large domestic and international corporations, where a growing distribution of profits and liquid asset operations is observed, independent of the production sector." Levy-Orlik (2014: 125) notes that the Mexican banking sector "underwent profound institutional changes as bank ownership was transferred to foreign multinational corporations that took advantage of the oligopolistic banking market structure, even though they diversified their activities".

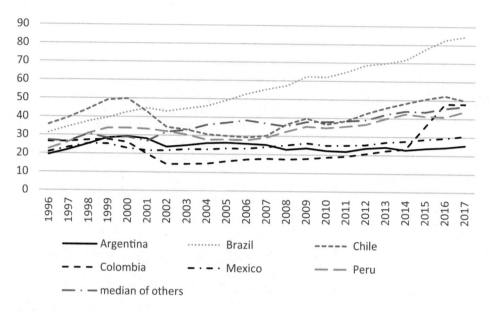

Figure 5.6 Bank deposits to GDP (per cent): Latin and South America
Source: Based on data from Financial Development and Structure Dataset, compiled by Aslı Demirgüç-Kunt *et al.* (2019)

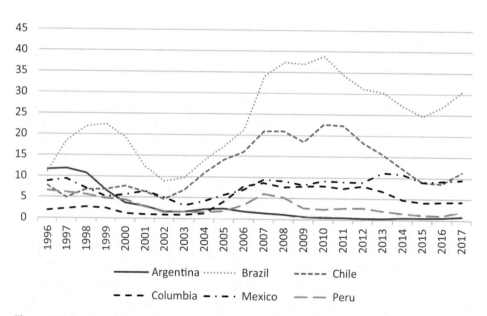

Figure 5.7 Stock market capitalization to GDP (per cent): Latin and South America
Source: Based on data from Financial Development and Structure Dataset, compiled by Aslı Demirgüç-Kunt *et al.* (2019)
Note: The countries included in this figure were those that had stock market capitalization above 5 per cent at some point. Hence the scale of stock market is overstated here.

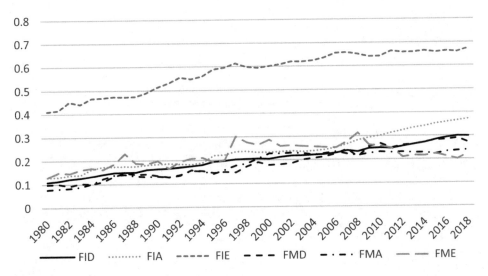

Figure 5.8 FDIs: Asia and Pacific
Source: calculated from FDIndex database, IMF

Asia and Pacific

The Asia and Pacific countries show (Figure 5.8) a rising trend in each of the sub-indices with the exception of FME, which rises from 1980 through to 2008 but declines thereafter.

The experience of seven large Asian countries on bank deposits relative to GDP is illustrated in Figure 5.9. There is a mixture of rapid increases (in Hong Kong, China and Korea over a much shorter period) and no clear trend. The median figure for those countries not included in the "big seven" and for which data are available shows a substantial increase, particularly after 2012.

The scale of stock markets in eight of the larger countries is illustrated in Figure 5.10. The large differences between countries (with Hong Kong as a financial centre) and the large fluctuations in stock market values and the major crashes are readily seen. There are general upward trends in the stock market ratio across countries but with some noticeable exceptions in India, Pakistan and Singapore.

Africa

The FDIs for Africa are illustrated in Figure 5.11 and tend to show an upward trend from a low base. The indices relating to financial markets in particular are low by international comparisons and show little by way of a trend.

The bank deposits to GDP ratio figures in Figure 5.12 refer to the largest (by population) ten African countries for which there is sufficient data. The general upward trend along with the large differences between countries are readily apparent.

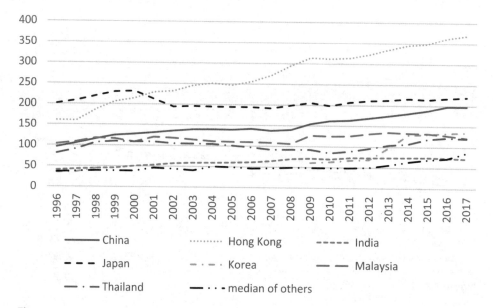

Figure 5.9 Bank deposits to GDP (per cent): Asia
Source: Based on data from Financial Development and Structure Dataset, compiled by Aslı Demirgüç-Kunt *et al.* (2019)

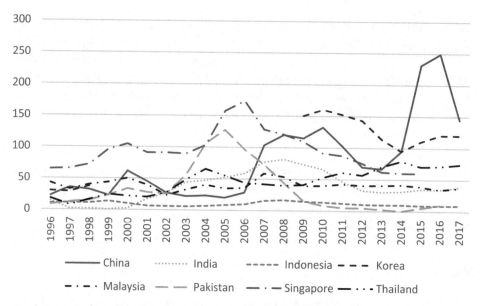

Figure 5.10 Stock market capitalization to GDP (per cent): Asia
Source: Based on data from Financial Development and Structure Dataset, compiled by Aslı Demirgüç-Kunt *et al.* (2019)
Note: Of countries for which data available, Hong Kong not included; Sri Lanka less than 5 per cent in every year but one; Vietnam rises from virtually zero to 15 per cent; Pakistan experiences large fluctuations with tendency to fall.

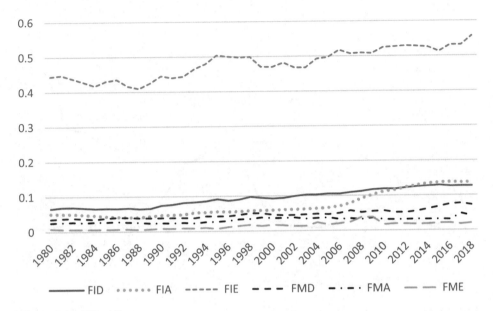

Figure 5.11 FDIs: Africa
Source: calculated from FDIndex database, IMF

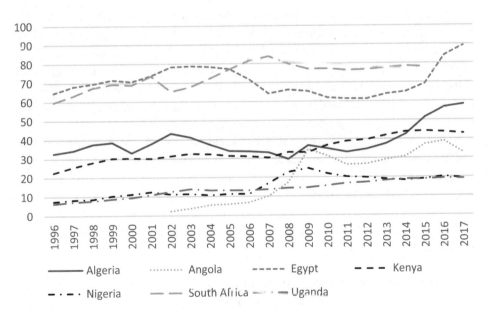

Figure 5.12 Bank deposits to GDP (per cent): sub-Saharan Africa
Source: Based on data from Financial Development and Structure Dataset, compiled by Aslı Demirgüç-Kunt *et al.* (2019)

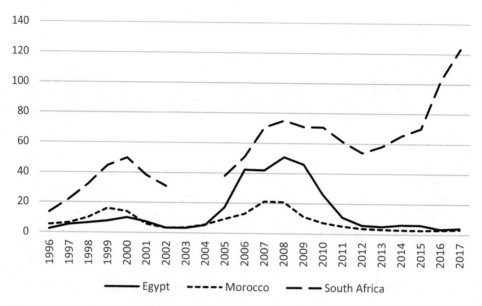

Figure 5.13 Stock market valuations to GDP (per cent): Africa
Source: Based on data from Financial Development and Structure Dataset, compiled by Aslı Demirgüç-Kunt *et al.* (2019)

The financial systems in most African countries are generally recognized to be relatively small by comparison with most other countries, both developed and emerging and developing economies. In the past four decades or so, there has been a near-global growth in financial institutions and financial markets. In respect of stock markets, only three countries have substantial stock market to GDP ratios, and they are illustrated in Figure 5.13. The financialized nature of the South Africa economy can be readily seen from this and the previous figure.

As Beck *et al.* (2011) indicate, the African banking systems are small and concentrated and it is the region with the highest share of foreign-owned banks. Privatization programmes in the 1980s saw many banks returned to private ownership that had been nationalized in the previous years.

Middle East

The FDIs for the Middle East and North African countries are displayed in Figure 5.14. There is a strong upward trend in financial institution efficiency, with financial market efficiency trending upwards until 2008, followed by declines thereafter.

Figure 5.15 portrays the growth of the banking sector over two decades from the mid-1990s. In general, private bank credits relative to GDP show general growth.

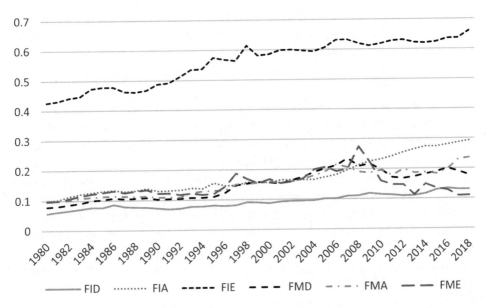

Figure 5.14 FDIs: Middle East and Central Asia
Source: calculated from FDIndex database, IMF

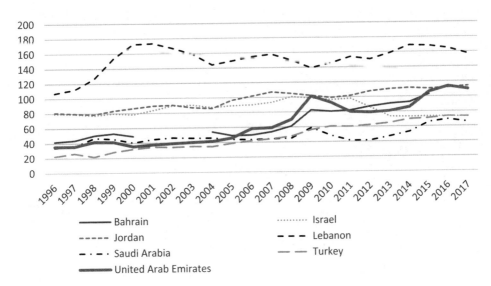

Figure 5.15 Bank deposits to GDP (per cent): Middle East
Source: Based on data from Financial Development and Structure Dataset, compiled by Aslı Demirgüç-Kunt *et al.* (2019)

The relatively little data on stock market valuations available are displayed in Figure 5.16. These figures indicate a strong tendency for "boom and bust", with rapid rises in the early to mid-2000s as many countries did in the build-up to the GFCs of 2008–09. But, in most cases, stock market capitalization (relative to GDP) was at a broadly similar level in 2017 and in the mid-1990s.

IMF (2018a: 4) reports on a "wave of reforms [in Gulf Cooperation Council (GCC) countries] to modernize financial stability policy frameworks and financial safety nets together with improvements in banking supervision also helped improve banking sector resilience and the development of banks' balance sheets. Financial market reforms have focused on strengthening stock market regulation and supervisory frameworks, enhancing corporate governance, and easing restrictions on foreign investment."

Further, banks and other financial institutions are central to the structures of the large business conglomerates. Hanieh (2016: 1240) reports that "all of the leading banks in the GCC have representatives of these business conglomerates sitting on their boards and as investors (alongside state capital)". He notes that ownership of GCC banks remain generally in national hands.

Sovereign wealth funds (SWFs) play a role in the processes of financialization as they become major allocators of funds, both domestically and, more importantly, internationally. Much of the engagement of GCC financial institutions in the global financial markets takes place through SWFs. The ways in which funds are allocated are strongly influenced

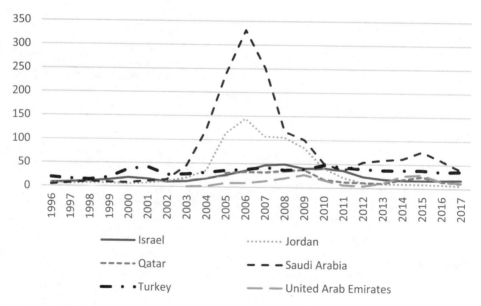

Figure 5.16 Stock market valuation to GDP (per cent): Middle East
Source: Based on data from Financial Development and Structure Dataset, compiled by Aslı Demirgüç-Kunt *et al.* (2019)

by the ways in which SWFs operate. The growth of SWFs could be seen as one dimension of financialization involving the growth of a particular type of financial institution, which has access to substantial funds, often based on natural resources and state-owned.

The GCC Islamic banks and other IF (Islamic finance) institutions are among the largest and most influential of their kind in the world. As of 2018, approximately 44.9 per cent of global assets in Islamic banks are in the GCC countries but also the weight of IF in the Gulf is growing significantly and is explicitly projected in national plans and "vision" documents as a key priority of future development policies (Hanieh 2020). Consequently, financial markets in the Gulf are closely interwoven with the accumulation of Islamic banks, the influence of which extends across a wide range of economic activities. Gulf governments also highlight IF as an essential strategic element to the region's evolving linkages with other international markets (particularly across South-East Asia, the Middle East and Africa). In this manner, IF in the Gulf not only provides illuminating insights into the variegated nature of financialized capitalism outside of the core, but also holds important implications for the future patterning of South–South relations (Hanieh 2018).

The basic Shari'ah tenets in relation to IF, as part of negative screening, include nonengagement in interest-related transactions; no financing in non-Shari'ah compliant businesses; and no investment in non-Shari'ah compliant companies, bonds, stocks and equities; whereas it promotes profit-loss sharing and risk-sharing business models by prohibiting speculative and non-asset-based transactions.

Central and eastern Europe

The countries of central and eastern Europe were part of COMECON, with forms of central planning (with exceptions), until the fall of the Berlin Wall in 1989. The sharp upswing in financialization can be clearly seen in the Figure 5.17. The indices are all below 0.1 before 1990. FIE and FIA rise sharply through the 1990s and early 2000s and then level off. The financial market indices rise much more slowly.

In Figure 5.18a, the ratio of bank deposits to GDP is tracked since 1994 for eight central and eastern European countries. From a generally low base, reflecting the small-scale financial system under the communist regimes, there has been a familiar rapid growth in these countries.

Figure 5.18b provides similar data for the Baltic states, Belarus, Georgia and Ukraine, and follow a broadly similar pattern.

Stock markets were introduced in these countries (Hungary had done so prior to 1989). The growth and volatility of stock markets is illustrated in Figure 5.19, with data on stock market capitalization relative to GDP for four countries. The other countries for which data are available have a capitalization ratio that is generally below 5 per cent.

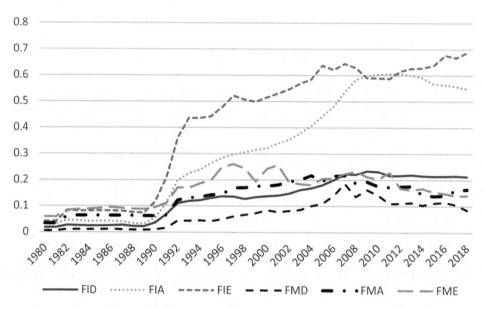

Figure 5.17 FDIs: central and eastern Europe
Source: calculated from FDIndex database, IMF

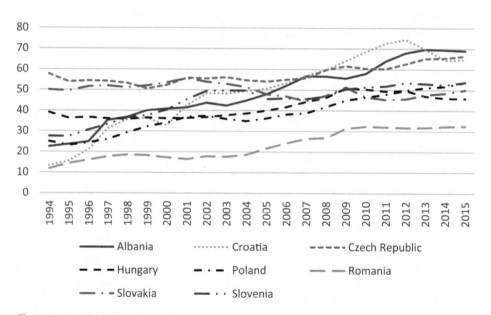

Figure 5.18a Bank deposits to GDP: central and eastern Europe

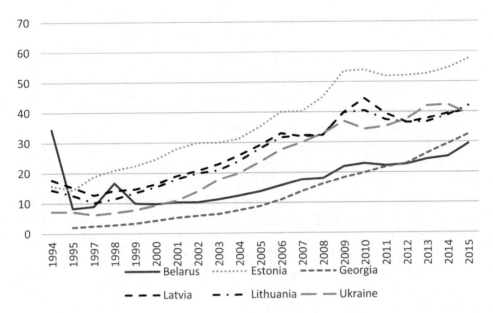

Figure 5.18b Bank deposits to GDP: Baltic states, Belarus, Georgia and Ukraine
Source: Based on data from Financial Development and Structure Dataset, compiled by Aslı Demirgüç-Kunt *et al.* (2019)

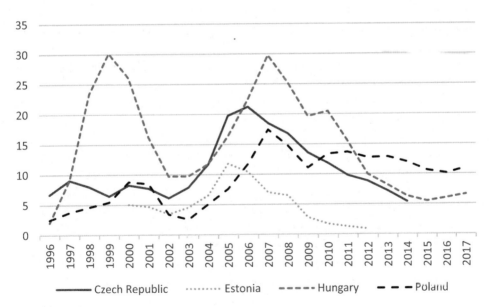

Figure 5.19 Stock market capitalization to GDP: central and eastern Europe
Source: Based on data from Financial Development and Structure Dataset, compiled by Aslı Demirgüç-Kunt *et al.* (2019)

Becker and Cetkovic (2015) view financialization as the main driver of growth prior to the GFCs, whereas the Visegrád countries (Czech Republic, Slovakia, Hungary, Poland) and Slovenia had growth models which were based on both financialization and export industrialization. They see financialization in these countries characterized by dependent financialization, which involves reliance on external funds and control of key components of the financial sector by foreign companies.

Becker and Cetkovic (2015: 85) argue that the Visegrád countries and Slovenia followed a growth model that was not solely dependent on financialization. "A characteristic feature of financialization in Slovenia was the high dependency on external funding of loans of the non-financial enterprise sector. On the other side, the Czech Republic, Poland and Slovakia have been faced with upcoming signs of financialisation since private households have increased their debt steadily. A fast increase in household debt was one key feature of financialization in Hungary. The other one is the high fraction of foreign currency loans. The case of Hungary is thus very similar to the second group of countries considered here, namely Bosnia and Herzegovina, Croatia, Montenegro and Serbia. These countries experienced enormous growth rates in household credits which were partially financed by foreign capital."

Global financialization

The previous sections of this chapter have sought to outline the processes of financialization within development and emerging economies. What may be termed "international financialization" moulds the internal processes of financialization as well as having impacts of the domestic economies more generally.

Lane and Milesi-Ferretti (2007: 223–4), covering the period 1970–2004, with statistics on 145 countries, note that:

> the dramatic increase in international financial integration has been one of the salient global economic developments in recent years. Countries have accumulated substantial cross-border holdings, and there have been sizable shifts in the composition of asset and liability positions, with attendant revisions in the risk profiles of individual economies. In particular, the side of countries' external portfolios in the risk profiles of individual economies. In particular, the size of countries' external portfolios is now such that fluctuations in exchange rates and asset prices cause very significant reallocations of wealth across countries.

A measure of international financial integration for a country is defined as the sum of its stock of external assets and external liabilities expressed as a ratio of its GDP. The IFI ratio is reported as around 45 per cent for both industrial countries and emerging and developing countries in 1970, and there is rise in step through to 1988 when the ratios are around 110 per cent. Thereafter, the ratio for industrialized countries rises to around 320 per cent by 2004, hence almost tripling in 16 years. The ratio for developing and emerging countries reaches around 150 per cent by 2004.

The authors also compute for each country and each year the ratio of sum of stocks of portfolio equity assets and of liabilities and stocks of direct investment assets and of liabilities to GDP, and labelled GEQY. "For the industrial group, the figures show three phases – until 1985, the GEQY ratio was broadly stable; from 1985 to 1995, it gradually increased; since 1996, it increased much more rapidly, save for 2001–2002 reversal in global equity valuations. The trend has been reasonably similar for emerging markets and developing countries, with cross-border equity positions growing strongly during the 1990s" (*ibid*.: 235).

Lane and Milesi-Ferretti (2018: 191) state that "throughout the post-crisis period, the level and composition of capital flows have been substantially different relative to pre-crisis patterns. The shrinking of balance sheets for many large international banks has implied a substantial pullback from cross-border banking. This has been partly replaced by an increase in international bond issuance."

World external assets and also liabilities showed a "remarkable expansion in cross-border positions up to a peak in 2007, these have declined slightly in relation to world GDP" (*ibid*.: 194). Financial centres reported as accounting for around 10 per cent of world GDP in 2007 declining to 8 per cent in 2015 but accounting for over 43 per cent of global financial assets in both years. Emerging and developing economies held 10 per cent of cross-border financial assets in 2007, rising to 13 per cent in 2015, although accounting for around 30 per cent of world GDP in 2007, rising to around 40 per cent in 2015.

Akyüz (2017) sets out how emerging and developing economies have become even more closely integrated into an international financial system. He states that a key factor in the acceleration of integration has been substantial increases in capital inflows starting in the early 2000s and largely continuing through into at least the mid-2010s. He identifies this as the third postwar boom in capital inflows to emerging and developing economies, with a first boom from the late 1970s ending in 1982 with the Latin American debt crisis. The second was in the first half of the 1990s, culminating in financial crises of Mexico in 1994/95, the East Asian crisis of 1997 and then crises in Brazil, Russia, Turkey and Argentina. The third boom surpassed the first two both in terms of the absolute scale of the flows and relative to GDP. He ascribes the boom to the liberalization of international capital flows and greater openness to foreign financial institutions in DEEs.

Banking has come under foreign ownership in many countries (as noted above), which the "World Bank has been particularly active in promoting foreign ownership of banking in developing countries" (Akyüz 2017: 86). The internationalization of finance in emerging and developing economies comes in two overlapping ways: the "rapid expansion of international assets and liabilities as conventionally defined on the basis of residence – that is, the balance sheet positions of residents of EDEs vis-à-vis non-residents" and "the balance sheet positions of nationals of EDEs vis-à-vis foreigners including debt to foreign banks located in EDEs and the external debt of overseas subsidiaries of their corporations" (*ibid.*: 87).

However, as Bortz and Kaltenbrunner (2018: 375) argue, international financialization more than increases in these cross-border capital flows and it "also involves qualitative changes in the way in which people, corporations, banks and governments are integrated into international capital markets". The DEEs have a subordinated position in the international economic and financial system. "As with their integration in the global economy, financialization in developing countries will be shaped by their subordinate position in the world" (Bonizzi 2017: 20).

UNCTAD (2015: 39) argues that "financialization and open capital accounts, and the higher interest rates they often require to maintain stability, compromise domestic investment and the ability of governments to support it, independently of whether any inflows or outflows have taken place. …When inflows or outflows do occur, they can have deleterious effects on industrialization and development in various ways."

UNCTAD (2015: 43) concludes a review of the literature by indicating that the liberalization of capital accounts and domestic financial markets by DEEs led initially to surges in capital inflows, followed by sudden stops and reversals that increased the likelihood of financial crises.

Kaltenbrunner and Painceira (2018: 290) analyse "the recent changes in financial practices and relations in emerging capitalist economies (ECEs) using the example of Brazil. [It is argued] that in ECEs these financial transformations, akin to the financialization phenomena observed in Core Capitalist Economies, are fundamentally shaped by their subordinated integration into a financialised and structured world economy."

In respect of DEEs, Bortz and Kaltenbrunner (2018: 381) state that their international financialization has "been characterized by rising involvement of domestic economic actors in international financial markets". Specifically, they argue that non-financial corporations "have substantially increased their (international) financial exposure, mostly in foreign currency (usually dollars) and through bond issues by offshore affiliates (directing part of the borrowed funds to their home company".

National currencies are hierarchically positioned below the key currency (US dollar) according to their liquidity premium. The currencies issued by the other developed countries are in intermediate positions as they are also liquid currencies, yet with a smaller liquidity premium than the key currency, and these currencies can also be regarded as international currencies. The reduced liquidity premium of currencies at lower ranks of the hierarchy, as for currencies of DEEs, means that they have to offer higher interest rates, are subject to short-term speculative operations and subject to high degree of external vulnerability as changes in international liquidity preference can cause a flight to the currency with highest liquidity premium (see, e.g. Bortz & Kaltenbrunner 2018; Prates 2017).

Conclusions

This chapter has intended to convey a simple story, namely that financialization (at least on the quantitative measures deployed here) has been a near-universal phenomenon over the past four decades or so. It is clear from these simple quantitative measures that countries started from different levels of financialization and proceeded at different paces. There are major differences between groups of countries in regard to the size and scale of their financial sectors as illustrated by Figures 5.1 to 5.4. In subsequent sections I have provided some highly summary quantitative data on the scale of the financial sector in terms of bank deposits and the stock market, alongside the FDIs. The general picture continues of the rising scale of the financial sector, with in some cases a levelling off after the GFCs. Some rather brief indications of the qualitative effects of financialization have been given. The financialization of individual countries has gone alongside global financialization, with economies drawn into international financial markets.

6
FINANCIAL LIBERALIZATION AND FINANCIAL CRISIS

The processes of financialization over the past four to five decades has been spurred on by financial liberalization and the deregulation of the financial sector. The financial sector has lobbied and pushed for deregulation, as the interests of the financial sector press for removal of limitations on their activities, and the lifting of such limitations spurs the growth of the financial sector. Financial liberalization has been part of a much broader neoliberal agenda that promoted deregulation (and also privatization) more generally. It has been promoted by international organizations such as the IMF, and deregulation in terms of the abolition of regulations impeding market entry or restricting competition was one of the policies within the so-called Washington Consensus (Williamson 1990).

An intellectual climate for deregulation was created by academic writings portraying the expansion and evolution of the financial sector as potentially social efficient and in effect being held back by regulations (e.g., controls over the interest rates that could be paid on deposits and charged on loans, regulations on who could operate as a bank). Financial liberalization intends to slacken or lift what are perceived to be constraints on the operations of financial institutions and markets. It is undertaken in the belief that liberalized financial institutions and markets will promote the growth of finance, which in turn promotes savings and investment. Financial liberalization has domestic and external aspects – for example, domestically, the slackening of regulation and controls over interest rates and credit allocation; and, externally, in the reduction and removal of capital controls.

In this chapter, I begin by illustrating the nature and scale of financial liberalization in the past four decades. The intellectual and political support that aided the adoption of financial liberalization around the world and by the international organizations follows. The lifting of limitations on the financial institutions and their operations provided a strong stimulus for the expansion of the financial system. The pressures for financial liberalization arose from the financial sector itself, with intellectual backing provided by many economists and finance specialists and generally backed by international organizations. The promotion of financial liberalization, which often was undertaken by the ending of "financial repression", as the name suggests, involved repressing the development of the financial sector through controls over prices (notably interest rates charged by banks) and quantities (of loans). Financialization liberalization would bring, it was argued, improved economic performance, particularly in respect of economic growth as savings and investment rise. Financial liberalization (and financialization more generally) involves the rapid expansion of credit and rise in asset prices and, as such, financial liberalization readily feeds into the generation of financial crisis.

The pace of financial liberalization

In the first two decades or so after the Second World War there were the first signs of the lifting of restrictions on the financial sector, both domestically (e.g. limits on interest rates, control of credit allocation) and internationally (e.g. controls over capital movements). The World Bank (1989: 51) argued that high rates of inflation and developments in financial markets and institutions had, by the late 1960s and early 1970s, undermined many of the credit and banking controls then in use. Many countries, including the UK, Canada, France, the Netherlands and Sweden, enacted a series of wide-ranging banking reforms. These reforms included abolishing some of the distinctions between different types of institutions, the relaxation of selective credit controls (e.g. controls over the degree to which banks could lend to households, directions over the sectors of the economy to be favoured in the provision of loans), some lifting of exchange controls and the liberalization of interest rates on lending and wholesale deposits.

After an interruption during the 1970s, deregulation of the financial sector resumed in many countries and was in effect joined by wider moves towards deregulation of other industries, with the airline industry in the USA being one of the first. The forms of financial deregulation (often labelled financial liberalization or the lifting of financial repression) took a variety of forms ranging over the elimination or relaxation of controls on the volume of credit and its allocation, upper limits on interest rates, foreign exchange and capital controls, and also often encouraging the development of new types of financial instruments.

One set of forces leading to deregulation came from financial institutions finding ways of circumventing the prevailing rules and regulations. The World Bank, for example, argued that "deregulation was prompted by the growing realization that direct controls had become less effective over time. The growth of the Euromarkets, the development of new financial instruments, and the advent of electronic technology all made it easier to bypass the restrictions. Governments also recognized that the prolonged use of directed and subsidized credit programs would lead to the inefficient use of resources and hinder the development of better systems" (World Bank 1989: 51). The World Bank (1989: 52) was able to celebrate that "deregulation has eliminated many of the man-made barriers to global finance, and technology has lowered the barriers imposed by nature. Advances in computing, information processing, and telecommunications have boosted the volume of business by reducing transaction costs, expanding the scope of trading, and creating information systems that enable institutions to control their risk more efficiently." In other words, deregulation and technology were viewed as major factors in these processes of financialization.

The pace, nature and global reach of financial liberalization can be illustrated from the work of Abiad, Detragiache and Tressel (2008), who constructed indices of financial reforms based on seven elements, which serve as a useful summary of the range of policies that come under this heading of financial liberalization and of the ways in which the financial sector has often been regulated.

The first of the indices refers to the relaxation and removal of a range of controls over credit and loans provided by banks. Credit controls involve placing ceilings on the level and/or rate of expansion of credit and loans. They can also include the imposition of high reserve requirements, which are deemed excessive when judged against what would be required for prudential purposes. This heading would also include policies designed to channel loans into, for example, firms and sectors deemed priority for purposes of industrial policy and development, and limiting loans to other sectors, often private households.

There has been a long history of controls over interest rates and that forms the basis of the second of the indices. Usury laws, for example, placed limits on the level of interest rates. Government controls over bank interest rates, applied to bank lending and/or bank deposits, were widespread in the postwar world. The literature on "financial repression", discussed below, argued that placing such constraints on interest rates served to limit both savings and investment and thereby growth.

The third component relates to entry barriers into the banking and financial system. It is usual for forms of licensing of financial institutions that accepted deposits from the public and is often linked with the relationship of such financial institutions with the central bank (e.g. which financial institutions have access to borrowing of reserves from the central bank). The entry barriers may serve to limit the number of financial companies and the degree of competition. Entry barriers may involve restriction of entry of new domestic banks or foreign banks.

In their indices, Abiad, Detragiache and Tressel (2008) include ownership and, in part, the diminution of state ownership is regarded as part of financial liberalization as the fourth component. State ownership is deemed to involve the state being able to direct the allocation of credit towards favoured sectors, often to enhance industrial development. Indeed, advocates of enhanced roles for state development banks do so precisely for that type of reason – and often linked with what is termed "green investment"; that is, investments in environmentally friendly and low-carbon use activities, an issue to which I return in Chapter 11.

The fifth element refers to the lifting of restrictions on capital movements, particularly outward movements and more generally restrictions on access to foreign currency. These policy measures are often linked with having some control over the exchange rate of the domestic currency and to maintain a fixed exchange rate. As will be seen in the charts below, the general trend has been towards lifting capital and exchange controls, although in recent times the advocacy of the benefits of some capital controls has risen. Grabel (2016: 208) argues that "for now, though, there seems to be substantial momentum propelling increasing use of and experimentation with the flexible deployment of capital controls, in some cases with IMF support and most other cases without IMF resistance". As Chwieroth (2014: 445–46) notes that "while the IMF became more open to the use of capital controls after the Asian financial crisis, freedom of capital movements retained an enduring appeal among many of its staff".

The sixth component refers to the nature of prudential regulations and supervision of the banking sector. In this case, a greater degree of government intervention is coded as a reform. The nature of the regulatory system is viewed in terms of risk-based adequacy ratios based on the Basle 1 capital accord, the banking supervisory agency independent from the executive's influence and sufficiency of its legal power. Are some financial institutions exempt from supervisory oversight? How effective are on-site and off-site examinations of banks?

Seventh comes securities market policy, which is coded to reflect government policies to either restrict or encourage development of securities markets and openness of securities markets to foreign investors.

Each of the indicators is scaled between 0 and 3. In the database three measures are returned for the first indicator (split into directed credit, credit ceilings and credit controls). The general developments of financial liberalization over the period 1973 to 2005 are illustrated in Figures 6.1–6.3 (based on Abiad, Detragiache and Tressel 2008).

Figure 6.1 shows the general trends of the indices. It is noticeable that in the 1970s there were substantial controls over the financial sector in advanced economies, albeit at a lower level than in other economies. On the general indices, the industrialized (advanced) economies have the highest degree of financial liberalization and also displayed a rapid programme of liberalization from 1973 onwards with some flattening off from the late 1990s onwards, not surprisingly as in the advanced economies at least the indices had almost reached the upper limit. Latin American countries ended the period with one of the higher levels of financial liberalization, although the ups and downs of financial liberalization in Latin America can be seen, including decreases in the early 1980s. All the regions included in Figure 6.1 have substantially higher degrees of financial liberalization in 2005 as compared with the 1970s, and the general trend has been upward in most years. Financial liberalization is recorded as occurring in all regions in a continuous way over the period 1973 to 2005 and, on the basis of these indices, particularly focused in the period from mid-1980s to late 1990s, with a flattening off after that.

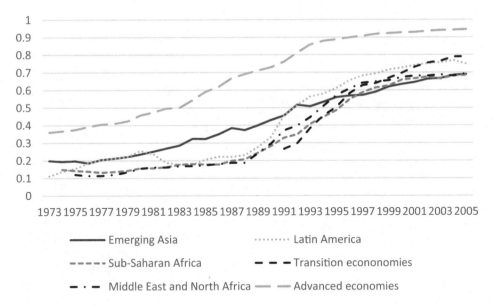

Figure 6.1 Financial reform index
Source: calculated from Abiad, Detragiache and Tressel (2008)

In Figure 6.2, the path of the financial reform index for each of the G7 countries is given. It can be readily seen that, by the early 2000s, three of the countries had recorded a "1" on the index and the others were over 0.85.

Figure 6.3 records the more detailed trends for countries included in the category "advanced". The statistics indicate the almost complete ending of interest rate controls and international capital controls, the reforms of banking supervision (reflecting Basel I and II), and trends towards privatization, although with significant retention of state ownership.

The trends towards financial liberalization are clear from the data in Figures 6.1 and 6.2. In nearly all cases (reforms to banking supervision could be an exception) these policies would foster the growth of the financial sector and its range of activities, which contributes to the processes of financialization. It is, though, relevant to enquire into whether these reforms have beneficial outcomes. In Chapter 10 the general literature on the effects of the larger-scale finance sector on growth and economic performance is examined. It is also relevant to note (and will be discussed below) that the lifting of interest rate ceilings and of credit controls on banks will lead to an expansion of credit and loans and also the issue whether such expansion, particularly if rapid, leads to credit booms and busts.

Alongside these trends towards financial liberalization, there are many questions of the effectiveness with which the remaining regulations were implemented. There are the

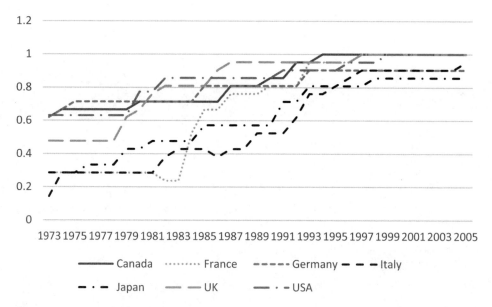

Figure 6.2 Financial reform index: G7 countries
Source: calculated from Abiad, Detragiache and Tressel (2008)

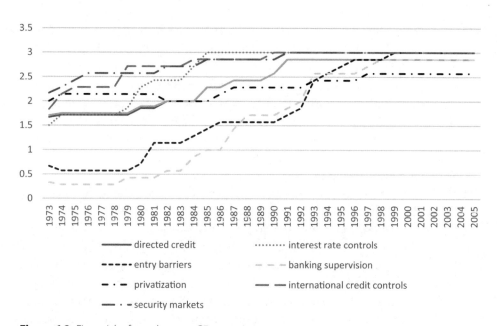

Figure 6.3 Financial reforms by type: G7 countries

well-known issues of regulatory capture, whereby the regulators come to operate more in the interests of those being regulated than the general public. Regulations designed to benefit consumers may lead to substantial benefits in aggregate but with relatively small benefits per person and benefits that the public may have little awareness of in terms of the differences between a regulated and a non-regulated situation. On the other hand, the perceived costs of regulations and their impact would fall on a relatively small number of producers, who would have incentives to lobby the regulatory agency for changes in the regulations. What has become known as "agency capture" may follow (Stigler 1971), whereby the regulatory agency comes under the power of those it seeks to regulate, aided by the movement of people between the agency and the industry.

There can be the doubts held by regulators and others in the value of regulation. If so-called free markets are believed to generate economically efficient outcomes, then why regulate markets? Hindmoor and McConnell (2015: 90), for example, argue that in the UK the key institutions such as the Bank of England, the Treasury, the Financial Services Authority, along with the major banks in the UK and USA shared this faith in markets and their efficiency and stability.

The ideas of a "great moderation" and stable financial markets were widespread among the financial establishment in the first years of the new millennium. As Hindmoor and McConnell (2015: 89–90) argue, there were few warning signals on instabilities in the financial markets. In the UK, "the Bank of England, the Chancellor of the Exchequer, MPs, leader writers on the *Times* and the *Financial Times*, bank executives and credit rating agencies failed to identify key vulnerabilities in the financial system".

The apparent stability of the 1990s and 2000s built up a widespread complacency. Kregel (2010: 6) quotes from a *Washington Post* article that the performance of the Federal Reserve as a regulatory agency "was crippled by the doubts of senior officials about the value of regulation, by a tendency to discount anecdotal evidence of problems and by its affinity for the financial industry". The "doubts of senior officials" and many others who praised the stability of the so-called "great moderation" can be closely linked with an approach to regulation where financial markets are viewed as inherently stable and any crisis arises from some outside forces ("exogenous shocks"). If crisis comes from outside shocks, then the appropriate policy response would not be regulation of the sector but instead adopting an approach of dealing with the crisis when it arises. The alternative perspective is, of course, to treat the financial sector (and the economy more generally) as inherently unstable and prone to crisis, which may be modifiable through appropriate regulation and implementation. The "affinity for the financial industry" is an expression of the well-known issue for regulatory agencies, not just those covering the financial sector of "regulatory capture".

The 1990s and the early 2000s have been described with particular reference to the USA but also extending to other industrialized economies as "the great moderation" (Bernanke 2004). The period was seen as one of stability and growth (in the words of

Mervyn King, governor of Bank of England, the NICE decade non-inflationary continuous expansion) by comparison with the 1970s and 1980s and the high and variable rates of inflation. The 1990s and early 2000s were generally free from financial crisis in the industrialized countries (although note Sweden in 1992), and severe recession (UK after 1992, USA recession in 2001 following the bursting of the dot-com bubble). Many have argued that the combination of the perception of a stable economic environment and relatively low interest rates provided an atmosphere for risk-taking – the perceived risks were low and high risk was associated with higher returns.

Alan Greenspan, head of the US Federal Reserve 1987–2005, and thereby heading the regulatory authority, had been viewed as a strong proponent of deregulation and adopting a relaxed stance on the implementation of the regulations. However, he "admitted to a congressional committee yesterday that he had been 'partially wrong' in his hands-off approach towards the banking industry and that the credit crunch had left him in a state of shocked disbelief. 'I have found a flaw,' said Greenspan, referring to his economic philosophy. 'I don't know how significant or permanent it is. But I have been very distressed by that fact.' He further conceded that the global financial crisis has exposed a 'mistake' in the free-market ideology which guided his 18-year stewardship of US monetary policy."[1]

Davis and Walsh (2016: 677) quote UK Labour MP Geoffrey Robinson to the effect that the then UK minister of the City, Ed Balls "went round preaching deregulation … 'light touch, light touch' everywhere he went … and the Treasury's light touch idea was to attract as much as we could of these [financial] activities to London, certainly we were successful there … [but] we definitely took our eye off the ball and paid a heavy price for it".

It is significant that a government minister was appointed specifically to defend the interests of the London financial centre. The UK Financial Services Authority, set up in 2001 to regulate financial service, "regulates diffidently, and was evidently intended as little more than window-dressing … in its covert and successful bid to attract US companies to London, allowed banks and insurance companies operating from the City to do so with much less capital than similar organizations in New York. Its commitment to light and limited regulation meant that to deal with British financials markets one-third the size of those in the US, it has eleven times fewer enforcement agents than that Securities and Exchange Commission" (Wade 2008: 13).

Another strand of argument downplaying regulation was the argument deployed particularly by US regulators that "that market discipline would support adequate levels of capital and liquidity at the major banks and investment banks, and that aggressive regulation was unnecessary or counterproductive" Duffie (2019: 82). But clearly,

---

1. See "Greenspan – I was wrong about the economy. Sort of", *The Guardian*, 24 October 2008; www.theg uardian.com/business/2008/oct/24/economics-creditcrunch-federal-reserve-greenspan

market discipline did not work to prevent the excessive risk-taking by banks and other financial institutions, which contributed to the GFCs. Lagarde (2018) argued that it was "financial innovation that vastly outpaced regulation and supervision". Financial institutions "went on a frenzy of reckless risk-taking", which included less reliance on deposits and more on short-term funding, loans being moved off balance sheet through securitization, and the shifts of activity to parts of the financial sector that were subject to less regulatory oversight. "Globalization also contributed to the problem through regulatory arbitrage – financial institutions were able to demand lighter oversight based on their ability to decamp to more favorable jurisdictions" (Lagarde 2018).

A major step on the path to financial liberalization in the UK came with the Competition and Credit Control Act 1971, which facilitated a credit boom feeding into a property boom in 1972–73, a subsequent collapse, then a secondary banking crisis of 1973–75 (Reid 1982). Oren and Blyth (2019: 615) report on a memorandum entitled "Final Steps" sent to Margaret Thatcher by Professor Brian Griffiths and David Willets from her Policy Unit (PREM 19/1718, 3 June 1986), which "fully acknowledge[d] the potential for boom-and-bust cycles engendered by liberalisation." However the Policy Unit and Treasury officials "claimed that 'this time is different' because much tighter monetary policy, better macroeconomic policy, and a more market-friendly regulatory framework made the financial system, as a whole, much safer for investors and borrowers".

Another major step in the UK to financial liberalization was what became known as the "Big Bang" in 1986, the deregulation of UK financial markets, including the abolition of fixed commission charges and of the distinction between stockjobbers and stockbrokers on the London Stock Exchange and a change from open-outcry to electronic, screen-based trading. Legislation that facilitated demutualization (and generally lead to the members of an institution that demutualized a substantial monetary windfall) encouraged many (mutual) building societies to become private companies.[2]

However, Golub, Kaya and Reay (2015: 684) argue that it is too simplistic to attribute the Federal Reserve's failure over regulation to free-market ideology, reliance on unrealistic models and regulatory capture. They argue that a combination of factors, "most prominently confidence in 'post hoc interventionism' as the best policy response to bubbles, and institutional routines that directed attention away from the crucial issues, were what blinded the Fed to mounting systemic risks in the pre-crisis period".

Duffie (2019: 81–2) argues the failures of financial supervision have now been widely recognized. He quotes Spillenkothen (2010), director of banking supervision and regulation at the Federal Reserve Board from 1991 to 2006, as writing that "prior to the crisis, career supervisors in the regions and at agency headquarters – primarily at the

---

2. The record of the former building societies is strewn with failures: see, for example, www.thenews.coop/85589/sector/big-bang-demutualisation-building-societies-failed/

Federal Reserve, Office of the Comptroller of the Currency (OCC), and SEC – failed to adequately identify and prevent the build-up of extreme leverage and risk in the financial system, particularly in large financial institutions".

Tarullo (2019) notes the ways in which developments in financial markets and in banking undermined the effectiveness of and rationale for the US regulatory framework, which had been put in place in the New Deal era of the 1930s. He argues that the removal of many restrictions on the activities and affiliations of banks allowed them to grow rapidly as well as "shadow banking", operating outside of most regulations, also growing rapidly. The Commodity Futures Modernization Act of 2000 ensured that OTC derivatives were unregulated. It clarified that most OTC derivative transactions between "sophisticated parties would not be regulated as "futures" or as "securities" under federal law but the major dealers of those products would have their dealings in OTC derivatives supervised by the federal regulators under general "safety and soundness" standards.

Mark Carney, when Governor of the Bank of England, spoke of the "three lies of finance" (Carney 2015: 3). The first lie is the notion that "this time is different", which he views in terms of initial successes from a policy framework "gradually building into a blind faith in a new era of effortless prosperity". He notes that price stability (which is and remains the major focus of monetary policy through inflation targeting) does not guarantee financial stability. "Most importantly – and this is the lie – complacency among individuals and institutions, fed by a long period of macroeconomic stability and rising asset prices, made this remorseless borrowing seem sensible."

The second lie is that "markets always clear". Carney argues that there was a deep-seated faith in markets, which flourished in the 1990s and 2000s. The myth that finance can regulate and correct itself spontaneously led the authorities to retreat from their regulatory and supervisory responsibilities. He argues that dangerous consequences flow from this "lie". If markets always clear and are in equilibrium (as is taken in the "efficient markets hypothesis" and the "rational expectations" approach more generally) then "bubbles can neither be identified nor can their potential causes be addressed. Such thinking dominated the practical indifference to the housing and credit booms before the crisis" (*ibid.*: 5). Further, markets are treated as stable and not requiring policies designed to monitor and address instabilities.

The third lie is that "markets are moral", whereas "the crisis showed that if left unattended, markets can be prone to excess and abuse" (*ibid.*: 8) – something of an understatement and to which we return in a later chapter.

Pressures for financial liberalization

Financial liberalization and deregulation have received strong intellectual support and advocacy from many economists and finance specialists. The central argument has been that freeing financial institutions and markets from government intervention and limits on their activities would enhance financial development and deepening (as it was often called), stimulating savings and investment and, more generally, improve efficiency; arguments clearly in line with a neoliberal agenda.

Goldsmith (1969) argued that the main transmission channel of financial liberalization was the effect on the efficiency of the allocation of capital with higher quality investment. McKinnon (1973), Shaw (1973) and many others argued that government regulations on the banking system restrain the activities of the banks with regard to interest rates and the allocation of credit, which in turn limit the funds allocated to investors and lower the quantity and quality of investment and thereby growth. The latter referred to a high degree of regulation of the banking and financial system in many countries and specifically control by the central bank and government of the level of interest rates and the allocation of credit. These were usually perceived to involve the enforcement of interest rates on loans below the "market level" and associated direction of loans towards those sectors given preferential treatment in the allocation of credit (and away from the sectors without such treatment).

Those policies involved financial regulations and state-owned or state-directed banks, all of which were used for a range of economic and social purposes. For example, subsidising housing, supporting financial infrastructure, development and industrial policy in more general terms, as well as promoting exports and small businesses (Grabel 1997). Central banks in both developing and developed countries supported those policies and activities through a variety of tools and mechanisms, most importantly through subsidising credit and regulating financial institutions to direct credit to specific sectors and for specific purposes (Epstein 2006). The recommendation of the financial liberalization proponents was the removal of ceilings on interest rates and scrapping of credit allocation policies, as these limits on interest rates were viewed as preventing an equilibrium between savings (taking the form of bank deposits) and investment (funded by loans) being established. With interest rates set relatively low, it is postulated that savings would be lower (than they would be in the equilibrium outcome) and that would constrain the availability of funds for investment, and lower investment. This was then seen as a major way in which "financial repression" with these limits would lead to lower investment, and thereby economic growth, and that the lifting of "financial repression" stimulating financial development would speed up economic development.

This approach in respect of banks treats savings as deposited in bank accounts and investment as funded by bank loans. It is based on a view of banks in which deposits make loans and the amount of loans provided is limited by the amount of bank deposits. Banks act merely as financial intermediaries between savers and investors. It is well recognized that this is not an accurate representation of the activities of clearing banks. Deposits by the public at clearing banks serve as part of the stock of money – bank deposits are the predominant way in which purchases are financed. When banks provide loans, deposits and hence money is created; when loans are repaid, money is destroyed. Decisions on how many loans and to whom are made by banks in response to what they deem credit-worthy demand for loans. Loans create deposits rather than deposits enabling the creation of loans. The limitation on the creation of loans comes from banks' willingness to become more illiquid in that a bank may be vulnerable from a withdrawal of deposits – whether in the form of cash withdrawal or through their customers making net payments to customers of other banks.

In the context of financial liberalization, the potential problems arise from rapid credit creation, which may be unleashed by financial liberalization and the relaxation of controls over the volume of credit. The processes of financial liberalization (and a general trend towards deregulation, although there are also changes in the form of regulation involved) may well exacerbate the tendencies towards instability. This was expressed as "financial liberalization produces an upward step-change in the intensity of the domestic drive towards financial innovation. ... It thereby speeds up the process by which debt ratios of commercial concerns and financial institutions rise, escalating financial fragility, and it hastens the day when banking and financial crises loom" (Arestis & Glickman 2002: 244–5).

World Bank (1989: 1) provides a good illustration of the promotion of financial liberalization by international organizations. They note the shift in many developing countries during the 1980s towards private sector and market mechanisms (in effect neoliberalism) – "To obtain all the benefits of greater reliance on voluntary, market-based decision-making, they need efficient financial systems." It refers to past "governments' efforts to promote economic development by controlling interest rates, directing credit to priority sectors, and securing inexpensive funding for their own activities have undermined financial development". It continues by praising the development of "a more robust and balanced financial structure [which] will improve the ability of domestic financial systems to contribute to growth". Under what is termed the interventionist approach, they argue that "under government pressure, banks did lend to state enterprises and priority sectors at below-market interest rates, but spreads were often too small to cover the banks' costs. Many of the direct loans were not repaid. Interest rate controls discouraged savers from holding domestic financial assets and discouraged institutions from lending longer term or to riskier borrowers. In some countries, public borrowing from commercial banks displaced lending to the private sector; in others, public borrowing financed by money creation led to rapid inflation" (*ibid.*: 3). It is acknowledged that "financial liberalization needs to be undertaken alongside macroeconomic reform. ... And to avoid the destabilizing capital flows that proved so difficult to manage in several countries attempting deregulation, care must be taken in opening the capital account."

The "Washington Consensus" was a neoliberal agenda largely promoted by government and agencies rather than by corporations (Williamson 1990; see Williamson 2004 for further discussion). It was closely linked with neoliberalism, including "financial liberalization, involving an ultimate objective of market-determined interest rates" (Williamson 2004: 196) along with a unified and competitive exchange rate. It covered fiscal policy invoking "fiscal discipline" and small budget deficits, plus a shift of public expenditure away from subsidies and towards education, infrastructure investment and a broadening of the tax base and lower marginal tax rates. It sought to promote liberalization of inward foreign direct investment, providing legal security for property rights; deregulation with the abolition of regulations that impede market entry or restrict competition and prudential oversight of financial institutions; and, further, privatization of state enterprises and trade liberalization with elimination of quantitative restrictions.

Stiglitz (1994: 20) noted that the spirit of deregulation had become a dominant theme in general economic policy discussions and increasingly in financial markets. "The claim is that market liberalization will enable the financial system to perform its main function of allocating scarce capital more efficiently and will thus benefit the rest of the economy." He argues that much of the rationale for liberalizing financial markets is based neither on a sound economic understanding of how these markets work nor on the potential scope for government intervention. Often, too, it lacks an understanding of the historical events and political forces that have led governments to assume their present role. He argues that much of the rationale for liberalising financial markets is "based on an ideological commitment to an idealized conception of markets that is grounded neither in fact nor in economic theory".

Beliefs that competitive market mechanisms driven by profit-seeking firms would generate socially optimal outcomes (a theoretical proposition closely associated with neoliberalism as discussed in Chapter 3) was a strong force behind deregulation. They also helped to create "an environment in which both complicated financial innovations and risky decisions made by financial institutions went unchecked" (Orhangazi 2014: 17). Further, "part of the rhetoric on financial deregulation included an emphasis on self-surveillance and self-policing of the financial sector. For example, assessment and regulation of sophisticated financial instruments such as derivatives, CDOs and structured investment vehicles were mostly left to financial market institutions, and they used highly sophisticated quantitative models of risk assessment for this purpose. This led to an underestimation of the real risks and created a situation in which it became increasingly more difficult to distinguish poor judgement from fraudulent behaviour" (*ibid.*), which became significant factors in the lead-up to the GFCs.

IMF (2012: 3) point out that "from a theoretical perspective, liberalizing capital flows can benefit investors in both source and recipient countries by allowing a better allocation of resources across countries. This result rests on the assumptions of perfect markets and full information", which have been widely challenged as applicable to financial markets where "full information" on a fundamentally uncertain future is unobtainable, and where (as argued by Stiglitz and many others) financial markets always involve credit rationing in some form and hence cannot approximate to the notion of a perfect market.

IMF (2012) highlighted that liberalization can "promote (i) cross-border risk-sharing; (ii) accelerated development of domestic financial systems due to greater competition; and (iii) policy discipline, thereby enhancing growth and welfare." IMF (2012a) goes on to say that financial liberalization can be associated with an increase in macroeconomic volatility and vulnerability to crises. It is then acknowledged that the empirical evidence on the benefits of liberalizing capital flows is mixed ranging from positive effects through to no significant effects.

Financial liberalization and financial crisis

Financial liberalization is promoted on the basis that it leads to expansion of the financial sector and the stimulation of savings and investment. It is also likely to involve expansion of credit and of household debt. A rapid expansion of credit linked with asset price inflation and risky loans is likely to be a forerunner of financial crisis. Arestis (2004: 254) pointed out the problematic nature of the theoretical framework of financial liberalization, noting that the financial liberalization thesis had encountered increasing scepticism over the years. It was promoted by the IMF and the World Bank as part of more general reforms and structural adjustment programmes but he argues that "events following the implementation of financial liberalization prescriptions did not justify the theoretical premises". In his view, this included the notion that financial liberalization enhanced economic growth and that deregulated banking leads to stability of the financial system. The financial liberalization thesis was also based on the view that savings precede and cause investment, rather than the Keynesian perspective that investment in a sense causes savings.

Many authors have investigated the links between financial liberalization and the generation of financial crisis. One of the first was Diaz-Alejandro (1985), who sought to understand how the financial sector reforms that had aimed at ending "financial repression", including lifting limits on interest rates and removal of what were viewed as government-induced distortions aimed at ending "financial repression", had led by 1983 to financial crises. He characterized the results as involving widespread bankruptcies, and government interventions and nationalizations had been responses to the financial crises. Low domestic savings were also involved, although the advocates of lifting financial repression had predicted higher savings, investment and growth as flowing from ending financial repression. His discussion of the experiences in Chile in the 1970s illustrates the ways in which financial liberalization can lead to credit booms, inadequate regulation and what becomes the political necessity to bail out failing banks.

The study by Demirgüç-Kunt and Detragiache (1998) of 53 countries in the period 1980–95 finds that financial liberalization increases the probability of a banking crisis, although the probability is lessened where there is a strong institutional environment.

Further, after liberalization, countries that had been financially repressed tend to have improved financial development following financial liberalization even if they experience a banking crisis.

Arestis and Stein (2005: 384) draw attention to the linkages between financial liberalization and subsequent financial crisis, fuelled by rapid credit expansion following deregulation and often asset price bubbles. They note the major crises in Argentina, Ecuador, Thailand, Russia, Turkey, Uruguay, Columbia, Indonesia, Kenya and South Korea over the preceding decade. They argue that "much of this instability has been associated with rapid financial liberalization, without exception".

Financial liberalization and economic performance

Financial liberalization has been viewed by many as developing financial markets and boosting savings and the linkages between savings and investment, thereby raising economic growth. Others have pointed to the potential role of financial liberalization policies in creating credit booms, leading into economic and financial crises. Bumann, Hermes and Lensink (2012: 268) note that academic research that has investigated the nature of the relationship between financial liberalization and economic growth has been inconclusive. They conduct a meta-analysis based on 60 different empirical studies of financial liberalization, whether of domestic financial systems or of capital controls. Their results indicate "a positive albeit weak effect of financial liberalization on growth. This result suggests that financial liberalization is not a panacea for achieving strong economic growth."

In a paper that examines the relationship between macroeconomic performance and financial stability, Creel, Hubert and Labondance (2015: 32) test whether financial stability affects economic performance. They find that "in most cases, the use of these indicators shows that financial instability has a negative effect on economic performance, and their inclusion does not affect the financial depth effect. Financial instability – independently from financial deepening – has a negative effect on the economy."

Caner (2010) asks the question: does financialization help the poor?. She notes that financial liberalization policies pursued during the present era of financialization form part of what may be termed a neoliberal agenda of marketization, privatization, flexibilization and deregulation. As such, it is not expected that financial liberalization policies would be particularly concerned with poverty alleviation, although its proponents would argue for "trickle down" effects eventually benefiting the poor. Caner argues that there is no conclusive evidence in favour of a positive effect of financial liberalization on growth. "Evidently, when [financial liberalization] is applied without first maintaining macroeconomic stability and establishing the supporting institutions and policies, even when it brings economic expansion, it often comes at the cost of devastating crises and increasing economic inequality. The poor appear to pay a higher price in the aftermath of these crises". She also argues that there is a lack of evidence that financial liberalization increases the availability of credit or financial services to the poor.

Arestis and Caner (2005: 122) identify channels through which financial liberalization may impact on the poor. There is the general channel that financial liberalization is argued to lead to financial and economic development and thereby have some effects of both poor and the rich. Financial liberalization has often led to financial crisis and the poor may well be more severely affected by such crises. The crisis channel works through increasing volatility and vulnerability to financial crises following liberalization. Another channel may come insofar as there is better access to credit and financial services for the poor following financial liberalization. They conclude that financial liberalization applied "without maintaining macroeconomic stability and establishing the supporting institutions and policies, even when it brings economic expansion, it often comes at the cost of devastating crises and increasing economic inequality. ... The poor appear to pay a higher price than the rich in the aftermath of these crises."

The GFCs were preceded by a long period of deregulation and also slack regulation. Several authors have focused on financial deregulation as a major contributing factor in laying down the conditions for the financial crisis, particularly in the USA. Orhangazi (2015) identifies five related channels through which financial deregulation provided a foundation for the crisis. These include the emergence and expansion of shadow banking with a minimum degree of regulation (and hence the effective decline of the reach of regulation). There were other failures of regulation that enabled the rapid expansion of financial innovations, including complex financial derivatives and the accompanying excessive leverage, increased securitization and increased risk-taking by financial institutions.

Arestis (2016) views financial liberalization in the USA as a major cause of the American source of the GFCs. He traces financial liberalization from 1977, with the deregulation of commissions for stock trading and investment banks being allowed to introduce unsecured current accounts. Regulation Q, which had placed ceilings on retail deposit interest rates in the 1980s, was removed during that same decade. The most significant liberalization was the repeal in 1999 of the Glass-Steagall Act of 1933, which had been introduced in response to the banking crises of 1929 to 1933, aimed to separate the activities of commercial banks and the risk-taking "investment or merchant" banks along with strict regulation of the financial services industry. The repeal of the Act in 1999 enabled investment banks to branch into new activities and commercial banks to encroach on the investment banks' other traditional preserves. The final step in the process was another major and relevant legislative phase, which was the repeal of the Shed-Johnson jurisdictional accord of 1982, which banned regulation of OTC derivatives.

Ghosh (2005: 16) regards the arguments in favour of financial liberalization as rather weak. She argues that "in many cases, the social and economic effects have been especially adverse for the poor and for farmers and workers, who have not only suffered more precarious conditions even during a so-called 'financial boom', but who have typic-ally also been the worst affected during a financial crisis or the subsequent adjustment". Ghosh argues that financial liberalization creates exposure to increased risks of financial crises, external and internal, deflationary impact on real economic activity and reduced access to funds. She concludes that "there is a strong case for developing countries to ensure that their own financial systems are adequately regulated with respect to their own specific requirements, which may vary substantially, depending upon the size and nature of their economies, the extent of external integration, the relative importance of the banking system vis-à-vis the capital market, and so on" (*ibid.*).

Eichacker (2015: 324) examines European financial reforms from the 1970s through the 1990s and argues that they increased vulnerability to financial crisis. This was added to by the Economic and Monetary Union, which involved a rapid opening of financial markets and unprecedented capital flows following elimination of capital controls. She uses and tests a model that relates the onset of financial crisis in 17 European countries between 1983 and 2011 to financial liberalization (measured by gross capital flows, bank liberalization and supervision), along with a range of control variables. She finds that "the model robustly supports the idea that financial liberalization has played a significant role in increasing the likelihood of financial crisis in these countries".

Conclusions

The financial sector has promoted financial liberalization, which in turn has been a sig-nificant factor in the expansion of the financial system and financialization more gener-ally. Financial liberalization, like the expansion of the financial sector more generally, is promoted along the lines that economic efficiency will be enhanced as regulations and restrictions are reduced and savings and investment are promoted. Examining finan-cial liberalization illustrates the academic intellectual support for deregulation and for the growth of the financial sector. It also illustrates the support from international organizations and many others in promoting financialization.

Financial liberalization, like financialization more broadly, can bring economic and social benefits but does so alongside economic and social costs. In this chapter, the ways in which financial liberalization and the lifting of financial repression aided financial instability has been highlighted, as well as some of the ways in which financial liberaliza-tion did not live up to the claimed effects of stimulating savings and investment.

7
FINANCIALIZATION OF THE CORPORATION AND THE PURSUIT OF SHAREHOLDER VALUE

In the present era of financialization, one of the defining dimensions has been the financialization of the corporation and the "pursuit of shareholder value" (see Chapter 2). One aspect of the financialization of the corporation is the degree to which non-financial corporations are becoming more involved with finance and financial transactions. While non-financial corporations are predominantly involved with production and distribution of goods and services, they have always been involved with finance, at least in the minimal sense of using money to buy goods and services and borrowing through loans and the issue of bonds and equity to fund investment. In the financialization era, non-financial corporations have become increasingly involved with finance. This includes the provision of loans to consumers to enable purchase of their products (a notable example being car companies with significant finance divisions). It also includes extensive financial dealing, ranging from holding and managing extensive financial assets through to the engagement in commodity market futures.

The "pursuit of shareholder value" is the promotion of the view that profits and dividends (and thereby the stock market valuation of the corporation) should be or are the primary purpose of the corporation. This has been variously argued along legal grounds and on efficiency grounds. This perspective of the central importance of the "pursuit of shareholder value" places the shareholders (and thereby financial interests) above those of other stakeholders such as employees, customers and the wider society. Financial markets and financial institutions exert, through a variety of routes, pressures on the managers of corporations to adopt business practices promoting shareholder value. The pressures for shareholder value come at the expense of other stakeholders of the corporation, workers, customers and the wider public.

Froud et al. (2006: 8) argue that "shareholder value was never a well-defined concept but a pliable rhetoric that was appropriated and inflected by different social actors". In their review of the evidence on giant company CEO pay over 20 years they show how top managers in both US and UK companies were able to become rich through what they term "value skimming". Further, they argue that it is growing pressure from capital markets that redefines company strategy and changes the work of management.

Capitalist firms have always been seen as pursuing profits for their owners, so in what respects is the notion of the pursuit of shareholder value based on the profit prospects and dividend payments anything more than an alternative label for pursuit of profits? In a small capitalist unincorporated firm, the manager, the key decision-maker and the owner may often be one and the same. The pursuit of shareholder value is at one level posed in terms of the shareholders enforcing their interests on the managers, where there is a separation of identity and of interests between the managers and the shareholders. Financialization has generally involved the growth of stock markets and hence more corporations with their shares traded on stock markets. It has also involved financial institutions becoming increasingly shareholders in non-financial corporations and hence the pursuit of shareholder value has been to the benefit of financial institutions.

Financialization often involves the growth of ownership and dealings in equity by the financial sector and the growth of financial markets. There has been the speed-up in the trading of equity (as with other financial assets) and emphasis on short-term share-price performance rather than on longer-term growth prospects. The particular significance of these developments here comes from the impact on decisions on investment, employment, output, etc., as made by corporations.

The basic idea that the pursuit of profits by firms is economically beneficial and efficient has a long history in economics and beyond. It would follow that the responsibility of those managing a corporation would be to shareholders and not to those (employees, customers and wider society) who could be viewed as stakeholders in the corporation.

Financial institutions, notably in the form of pension funds, insurance companies, investment banks, whether trading on their own account or on behalf of others, become owners of equity and have interests in the price of equity. The financial institutions and their managers have material interests in the corporate performance, at least as reflected in the equity price. At the same time, and in some ways paradoxically, the frequency of trading has speeded up and hence the average length of time for which an equity is held is reduced. The exercise of ownership interest in the performance of a corporation can be enhanced with the growth of financial institutions insofar as a large number of small individual shareholders is replaced by a small number of financial institutions with a sizeable interest. The higher frequency trading, though, means that a financial institution's portfolio is continuously changing and reliance on price changes for profits.

The arguments are examined on how such a "pursuit of shareholder value" by financial institutions impacts on the decisions of non-financial corporations in respect of investment, research and development, employment, etc. The "pursuit of shareholder value" can often be portrayed in terms of discipline on the managers of the corporations through the operation of financial markets, with markets presented in terms of a natural phenomenon. The reality is that it is the relatively small number of financial institutions and financial traders who are the "market forces". The empirical evidence is examined on these possible effects of financialization on investment and capital accumulation and thereby growth, with the general perspective that there has been a dampening effect on investment.

The relationships between financialization and neoliberalism features in Chapter 3. Neoliberalism includes the promotion of markets and, within the financial sector and elsewhere, the liberalization and deregulation of markets. It can also be associated with promotion of the idea of "flexible labour markets". At one level, flexible labour markets can be viewed in terms of ease of varying wages as demand conditions change and, according to the competitive theory, alleviating unemployment. At another level, flexible labour markets involve ease of "hire and fire", short-term contracts, etc. The pursuit of shareholder value has implications for the nature of employment relations, with not only emphasis on short-term profits coming at the expense of wages and a "hire and fire" mentality.

The pursuit of shareholder value: background

Minsky (1988, 1993) identified four stages of (American) capitalism, and the latter two are particularly relevant here (see Chapter 2). The third and postwar stage was labelled "managerial capitalism", succeeded by the stage of the "money manager". Under managerial capitalism the managers of corporations were viewed as relatively independent of shareholders and financial markets. Although the corporate management were legally the agents of shareholders, they were dominant in decision-making and control over cash flows. In Minsky's terminology an era of "managed money capitalism" emerged and this is broadly part of the era of financialization and the pursuit of shareholder value.

Capitalist firms have always been viewed in terms of the pursuit of profits and accumulation. As firms grew in size and as the formation of corporation was permitted, questions arose as to who the effective decision-makers within a corporation were and in whose interests they operated. Adam Smith raised the point when he wrote in 1776 in the *Wealth of Nations*: "The directors of such [joint-stock] companies, however, being the managers rather of other people's money than of their own, it cannot well be expected, that they should watch over it with the same anxious vigilance with which the partners in a private copartnery frequently watch over their own. ... Negligence and profusion, therefore, must always prevail, more or less, in the management of the affairs of such a company" (Smith 1776: 741).

The growth of corporations and the development of equity markets tended to lead to the number of shareholders in a company growing and some growing separation between those who managed the corporation and those who owned it. One of the earliest expressions of the idea that in corporations with a large number of shareholders the managers would pursue their own interests without significant control from the shareholders came with managerial theories of the firm).[1] In these theories, what were termed managers (in effect the board of directors) were portrayed as pursuing their own objectives, which could run counter at some point to the interests of shareholders.

Baumol (1959), for example, envisaged managers as being interested in the size of the firm (as measured by sales revenue) for a variety of reasons, including the relationship between their own salaries and the size of the company. Marris (1964) framed this in a more dynamic setting and aligned the interests of managers with growth of the company. In these theories managerial interests were portrayed as at some stage in conflict with owners' interests. Other theories (e.g. Williamson 1964) portrayed the interests and objectives of managers in different ways: the particular significance of the Marris approach is the focus on growth of the firm as the key managerial objective.

These theories recognized that shareholders had some residual power to constrain the activities of managers. The theory of Marris is particularly relevant in this context. The stock market price is treated as reflecting assessments of present and future profitability (and treating the stock market as efficient in incorporating available information into prices).[2] Insofar as the present managers do not vigorously pursue profits, then the share price will be lower than it would otherwise be. This led to the argument that a corporation with a relatively low share price would be vulnerable to the threat of takeover. Marris (1964) portrayed this in terms of the "valuation ratio" – the ratio between stock market price and the book value of the company. There are costs associated with mounting a takeover bid, which has to pay over the current price if it is to be successful (a premium of the order of 20 to 30 per cent being observed). The approach of Marris leads to the view that a manager-controlled firm would tend to grow faster than a comparable owner-controlled firm, have a lower stock market valuation but with a valuation ratio high enough to avoid being taken over.

A more formalised treatment came in Manne (1965: 112), who argued that "the market for corporate control gives to these [small] shareholders both power and protection commensurate with their interest in corporate affairs". He argued that when a company was managed in a way that was not making the scale of returns for the shareholder, which could be achieved by alternative management, then the market price of the shares declines relative to the shares of other companies. The relatively low returns may come from incompetent management and/or from use of retained profits to fund expansion rather than as pay-out to shareholders as dividends. Manne then notes that takeover would threaten the position of the existing managers. He also argues that there is no *objective* standard of managerial efficiency other than from stock market valuation.

---

1. See Sawyer (1979: ch. 7) for a review of the theories, and Sawyer (1985: ch. 11) for a survey of evidence.
2. The work of Shiller (e.g. 2000, 2003) has emphasized the volatile nature of equity prices and tendencies for periods of overvaluation and other periods of undervaluation. This is work for which he received a Nobel Prize in economics alongside Fama, whose work had stressed the efficiency of markets (e.g. Fama 1970); see also Malkiel (2003) on efficient markets.

Further, the threat of takeover provides some assurance of competitive efficiency among corporate managers and helps to protect the interests of small non-controlling shareholders. The interesting parts of this line of argument concern the view of takeovers as a route of enhancing efficiency and placing constraints on managers and their actions. The financial markets (in the form of what is here called market for corporate control) are seen as a mechanism for raising the interests of shareholders – those in a "failing company" receiving a premium if and when their company is taken over.

Fligstein and Markowitz (1993: 193) argue that the financial forms of reorganization, which have included mergers, divestures, leveraged buyouts, the accumulation of debt and stock repurchasing, which can be viewed as the financialization of the firm, were invented or perfected in the late 1950s and the 1960s. There can also be seen to be a shift (notably in the USA and then the UK) towards the type of activities mentioned by Fligstein and Markowitz. The decade of the 1960s and into the early 1970s was a period of intense merger and acquisition activity. However, in a similar vein, the 1900s and 1910s had also seen intense merger and acquisition activity, particularly in the USA with considerable involvement of banks and financial institutions such as J. P. Morgan.

It is more difficult to discern the changing motivations for mergers and acquisitions. One perspective on mergers and acquisitions ("takeovers"), which is often reflected in the competition policies in regard to takeovers, is that they are pursued to enhance the market power of firms involved. Two large firms operating in the same industry who merge will find their market share rising, their market power enhanced and an ability to lower costs and further exploit economies of scale. Such a merger would be anticipated to increase profits from market power and economies of scale (although whether increased profits are realized is debatable: e.g. Mccks 1977). The point here is that the anticipated increase in profits comes from production activities rather than through financial manipulation.

Friedman (1970: 123) was a fierce advocate of the view that the only responsibility of managers was the maximization of profits and denouncing any pursuit of corporate and social responsibility and of any regard for the interests of stakeholders other than the shareholders. Any business executives who pursued goals other than profits were "unwitting puppets of the intellectual forces that have been undermining the basis of a free society these past decades". One defence that Friedman and many others would raise is the view that the pursuit of profits leads to efficient outcomes. The maximization of profits as the difference between sales revenue and costs is an optimization of social welfare insofar as sales revenue is a reflection of social benefits and costs, although crucially in such an argument, costs include the cost of capital, and profits are what are deemed economic profits.

Rappaport (1998: 1) was able to argue that the idea "that management's *primary* responsibility is to increase value has gained widespread acceptance in the United States" (emphasis added), and was spreading to other industrialized economies. He anticipated the ideas of shareholder value to "become the *global standard* for measuring business performance". He argued that in the early 1980s there were very few companies that had strong and unambiguous commitment to the pursuit of shareholder value, and the take-over wave of the 1980s pressured managers to focus on shareholder value and equity price. He listed four major factors that induce managers to adopt a shareholder value orientation. These are managers having a relatively large ownership position, managerial compensation closely related with shareholder return performance, threats of takeover by another organization and competitive labour markets for corporate executives. He argued that, in a capitalist economy based on the rights of private property, "the only social responsibility of business is to create shareholder value and to do so legally and with integrity". And as others have done to claim that the pursuits of profits and share-holder value generally lead to socially desirable outcomes.

The notion of managerial controlled firms can be examined in terms of principal-agent issues and agency costs. The general principal-agent issue arises when one economic agent (the principal) contracts another (the agent) to undertake tasks on behalf of the principal. The general issues that arise are whether the contract can be specified in a way that the agent will act in the interests of the principal, how the principal can monitor the actions of the agent, and what assurances the agent can give that they will act according to the contract (e.g. Laffont & Martimort 2002). In applying this line of argument to the firm, the question arises as to who is to be regarded as the principal and who as the agent. Who hires whom? The managerial theories of the firm could to a degree be interpreted in terms of the managers' (the effective decision-makers in the firm) finance capital on which a return has to be paid – that can be in the form of an agreed rate of interest or in the form of dividends. A worker cooperative firm would make that point more forcibly as, in that case, labour would be hiring capital.

The next issue that comes out from this type of approach concerns the nature of the employment contract of the managers. Perhaps the obvious way is to tie the rewards of the managers in with profits, growth of profits and share values. A "distant" shareholder's main interest in the corporation would come from the performance of the share prices and dividends received.

From this perspective then, it can be asked what effects contracts will have along the lines envisaged in Jensen and Meckling (1976) and, more generally, within the "pursuit of shareholder" value paradigm. First, a closer linkage is established between managerial remuneration with profits and share prices. The realignment of management interests with shareholder value was advocated through the use of share options, profit-related bonuses, etc. The growth of inequality resulting from the high pay of "top" managers is one result of that attempted realignment. Mishel and Wolfe (2019) report that the average pay of CEOs at the top 350 firms in the USA in 2018 was $17.2 million (or $14.0 million using a more conservative measure of the value of stock options). The ratio of CEO compensation to typical worker compensation was 278 to 1 (or 221 to 1 using other measure of value of stock options). The ratio had been 20 to 1 in 1965 and 58 to 1 in 1989. From 1978 to 2018, CEO compensation grew by 1,007.5 per cent (940.3 per cent under the options-realized measure), far outstripping S&P stock market growth (706.7 per cent) and the wage growth of very high earners (339.2 per cent). In contrast, wages for the typical worker grew by just 11.9 per cent. Statista (2019) provides figures for 2018 when the CEO to average pay ratio was 201 in the UK, the Netherlands 171, Switzerland 152, Canada 149, Spain 143 and Germany 136.

Second, there are the pressures on securing and maintaining a high share price. The argument (Marris, Manne) is that a relatively low share price may trigger a takeover bid, although the evidence (Singh 1971) is not fully supportive of that. More generally, the shareholders will judge the managers by the share price. When financial institutions are the major shareholders, the abilities of shareholders to organize and pressure managers is greatly enhanced as compared with when there are millions of individual small shareholders.

Third, there is the question of how managers respond to the incentives and pressures to raise profits and perhaps more significantly dividends, which are a strong influence on share price. A major line of argument here (and much influenced by the comparison with the managerial firm) is that managers/corporations will emphasize short-term returns (which boost share price) and dividend pay-outs (which again would boost share price). Higher dividend pay-outs reduce retained earnings, and investment and research and development, heavily dependent on funding from retained earnings, may well be lower (than they otherwise would have been). Since the cost of retained earnings is lower than the cost of external loans (in general), they are not likely to be replaced by borrowing. Investment and research and development would themselves be anticipated to lead to higher profits (and thereby dividends) in the future, although in the case of research and development a perhaps distant and uncertain future.

Zorn (2004) documents the rise of the chief financial officer (CFO) position in American firms over the period 1963 to 2000. He notes that the "CFO has been commonly linked to the shareholder value movement and represents firms' increasing orientation towards investors" (*ibid.*: 362), with the CFO being "one of the most powerful players in corporate America today" (*ibid.*: 346). In his sample of 400 firms, at the beginning of the period none had a CFO, whereas by 2000 more than 80 per cent did.

The advocacy of the pursuit of shareholder value is a route through which shareholder interests are imposed on managerial interests and, more generally, interests of other stakeholders, including employees and customers. It also acts in the interests of the financial sector, which gains from increasing stock market valuations. It is interesting to note that the "managerial theories" of the firm would "predict" that growth would be slower under shareholder value maximisation than previously. In the managerial theories of the firm (and elsewhere), the "top managers" were viewed as pursuing growth of their company as being in their interests (e.g. rewards tied to the size and growth of the company) and in the organizational interests. In order to grow, the company sought to ensure the

growth of demand for its products through advertising and marketing, through diversi-
fication into new territories and new products, etc. To grow, the corporation would need
to invest and to expand its capital stock and it needed to fund that investment; over a
range it could do so through retained earnings, which were a cheaper source of funds
than resorting to external borrowing. Although there were limits, it was argued that
a corporation would seek relatively high retained earnings and relatively low dividend
pay-outs. In that sense shareholders received relatively low dividends and their interests
would be served by higher dividend pay-out and thereby lower retained earnings, lower
investment and lower growth of the corporation. One particular aspect of the pursuit
of shareholder value is emphasis on dividends at the expense of retained earnings and
thereby lower investment.

The pursuit of shareholder value has not been universally welcomed even within the
business and financial communities. Jack Welch, former CEO of General Electric, argued
that "shareholder value is the dumbest idea in the world. Shareholder value is a result,
not a strategy … your main constituencies are your employees, your customers and your
products. Managers and investors should not set share price increases as their overarching
goal. … Short-term profits should be allied with an increase in the long-term value of a
company" (interview with Francesco Guerrera, *Financial Times*, 12 March 2009).

Stout (2012) seeks to debunk "the myth that corporate law mandates shareholder
primacy". The effects of the pursuit of shareholder value is that managers are seen as
focusing myopically on short-term earnings, which discourages investment and innovation, and she argues that harms employees, customers and communities.

The advocacy of the pursuit of shareholder value is a route through which shareholder interests are imposed on managerial interests. It also acts in the interests of
the financial sector, which gains from increasing stock market valuations. Lazonick
and O'Sullivan (2000) provide an historical account for the USA of the rise of shareholder value as the guiding principle of corporate governance, with a shift of corporate strategy from focus on retention of corporate profits and their reinvestment
in corporate growth in the 1960s and 1970s to a strategy of distribution of profits to
shareholders with pressures for reduction of labour employment. This leads to the
other major issues arising from the pursuit of shareholder value, namely the impacts
on the other stakeholders in a corporation. The focus in the discussion below is the
impacts on employment and wages, although there are other considerations, notably
on customers, government and wider society.

The pursuit of shareholder value, investment and growth

The thrust of the argument above is that the pursuit of shareholder value pushes managers and directors of corporations to pay heed to the share price, through tying their

salaries, bonuses, etc. to profits and the share price and, more generally, reviewing performance in terms of financial returns. Particularly by comparison with the managerial perspectives on the firm, the pursuit of shareholder value is often perceived to lower investment and growth.

The managerial firm has been described in terms of "retain and reinvest", whereas under the pursuit of shareholder value it becomes "downsize and distribute earnings". Under the former, the emphasis is on growth funded by retained profits, whereas under the latter the emphasis is placed on the distribution of profits through dividends (and through share buy-backs) at the expense of internal investment.

A post-Keynesian approach to the analysis of financialization distinguishes between workers, management and rentiers. I return to this analysis is Chapter 8 in connection with the distribution of income between those classes. Here the focus is on investment and profitability decisions. "Managerial capitalism" was represented by a relatively autonomous management pursuing growth rather than profits. The rise of the pursuit of shareholder value and the alignment of management interests with those of the shareholders who have a stronger preference for profits rather than growth leads to lower investment (related with growth) at the firm level (Stockhammer 2004).

Hein (2012: 116), adopting a post-Keynesian perspective on the overall effects of financialization on investment and on growth of capital stock, argues that "financialization has been associated with increasing shareholder power vis-à-vis management and labourers, an increasing rate of return on equity and bonds held by rentiers, and decreasing managements' animal spirits with respect to real investment, which each have partially negative effects on firms' real investment".

Hein (2012) summarizes a range of arguments on the effects of shareholder value under financialization on investment. It is argued that shareholders (most of whom are financial institutions) impose on corporations a larger distribution of profits and hence a higher dividend payment ratio. The lower retention of profits ratio and, on occasions, share buy-backs mean reduced internal finance for real investment. Hein labels this the "internal means of finance channel". A further channel, labelled the "preference channel", arises from the weakening of the preference of managers for growth (which translates into firms pursuing growth), as managerial remuneration schemes are based on short-term profitability and share price.

It has often been observed that in many industrialized countries over recent decades there has been a tendency for higher levels of profits to be accompanied by lower levels of investment, whereas the general presumption had been that investment and profits would be positively related. Profits are a spur to investment, and the level of investment is itself a determinant of the level of profits. As Van Treeck (2009: 908) observes, a popular microeconomic explanation of that association is the pursuit of shareholder value, which "has induced firms to develop a larger preference for profitability at the expense of investment (and potentially jobs and growth)".

One suggestion advanced by Cordonnier *et al.* (2019: 407) is that financialization raises the effective cost of capital. They argue that "financialization in France has increased the cost of capital for non-financial corporations with new standards of financial profitability". They label this "the over-cost" of capital and consider how this additional financial burden may explain the slowdown of the pace of capital accumulation.

Durand and Gueuder (2018: 147) discuss four competing hypotheses concerning the impacts of financialization, globalization and monopolization on investment, and investigate related stylised facts for France, Germany, Japan, the UK and the USA. They note that the relationship between profits and investment is historically contingent and find "some stylised facts supporting, at least to some extent, each of these four narratives". The four narratives are identified. First, what is termed "the revenge of the rentiers", which is a squeeze on available funds for investment arising from increase of financial payments by non-financial corporations. Second, "financial turn of accumulation", describing a change in managerial preferences for financial investment as the expense of domestic productive investment. Third, "globalization", giving rise to the substitution of foreign investment for domestic investment and the increased cost mark-up from cheaper inputs from low-wage countries. Fourth, "monopolization" hypothesis, under which declining competitive pressures lead to reduction in incentive to invest while raising profits, leading to firms looking to financial markets or foreign expansion, and market power enabling non-financial firms located in the industrialized countries to benefit from higher mark-ups in global value chains (GVCs).

Fiebiger (2016), however, argues that the managers of US national non-financial corporations did not abandon growth objectives in light of the rapid expansion of majority-owned foreign affiliates from the mid-1990s onwards. However, the rise of the power of the CEO, along with what he terms "a manager-friendly pay regime", pushed down wages.

Asker, Farre-Mansa and Ljungqvist (2015) compare the investment behaviour of publicly listed companies and privately held companies. Their results indicate that public firms invest considerably less than comparable private firms and are less responsive to changes in investment opportunities (measured by sales growth and Tobin's q ratio as the ratio of a firm's market value to book value, where the market value for private firms is imputed). They interpret their findings as consistent with the idea that short-termist pressures increase the "hurdle rate of return" that public firm managers use to evaluate investment projects. They highlight that short-termist pressures can be a significant cost of a stock market listing and end by noting the decline in the number of listed companies in the USA, with a more than halving in the number since 1997.

Do Carmo, Sacomano Neto and Donadone (2019) analyse the five largest car manufacturers (Toyota, Volkswagen, Hyundai, General Motors, Ford). Their results find that the dividend payments conform to shareholder value maximization principles. The increase of more financial activities is seen as fundamental to businesses dominated by major shareholders. The compensation of executives is shown to be hundreds of times the average salary.

It has been seen above that there are many definitions and perceptions of "financialization". In Chapter 4, it was indicated that there are many dimensions along which the expansion of the financial sector can be measured. It can further be recognized that in empirical work, which uses statistical and econometric methods, the statistics used to measure dimensions of financialization may not be good proxies. In the empirical work on the relationship between financialization and measures of economic performance, many ways of seeking to measure financialization have been used. Davis (2017) notes, in the context of empirical work on the financialization-investment nexus, the different aspects of financialization and different measures that are deployed. This is a general issue in relation to empirical work on financialization, as will be particularly seen in Chapter 8 on income distribution.

Davis (2017) surveys the literature on financialization and fixed investment. She provides a detailed survey of the theoretical arguments as well as the empirical results. In this literature, financialization has been approached through: first, the financial flow-based indicators of financialization and changes in the relative stocks of fixed and financial assets, debt and equity on firm balance sheets; and second, the pursuit of shareholder value on investment. The results from investigations of relationship between nonfinancial corporations' (NFCs') financial incomes and investment are mixed, although a negative relationship was found in some specifications. Davis (2017: 1352) concludes that "evidence of 'crowding out' [of fixed investment by financial investment] is not clearly robust across contexts and specifications". She concludes that "there is growing consensus that certain features of financialization – in the USA context, most notably shareholder orientation and corporate short-termism – depress physical investment". The empirical literature "provides econometric support for the hypotheses that growing shareholder orientation among NFC managers is associated with declining firm investment rates" (*ibid.*: 1350).

Stockhammer (2004: 739) finds some support for the hypothesis that financialization leads to lower investment, where the interest and dividend income of the non-financial business sector divided by its value added is used as the proxy for financialization. He reports "strong support for our hypothesis in the USA and France, some support in the UK, but none in Germany. Financialization occurred in the UK, but there was no general slowdown in accumulation because the UK already had rather low accumulation rates in the Golden Age. The insignificant findings for Germany are consistent with our story, since the literature indicates that shareholder value orientation is a very new phenomenon in German."

A similar view comes from Dallery (2009: 513), who argues from a theoretical analysis in the post-Keynesian tradition that financialization as a constraint for managerial behaviour leads to a relatively small drop in accumulation. But, where there is shareholder control, he finds "that the decrease in accumulation is far greater, but the scale of this reduction is dependent on what is assumed to be shareholders' objectives and time horizons (the longer it is, the more need for growth)".

Tori and Onaran (2018) explore the effects of financialization on physical investment for non-financial publicly listed companies in the UK over the period 1985–2013. The effects of financialization in terms of shareholder value orientation are represented in their investment equations through the ratio of profits minus cash dividends, financial inflows (dividends and interest received by non-financial corporation) and financial outflows (interest and dividend payments), all scaled against capital stock. They find strong evidence of an adverse effect of financial payments and financial incomes on the rate of investment.

Tori and Onaran (2020) estimate the effect of different financial channels on physical investment in 14 European countries (the 15 members of the EU prior to 2004 other than Luxembourg) over the period 1995–2015, using the balance sheets of publicly listed non-financial corporations. They find evidence that both financial payments and financial income have adverse effects on fixed asset investment. However, the negative impacts are non-linear in terms of company size, such that increasing financial income crowds out investment in large companies and has a positive effect on investment by relatively smaller companies (see also Tori & Onaran 2017).

Barradas (2017) finds that financialization has damaged real investment in the 27 EU countries examined over the period 1995–2013, where financialization was viewed in terms of financial receipts and financial payments. The paper concludes that financialization slowed down investment by 1–8 per cent and that it was to be seen as the main driver of the slowdown of investment in the European Union. Barradas and Lagoa (2017) find a similar result for investment by non-financial corporations in Portugal over the period 1979–2013.

Orhangazi (2008), using firm-level data for the USA over the period 1973–2003, found a negative relationship between financialization and capital accumulation, especially for large firms. Davis (2016) found confirmation of the notion that what are termed non-financial corporations engage in financial activities (over and above what would be required to finance production).

Milberg and Winkler (2010: 290) argue that the pursuit of shareholder value has led to the US non-financial corporate sector behaving increasingly like the financial sector in purchasing more financial assets and raising dividends and executive compensation rather than investing in the real economy. They "found that offshoring in the US did raise the share of profits in income, but that the gains from offshoring have likely not been fully realized because firms have purchased financial assets rather than investing in productive assets that raise productivity, growth, employment and income. The financialization of non-financial firms is a leakage from the system, which reduces the dynamic gains from offshoring by reducing reinvestment out of profits."

Davis (2018) found a small but positive relationship between cash holdings and shareholder value ideology among large corporations. She viewed this as supporting the view that *non*-financial firms are increasingly engaged in borrowing and lending for profit.

Kliman and Williams (2015), in contrast, seek to show "Why 'financialization' hasn't depressed US productive investment" (part of the title of their work, quote marks in original). They argue that there need not be a trade-off between the use of funds for financial investment and for real investment when borrowed funds are an additional source. It is rather, they argue empirically, that it is the fall in the rate of profit of US corporations that fully accounts for the fall in the rate of investment.

Shareholder value, technological change and innovation

Investment in research and development may in many respects be analysed in a similar manner to investment in plant and equipment. Firms may undertake such investment (noting that most firms do not actively engage in research and development) in pursuit of profits and growth, although the gains from research and development are subject to considerable uncertainty and take many years to come to fruition. It is through those features, combined with the degree to which the gains from research and development are captured by the firm initiating the research, that much research and development is funded by government. The short-termism associated with the "pursuit of shareholder power" discussed above in connection with investment can be exacerbated in the case of research and development.

Lazonick (2013: 860) identified an organizational failure in which "US business corporations have failed to use their substantial profits to invest in new rounds of innovation that can create new high value-added jobs to replace those that have been lost" to the financialization of the US corporation. US corporations are pursuing employment strategies solely for financial gain, which includes manufacturing plant closure, offshoring production to low-wage areas. He particularly identifies the use of corporate funds to buy back company equity for the purpose of boosting the company's stock market price, which is legitimized by the "maximize shareholder value". Through their stock-based compensation, corporate executives who make these decisions are themselves prime beneficiaries of this focus on rising stock prices as the measure of corporate performance. Lazonick (2017: 1) indicates how maximizing shareholder value "undermines the social conditions of innovative enterprise: strategic control, organizational integration, and financial commitment".

Tulum and Lazonick (2018: 281) focus on the productivity crisis in the US pharmaceutical industry. They argue that the financialization of that industry helps to explain this crisis against a background of an institutional environment, which is conducive for research and development in drug development. They argue that the industry has adopted a "highly financialized business model" where the key measures of performance are stock price and dividend yield and distributions to shareholders through large-scale stock buy-backs and dividends. "With this financial behaviour incentivized by stock-based executive pay, value extraction from corporations for the sake of distributions to shareholders comes at the expense of drug innovation."

Pursuit of shareholder value and labour

Slater and Spencer (2014: 142) have highlighted four routes through which financialization has consequences for work and work relations. The first is the direct impacts of financialization on the employment relationship, which has enabled employers to increase their power over workers. "As workers have accumulated financial assets and taken on greater amounts of debt, they have become less able and willing to push for higher wages and better working conditions. To the contrary, their weakened economic position has made them more vulnerable to real wage cuts, longer work hours and more precarious forms of employment (Glyn 2006)".

The second echoes the shareholder value route with the interests of shareholders elevated above those of other stakeholders including workers. "Pressurized by financial markets to maximize short-term profits and to raise dividends for shareholders, managers have looked to reduce wages, lay off workers, and downsize production (Lazonick & O'Sullivan 2000; Froud *et al.* 2006; Thompson 2011)" (*ibid.*: 142). The private equity business model "creates and sustains investor value but requires a 'downsize and distribute' approach to business strategy, corporate governance and the management of employment relations" (Clark 2009: 782). The rationale provided by agency theory "legitimizes the extraction of value from a wide group of stakeholders, redistributing it across a narrower group of key private equity fund managers and investors" (*ibid.*). The private equity business model leads to "higher leverage, a shorter-term focus and requirement to service debt before any exist, and are more likely to sell and downsize assets (including business units and pension schemes) by around 10 per cent" (*ibid.*: 783). Batt (in Batt & Morgan 2020: 86) portrays that the general effects of private equity companies are to "reduce staffing levels or wages and benefits as needed; outsource or offshore work; or identify less profitable units to be closed – even if they still make a profit – rather than investing in and upgrading them".

The third issue that (Slater & Spencer 2014: 143) discuss is the impact of the financial crisis of 2007/09, which "has its origins in the financialization process and among its outcomes has been a decline in employment, job security, wages and working conditions", to which could be added that financial crises have become more frequent under financialization, and these costs are further discussed in Chapter 10).

The fourth impacts on the organization of work, where it is argued that "financialization impedes the adoption and sustainability of forms of participatory work practices that rely on the elicitation of commitment and flexibility from workers. Despite their perceived economic benefits ... these practices have not been adopted to any great extent (Godard 2004), in part because they represent too high a cost for firms, but also because they pose a challenge to employers' 'right to manage'. ... Managers demand commitment and flexibility from workers but their drive to maximize shareholder value means that they cannot maintain the conditions required to secure the continued cooperation of workers." (Slater & Spencer 2014: 142–3).

Fligstein and Shin (2007) argue that the maximization of shareholder value and minimization of the role of employees seeks to increase profits by reducing the power of workers. They argue that mergers and acquisitions were pursued as a way to raise profitability but find, as many previous studies have done, that mergers and acquisitions do not in general succeed in raising profitability. It has also generally been found that it is the shareholders of the company acquired who stand to gain financially. The pursuit of profits also involved the use of computer technology "to reorganize and remove unionized labor forces" (*ibid.*: 420).

Assa (2012) finds that each percentage increase in financialization is associated with between 0.49 and 0.81 per cent more inequality (depending on which indicator of financialization is used). A similar increase in financialization is related to a 0.2 per cent slower growth of GDP, and between 0.12 and 0.74 per cent higher unemployment.[3] Palladino (2021) finds evidence for the USA that the growing power of shareholders has depressed workers' wages.

Batt and Appelbaum (2013: 1) argue that financialization represents "a shift from managerial capitalism, in which the returns on investments derive from the value created by productive enterprises, to a new form of *financial capitalism*, where companies are viewed as assets to be bought and sold and as vehicles for maximizing profits through financial strategies". One of the questions on which they focus is whether the specific mechanisms through which new financial intermediaries and the financial strategies of non-financial corporations affect the management of firms and employment outcomes. Their particular focus is on private equity companies as an example of financial capitalism. They argue that as firms increasingly make profits from financial activities rather than from productive activities, "their welfare is less intertwined with the welfare of employees" (*ibid.*: 6). Management has reduced incentives for investing in workforce skills and in developing productive labour-management relations. Trade unions were

---

3. His measures of financialization are: value added in finance as a percentage of total value added and employment in finance as a percentage of total employment, where finance sector is the broadly defined FIRE. The estimation is panel for OECD countries, and for the years 1970–2008 for growth and unemployment, and six period observations for inequality (Gini coefficient).

viewed by "purely rent-seeking agents of workers and an obstacle to maximizing share-holder returns" (*ibid.*: 13).

They consider the impacts of private equity companies on management and workers under four headings. The first comes from the concentration of ownership and the ways in which the private equity owners drive corporate strategy and decisions. The company is loaded with debt, which places managers under intense pressure to report high returns and to cut costs. The time horizons of managers are much shorter and they are under constraint in being able to invest in or manage their relations with labour, suppliers or customers. The second arises from the cost pressures leading to job losses. Third, there are differences between private equity companies and publicly traded companies in respect of their higher risk of financial distress and bankruptcy. A fourth is the effect of private equity on labour-management relations and collective bargaining, although they argue that there is little evidence that American private equity owners are more hostile to labour unions than American corporations generally.

Private equity firms raise investment funds from institutional investors such as pension funds and insurance companies and wealthy individuals. These investors, known as limited partners, account for about 98 per cent of capital in the fund, with the private equity partners who manage the fund putting in the other 2 per cent. The majority of private equity funds are used to buy out companies and then take them private, with the aim to resell in a three-to-five-year period. The high use of debt, loaded on the company itself, is a "leveraged buyout".

Appelbaum, Batt and Clark (2013: 514) study the effects of the operations of four private equity companies, where they argue "at least an important part of shareholder gains come from the losses that existing stakeholders experience in the form of lower returns to relationship-specific investment", which may be in addition to gains from "value creation strategies". They argue that the focus on the shareholder maximization involves incentives for the private equity firms to renege on the implicit contracts, which are critical to the company's successful dealings with its stakeholders. "Research has demonstrated the importance of trust-based relations to sustain competitive advantage, the centrality of trust in supplier relations in lean production networks and the import-ance of trust to the successful implementation of performance-enhancing practices. Breach of trust in organizations may facilitate financial restructuring, but it undermines long-term investments to improve cost, quality and innovation.".

Davis *et al.* (2014) use datasets that cover US buyouts by private equity from 1980 to 2005. It tracks 3,200 target firms and their 150,000 establishments before and after acqui-sition, making comparisons to the control group defined by industry, size, age and prior growth. It finds that buyouts lead to large increases in gross job creating and destruction, with modest net job losses. There is some gain in total factor productivity in the target firms, coming mainly from the accelerated exit of less productive establishments and greater entry of highly productive ones.

Cushen (2013: 327–29) draws on data from a six-month mixed method ethnographic study undertaken in 2007 in Avatar Ireland, a financialized knowledge intensive firm. The top management at Avatar "were facing a dilemma that typifies financialized capitalism namely financial actors sought levels of financial returns beyond what the product market could deliver". This case "identifies how budgets enable the structures and narratives which prioritize capital interests at the corporate governance level to be replicated inside the organisation". The paper documents "how performative interventions created the employment outcomes associated with financialization. [This case] highlights that financialization, in addition to creating employment insecurity, financial insecurity and work intensification, can also prompt role insecurity, suppression of voice and enactment of falsely optimistic behaviour".

Fligstein and Shin (2007) use data from 62 US industries over the period 1984–2000. They explore the connections between mergers and layoffs (viewed as shareholder value strategies) and changes in deunionization, computer technology and profitability. They find mergers occurring in industries with low profits and leading to increase in layoff of workers. Industries with a high level of mergers did, though, increase investment in computer technology, which displaced workers and was focused on reducing unionized workforce. They also report, as many other studies have done, that mergers did not raise profitability.

Darcillon (2015) investigates the impact of financialization on workers' bargaining power and on employment protection legislation in 16 OECD countries over the period 1970–2009. He argues that "the process of financialization will exert strong pressures on labor markets towards more eroded/decentralized bargaining institutions and more flexible employment relations" (ibid.: 477). Financialization is measured in terms of valued added in financial intermediation and in FIRE, employment in financial intermediation and in FIRE (all as percentage of total). His results "clearly indicate that the rise of the financial sector has affected workers' bargaining power in the sense of an erosion/ decentralization of collective bargaining institutions. ... [T]he rise of the financial sector in the economy is associated with higher levels of employment legislation protection" (ibid.: 497).

Meyer (2019: 477) focuses on the effects of equity market development, which is measured by the average of stock market capitalization/GDP and stock market value traded/GDP. Data refers to 21 OCED countries over the period 1970–2010. He finds "a negative effect of equity market development on unions' institutional structures, but not on union membership. Contrarily, I find that routine-biased technological change has a negative effect on union density, but an inconsistent relationship with the strength of unions' institutional structures."

Jung (2015) looks at downsizing announcements for a sample of 714 US firms between 1981 and 2006 and finds that pressures from institutional investors and a new decision context encourage firms to downsize more frequently than otherwise. He suggests that firms' growing dependence on equity financing makes them vulnerable to pressure from institutional investors and such pressures lead firms to downsize more frequently in their attempt to enhance stock performance.

Kollmeyer and Peters (2019) argue that trade unions are weakened through several channels by the growing dominance of finance and that financialization plays a significant role in the deunionization of national workforces. They use data from 18 advanced capitalist countries from 1970–2012. Financialization is measured through four variables: a stock market index, which itself combines stock market capitalization as a percentage of GDP and stock market trading activity; an inward portfolio index based on market value of inward portfolio investment as a percentage of GDP and measure of the liberalization of regulatory constraint on cross-border capital flows; value added in finance and insurance as a percentage of total value added; corporate indebtedness in terms of the book value of outstanding debt held by non-financial corporations as a percentage of GDP. Their results support the view that financialization is an important cause of union decline, with its particular effects varying between different forms of capitalism.

Dupuis, Peters and Scrimger (2020) find evidence for Canada over the period 1997–2007 for a negative relationship holding between financialization and union density when controlling for economic context and sectoral characteristics. They conclude that the sectoral impacts of financialization on union density, particularly in what they label highly financialized sectors such as manufacturing, extractive resources, transport and warehousing, are critical to the understanding of union decline and recent changes to employment relations. Financialization is measured by share equity as a percentage of total equity and assets, and financial assets as a percentage of total equity and assets.

Peters (2011: 73) reports on comparative changes and qualitative reforms to both finance and labour in 13 OECD countries between 1980 and 2005. There is a focus on three political economic changes: "rise in finance and adoption of corporate 'shareholder' systems"; "the expansion of mergers and acquisitions and their negative effect on unionisation and manufacturing jobs"; and "the effects of financial pressures and corporate reform on collective bargaining and wages" (*ibid.*: 73). Peters (2011: 94) finds that "for organised labour, the impact of these changes to finance and corporate management were largely negative. It certainly was true that despite the pressures of finance, unemployment and economic competition, political institutions alongside market regulation and wage-bargaining institutions continued to shape firm behaviour and economic change."

Carvalho and Cerejeira (2019) produce results that suggest the existence of a negative and significant effect of leverage on average employee wages.

Heil (2021) reviews a large number of studies on the influence of finance on labour market outcomes. He concludes that the studies indicate that finance has an impact on job quantity and job quality. Financial development is found to aid employment growth in non-OECD countries but not in OECD countries – a similar finding to the relationship between financial development and growth of output (see Chapter 10). Financial globalization is found to contribute to higher wages in emerging markets but tends to reduce wage share in OECD countries (as reported in Chapter 8). Employment in highly leveraged companies may be more sensitive to fluctuations in industrial production. Firms acquired through leveraged buyouts tend to slightly lower job growth rates and lower wages (cf. discussion on private equity).

Heil (2021: 1201) further finds that "certain types of bank deregulation can reduce income inequality and raise employment opportunities in countries with well-developed institutions". Higher earnings by financial sector workers are generally found to be higher compared with workers with similar skills (see Chapter 8). Heil (2021: 1226) finishes by arguing that "the evidence suggests that finance can contribute both positively and negatively to *resilience and adaptability*". Finance is related with increased realloca-tion of labour, which the paper reports may weaken or enhance productivity growth. A downturn in house prices can create mortgage lock-ins, thereby reducing the mobility of homeowners and contributing to labour market inefficiency.

Conclusions

The pursuit of shareholder value has been viewed as one of the major dimensions of the processes of financialization. That pursuit of shareholder value is the promotion of the interests of the owners of a company and the extraction of financial returns to those owners. This is then the promotion of the interests of shareholders at the expense of the interests of other stakeholders, including employees. The pursuit of shareholder value has been viewed as having a range of possible and other adverse effects on the other stakeholders and of the real economy more generally.

The focus of attention has been on the pressures on managers to pursue short-term profits even when it is at the expense of investment and longer-term profits. In this chapter I have outlined how these pressures to pursue profits may have effects on the levels of investment in research and development, employment and labour relations. The empirical evidence of these effects has also been surveyed and points in the direction of generally negative impacts.

8

FINANCIALIZATION: A DRIVER OF INEQUALITY OR AN ENABLER?

During the present era of financialization, there has been a widespread tendency towards higher economic and social inequality. United Nations (2020: 1) summarize this in the following terms: "Since the 1990s total global inequality (inequality across all individuals in the world) declined for the first time since the 1820s." The United Nations notes that income inequality between countries has improved in the past quarter of a century, with average incomes in developing countries increasing at a faster rate than developed industrialized countries, much of which comes from the rapid economic growth in China and other emerging economies of Asia. However, since 1990, income inequality has increased in most developed countries and also in emerging economies such as China and India. It reports that, while income inequality between countries has declined, income inequality within countries has risen. The report finds that, in the late 2010s, 71 per cent of the world's population lived in countries where inequality had grown in the preceding three decades.

"While inequality has increased within most countries, over the past two decades, global inequalities between countries have declined. The gap between the average incomes of the richest 10% of countries and the average incomes of the poorest 50% of countries dropped from around 50x to a little less than 40x. At the same time, inequalities increased significantly within countries. The gap between the average income of the top 10% and the bottom 50% has almost doubled, from 8.5x to 15x." (World Inequality Lab 2021: 10).

On a global level, at the beginning of the 2020s, the share in income (on a purchasing power parity basis) of the bottom 50 per cent is estimated at 8.5 per cent, the middle 40 per cent and top 10 per cent have shares of 39.5 per cent and 52 per cent, respectively. Inequality of wealth is much sharper, with the bottom 50 per cent having a 2 per cent share, the middle 40 per cent a 22 per cent share and the top 10 per cent a 76 per cent share.

There have also been shifts in the distribution of income in general away from wages and towards profits. These trends are briefly illustrated in the next section.

In the background to this chapter is the general belief that the degrees of inequality in a society are rather important dimensions of economic and social well-being. Pickett and Wilkinson (2009) are leading proponents of the idea that economic inequality has detrimental effects on wider economic and social well-being, ranging over education attainment, crime and drug addiction. Some may defend inequality from the structure of incentives to work hard and take risks, where some succeed but others fail, but where the resulting higher levels of effort and risk-taking benefit all.

Whatever the merits of that argument, it is not self-evident that the higher levels of inequality observed over the past three to four decades in western industrialized countries have been associated with economic success (insofar as that is measured in terms of economic growth of GDP). The attitudes that may be taken towards inequality, and particular high incomes, may come from ideas of how far those incomes are deemed to be deserved and merited.

The central issue in this chapter is whether the processes of financialization and rising inequality coincident trends or whether there are forces through which financialization promotes inequality and/or inequality adds to financialization. This issue is explored from theoretical perspectives and through reviewing empirical evidence on these matters.

There are many routes through which the processes of financialization may have impacts on income and wealth inequality and on the distribution of income (between wages and profits). One route would be what may be termed the direct contribution of the financial sector to higher inequality. The extent to which earnings in the financial sector itself are more unequally distributed (than in the rest of the economy) and the degree to which inequality in the financial sector has grown in the present era of financialization are considered.

Financialization has been seen to involve the pursuit of shareholder value and the rise of rentier income (as discussed in Chapters 2 and 6). These forces can be linked with a shift in the distribution of income away from wages and towards profits. I then examine the evidence that financialization has been involved in the general economy-wide shift away from wages towards profits.

The nature and source of earnings in the financial sector by comparison with earnings elsewhere is investigated, particularly to discover how far earnings in the financial sector include the extraction of rent (rather than reward for productivity). There are complex links between inequality and the financial crisis, which are examined in the final main section. There are also remarks on the empirical findings between inequality and debt expansion.

Most of the research reviewed here has used econometric analysis, hence it is only those dimensions of financialization for which quantitative proxies are available for inclusion. And then simple statistical measures may provide relatively poor proxies for the complexities of financialization. The nature and dimensions of financialization have been discussed in earlier chapters. In the empirical studies (and reflecting the theoretical background), authors have varied in terms of which dimensions of financialization are included and how those dimensions are to be measured. At best the simple measures included in the econometric exercises, which are labelled financialization (or similar), are reflecting a few of the dimensions of financialization and are limited to those dimensions for which a proxy is available.

Inequality can be conceptualized and measured in many different ways. In the work summarized here, inequality of income is the main dimension of inequality that is considered. Income can itself be measured in a range of ways, including income received from labour and capital (pre-tax income) and disposable income (post-tax and transfers). Income can be measured at the individual level (particularly when income is viewed in terms of labour earnings) or at the household level, often with adjustments for the size and composition of the household and assumptions on the degree to which income is effectively shared within the household.

The full distribution of income (however measured) has to be summarized in terms of the degree of inequality. A widely used indicator is the Gini coefficient, which can be viewed as a summary of the degree to which the actual distribution of income diverges from complete equality (for which the Gini coefficient would be zero) and complete inequality (for which the Gini coefficient would be unity). Other measures frequently used in the studies to which I refer below include share of the richest (including 0.1, 1 and 10 per cent) and the ratio of the income share of top income groups to the bottom income groups. There are many summary indices of inequality, which differ in the relative importance assigned to different parts of the income distribution.

The functional distribution refers to the shares accruing on the basis of different functions such as the provision of labour (hence the share of wages and salaries). In presenting statistics on the functional distribution, decisions have to be made on how self-employment income is regarded (how far it represents labour income, how far profits) and how payments such as rent are to be regarded.

The present era of financialization has occurred alongside rising inequality of income and wealth. The trends of inequality have by no means been uniform across countries but for many countries inequality was higher in the mid-2000s than in 1980. In the USA in particular, the share of income of the top 1 per cent was higher than at any time since the 1920s. This high and rising level of inequality can be viewed as a significant contributory factor in the generation of financial crises, an argument that is examined below.

The (World Inequality Lab 2019: 9) reports that "since 1980, income inequality has increased rapidly in North America, China, India, and Russia. Inequality has grown moderately in Europe. … From a broad historical perspective, this increase in inequality marks the end of a postwar egalitarian regime which took different forms in these regions." The report's Table E3a indicates the share of the top 10 per cent rising from 35 per cent in 1980 to 47 per cent in 2016. Figures covering Europe as a whole rose from 33 to 37 per cent. Russia displayed a particularly sharp rise from 24 per cent in 1990 to 48 per cent in 1997, and broadly flat since. China rises from 28 per cent in 1980 to 42 per cent in 2016, and India from 32 to 55 per cent. "In the Middle East, sub-Saharan Africa, and Brazil, income inequality has remained relatively stable, at extremely high levels" (*ibid.*: 40). The top 1 per cent on a global basis share rose from 16.5 per cent in 1980 to 22 per cent in 2007, with a slight decline thereafter but share maintained above 20 per cent. The bottom 50 per cent share rose from 6 per cent to just under 10 per cent.

There have also been marked shifts in the distribution of income between labour and capital, with a general downward trend in labour's share and corresponding rise in profits. For evidence on these trends in the distribution of income, Pariboni and Tridico (2019) cite numerous sources that support the statement of generally falling share of labour and also produce their Figure 2 in support.

With these broad trends in mind, I now explore the relationships between the financial sector and the generation of inequality and then move on to consider some of the effects of rising inequality on matters such as household debt and on financial crises.

The financial sector and inequality of income and earnings

The financial sector has acquired the reputation of paying high incomes to bankers, for the financial sector having high levels of income equality within it and for paying much higher salaries and bonuses than other sectors. The enlargement of the financial sector can contribute directly to the overall level of the inequality of earnings and incomes through two routes. First, insofar as employment in the financial sector expands and the financial sector displays higher than average levels of inequality, then overall inequality of earnings will rise. Second, as there is rising inequality of incomes within the financial sector, there could be a further contribution to higher inequality. This section examines how far those two routes of the financial sector contribute to inequality.

The nature and source of high earnings in the financial sector are also highly significant, particularly in consideration of the efficiency of the financial sector. If there are higher and rising earnings, do they represent payment for enhanced productivity and effectiveness, with links between wages, productivity and performance? Alternatively, do higher earnings in the financial sector reflect the power and ability of the top earners within the financial sector to extract economic rents, which would be rather in line with ideas on financialization and the power of the financial sector?

Bakija, Cole and Heim (2012) report that executives, managers, supervisors and financial professionals accounted for about 60 percent of the top 0.1 percent of income earners. Further, those groups account for 70 per cent of the increase in the share of national income, which went to the top 0.1 per cent of the income distribution between 1979 and 2005. They identify that 13 per cent of the top 1 per cent of earners were in the financial sector and 18 per cent were in the top 0.1 per cent. In their data, the share of the top 1 per cent rises from 9.72 per cent in 1979 (income including capital gains; 8.93 per cent excluding capital gains) to 20.95 per cent in 2005 (16.3 per cent excluding capital gains). Income of financial professionals accounted for around 9 per cent of the income of the top 1 per cent in 1979, rising to 16 per cent in 2005 (figures are little different whether capital gains included in income or not).

Philippon and Reshef (2012) investigate wages in the financial sector relative to the non-farm sector over the near century from 1909 to 2006. They find a decline for the first six decades through to 1970 and then a rise. In 2006 average incomes in the financial sector were 70 per cent above those in the rest of the private sector. After adjustment for education, incomes were comparable in the financial sector and the rest of the private sector but the premium in the financial sector averaged 50 per cent. The differences were more pronounced at the top of the income distribution where the wages of the top decile in finance grew to become 80 per cent more than the wages of top decile of earners elsewhere. They ascribed around half of the increase in the average premium to earnings risk and one-fifth to changes in the size distribution of firms. They argue that changes in financial regulation are an important determinant of these changes in earnings in the financial sector.

Godechot (2012) examines the rise in top income shares in France from 1996 to 2007. The financial sector is calculated to make a large contribution to the rise in the top income shares, with 51 per cent of the rise in the incomes of the top 10 per cent from 26.5 per cent in 1996 to 27.7 per cent in 2007, and 89 per cent of the rise of the share of the top 0.01 per cent from 0.27 per cent to 0.65 per cent.

Sum et al. (2008) report that there was no increase in the weekly earnings of typical full-time wage and salary workers in the USA over the period 2002–07, despite rising productivity and generally increasing employment opportunities. In contrast, the mean weekly earnings in investment banking and securities industries rose by $2,408, a 54 per cent increase. The weekly earnings (including bonuses) of wage and salary workers, including manager and executive in the investment bank and securities industries in Manhattan ("Wall Street"), rose by $8,028, a 90 per cent increase.

Kaplan and Rauh (2010) study the earnings of four groups: non-financial-firm top executives; investment bankers, private equity and mutual funds investors; corporate lawyers; and sports stars and celebrities. They calculate that these groups represent 15–26.5 per cent of the individuals who are in the top 0.1 per cent of adjusted gross income. Their estimation is that Wall Street-related individuals form a higher proportion of the top gross income brackets than is the case for non-financial executives of public companies. In contrast to the representation of top public company executives in the top fractions of the income distribution, they find that the contributions of hedge fund managers, private equity investors, venture capitalist investors and corporate lawyers have increased substantially over the past ten to twenty years, and likely by a greater amount than the top executives.

Hyde, Wallace and Vachon (2018: 206) look at the long-run effects of financialization on income inequality in 18 affluent democracies from 1981 to 2011. They examine the effects of financialization in conjunction with globalization and conceptualize financialization as multidimensional – FIRE employment, credit expansion and financial crises. Their findings show that financial crises significantly increased inequality of income before taxes and transfers and of income after taxes and transfers but also increased redistribution. They suggest that, while financial crises do increase income inequality, "welfare state policies that offer security and insurance to workers during crises kick in to reduce some, but not all, of the inequality" (*ibid*.: 207). Credit expansion is found to positively influence inequality (pre and post taxes and transfers). FIRE employment also increases inequality, which they interpret in terms of financial sector workers receiving higher pay than non-financial sector workers and thereby more employment in the financial sector increases inequality.

Earnings in the financial sector

The financial sector has the potential to extract economic rents. Economic rent is viewed as payment to those in a firm or industry over and above that required to secure the employment of the people and the capital deployed by the firm or industry. Economic rent can arise from privileged access. It is difficult to measure with precision the extent of economic rent in a specific sector as it requires identifying an appropriate benchmark. In regard to salaries, bonuses and other renumeration paid to workers in the financial sector, a comparison can be made between the salaries of workers in the financial sector with the salaries paid to other workers with comparable skills, training, education, etc. The difference can be labelled as a "wage premium".

Bell and Van Reenen (2014: F19) find that "in 2008, 28% of all top percentile earners in the UK were London bankers. But this dramatically understates their importance in the rise in overall wage inequality during the last decade. We estimate that somewhere between two-thirds and three-quarters of the overall increase in the share of wages taken by those in the top percentile have accrued to bankers." The term "bankers" is used in Bell and Van Reenen (2014) to refer to the employees in the financial intermediation sector, which also includes fund management and insurance businesses.

Philippon and Reshef (2013) find that wages in the financial sector are generally higher than in other sectors and have been rising in relative terms. There is an increasing trend, over the period 1970–2005, of average wages in the financial sector relative to other sectors in the USA, Netherlands, France, Germany, Denmark, Canada and Finland, and a mixed trend in Austria, Belgium, Japan, the UK and Sweden. Throughout, the relative wage of workers in the financial sector is above 1 and as high as near 1.8. They argue that the increase in skill intensity cannot explain wages in the financial sector. For the relative wages of skilled workers in the financial sector, six countries are reported to have an increasing trend and five a mixed trend (and one, Canada, for which data are not available). With the exception of France, in the first half of the period examined, the average wage of skilled workers in the financial sector is greater than the average for other skilled workers.

Bivens and Mishel (2013: 66) calculate that for the USA the unadjusted ratio of financial sector pay (annual compensation per full-time employee) relative to the pay of workers in the rest of the economy fluctuated below 1.1 between 1952 and 1982, and then gradually rose to reach 1.83 in 2007. They point to the rise in top incomes in the financial sector alongside its general expansion, coinciding with regulatory changes in the direction of deregulation and rising concentration in the financial sector. They argue that the rise in the incomes of the top 1 per cent in the USA "should be interpreted as driven largely by the creation and/or redistribution of economic rents". They further argue that "in some cases (particularly in the financial sector, evidence suggests that have been increased opportunities for shifting rents to boost incomes and wages in recent decades" (*ibid.*: 70).

Tomaskovic-Devey and Lin (2011) report that in the American financial sector employee compensation rose from being close to the average in 1980 to around 60 per cent higher by 2008. They ascribe this shift as happening through decreases in market competition and regulation, which provided the conditions of enhanced institutional market power to enable such a transfer of income.

Denk (2015: 6) finds that employees in the financial sector are heavily concentrated at the upper end of the overall earnings distribution. He finds that workers with similar observable characteristics, including age, gender, education and experience, are paid more in the financial sector than in other sectors, which can be seen as indication of rent extraction by financial sector workers. Two-thirds of the "wage premia" in the financial sector is received by financial sector employees who are among the 10 per cent of all workers with the highest earnings. Denk (2015) argues that it is these wage premia that account for most of the contribution of the financial sector to inequality of earnings.

Lindley and McIntosh (2017) report that the wage premium in the UK finance sector is large (of the order of 40 per cent) and increasing. They find that the largest returns within the financial sector are received by London-based male graduates in their 40s who are employed as dealers or brokers in the security broking sector. The premium is observable across different sub-sectors of finance and different occupations and different qualification levels. The wage premium is found across most other OECD countries. The wage premium "seems to be a pervasive feature of remuneration in the financial sector" (Lindley & McIntosh 2017: 589). They find that the UK financial wage premium has continued to rise after the 2007–09 financial crisis. They also consider explanations of the financial sector wage premium, including task-biased technical change with substitution of routine labour by capital equipment, skill intensity and cognitive abilities. They "propose that the finance sector pay premium is, at least in part, due to the rent-sharing of that sector's profits" (*ibid.*: 589) and argue that such a conclusion is supported by the prevalence of the pay premium across jobs at "all points of the occupation hierarchy, for workers of all skill types, and at all points of the wage distribution" (*ibid.*).

Nau (2013) labels those households that receive some portion of their income from wealth as "investors", although they may be more akin to rentiers. In his empirical work, the focus is on the two decades of the 1990s and the 2000s in the USA. He argues that the importance of investment income has increased greatly in recent decades. Over the period 1992–2010, non-investment income among the top 1 per cent was generally stagnant. He finds confirmation for the hypothesis that "elites have depended upon their investments to realize income growth, and that such windfalls were not shared with most other households" (*ibid.*: 451). His Figure 5 reports that by 2008 those with more than $2 million in financial investments accounted for over half the income of the top one per cent.

Arestis, Charles and Fontana (2014: 1488) argue that the income distribution effects associated with financialization have also gone alongside an occupational stratification process that has raised income of the managerial and financial occupations to the top of the income scale, while leaving service occupations at the bottom of the USA society. "The role of race norms seems to have been particularly strengthened by financialization in the high-status managerial and financial occupations." Further, the stratification of the USA labour market has been exacerbated by financialization operating through the effect on social norms.

In an earlier paper (Arestis, Charles & Fontana 2013), these authors had explored whether financialization in the USA had created identity preference effects by linking managerial and financial occupations to high earnings and, in turn, the high earnings of white men as the dominant demographic group in the workforce. Their empirical results covering the period 1983–2009 period confirmed that not only was there a wage premium for those working in managerial and financial occupations but also that the wage premium received by financial occupations is not equally distributed among all gender and ethnic groups. Within each ethnic group, men took an increasing share of the finance wage premium at the expense of women.

The work reviewed here refers to the financialization era from circa 1980, although the evidence does not yet extend past the GFCs. The dominant finding is that the financial sector itself tends to exhibit higher levels of inequality than other sectors, although it has to be noted that the number of countries covered is limited. The growth of the financial sector and the rising inequality within the financial sector have contributed markedly to the general rise in inequality. The financial sector is also seen to have higher earnings that the non-financial sector, with the earnings gap between them tending to widen. The evidence that has been brought forward here supports the view that the higher earnings in the financial sector reflect economic rents being gained by those in that sector rather than representing enhanced efficiency or productivity.

Financialization and income inequality

Evans (2014) considers the trends in inequality in four countries. He concludes that the worsening of the distribution of income in Germany primarily arose from the labour market reforms introduced by the Social Democratic-Green coalition government in the early 2000s. There were a range of financial liberalization measures introduced in Germany with diverse effects. In the USA, he finds that extensive liberalization in the 1980s and the 1990s was closely associated with a major increase in inequality, arising from a combination of high incomes paid in the financial sector and the pressures coming from financial institutions on non-financial corporations to reduce wage costs and employment. However, in Brazil, government policies from 2003 onwards raised the minimum wage and pensions and, through new credit programmes, lower income groups acquired greater access to housing and consumer durables. Although incomes in Brazil remain highly unequal, inequality has declined. In India, there was a marked rise in inequality as the financial liberalization of the early 1990s led to a reduction of credit programmes, particularly in rural areas, designed to counter inequality. There was an acceleration of economic growth but with the benefits accruing almost exclusively to middle- and upper-income sectors.

Flaherty (2015) examines the impact of financialization on inequality (income share of the top 1 per cent) using a panel analysis of 14 OECD countries over the period 1990–2010. Market capitalization, private sector credit (both as a percentage of GDP) and the gross operating surplus of FIRE in gross operating surplus, along with financial globalization (external assets and liabilities as a percentage of GDP) are used to measure financialization. The first and third of those variables are found to have a statistically significant effect in raising inequality. The extent of banking sector liberalization, the extent of banking sector supervision and a financial reform index are used as measures of the regulatory environment. Flaherty (2015) finds that these measures of aspects of financialization are all associated with growth in the top income share.

Zallewski and Whalen (2010) review the institutional routes through which financialization can impact on inequality. They use an index of financial deepening (see Chapter 3). They report a correlation coefficient across countries between the financial index and the Gini coefficient as a measure of income inequality of 0.184 in 1995 and 0.254 in 2004.

Tridico (2018) finds support from his econometric analysis for the proposition that financialization (measured by market capitalization of listed domestic companies as a percentage of GDP) encouraged inequality in OECD countries (measured in terms of personal distribution of income, using a range of measures, including the Gini coefficient, the Palma ratio).

Westcott and Murray (2017) focus on the ways in which the expansion of the financial sector and changes in financial institutions may impact on inequality. Increases in financial activities, alongside rising asset prices, suggest that financialization made an important contribution to the increase of wealth for financial asset owners. Financial deepening and development of new types of financial institutions were seen as allowing those in possession of financial assets to increase their income and their wealth at a faster rate than those dependent on labour earnings.

Roberts and Kwon (2017), using a panel analysis of 17 OECD countries from 1980 to 2007, find that growth in financial sectors and in financial sector employment associates with higher income inequality, greater wage disparities and a greater concentration of income in the more affluent households. The size of those effects is found to be stronger in liberal market economy countries.

Denk and Cournède (2015) use data from OECD countries over the past three decades and show that financial expansion has fuelled greater income inequality. They find higher levels of credit intermediation and of stock market capitalization are both related with a more unequal distribution of income. They use numerical simulations to indicate that expansion of the financial sector restrains the income growth of low- and middle-income households. The authors use three measures of financial size, all measured relative to GDP, which are the value added of the financial sector, credit by banks and other financial institutions to the non-financial private sector and stock market capitalization. They find that, in general, more finance has been associated with higher income inequality, although no relationship was detected for the value added of the financial sector (which was indicated above to be often not growing relative to GDP).

Dávila-Fernández and Punzo (2021: 520) investigate financialization and income inequality in the US economy over the period 1947–2013. Income distribution was measured by the Gini coefficient of household income and financialization measured in terms of share of financial sector employment and share of financial assets in corporations' total assets. "Causality goes from employment to income inequality and from the latter to wealth. Non-linear estimators suggest the existence of certain asymmetric effects such that changes in income distribution cannot be reverted by simply reverting financialization."

Jauch and Watzka (2011) investigate the link between financial development (measured by the ratio of credit to GDP) and inequality (measured by the Gini coefficient) using an unbalanced dataset of up to 148 developed and developing countries over the period 1960–2008. Within countries they find that financial development increases income inequality. They also report that more developed financial markets lead to higher income inequality. Control variables used include GDP per capita and its square, inflation rate, government expenditure and size of the agricultural sector. A range of robustness checks are included. They conclude that the positive relationship between inequality and financial development is highly significant but relatively small. With the Gini coefficient measured on a scale of 0 to 100, they report that an increase in the provision of credit by 10 per cent would lead to an average increase in the Gini coefficient of 0.22.

Kwon, Roberts and Zingula (2017) consider 20 developed economies during the years 1988–2009 and find that the scale of financial activities are closely related with income inequality measured in terms of the ratio of income of the 90th percentile (that is income of someone who is on the edge of the top 10 per cent) and the median income.

Gouzoulis (2021) focuses on France and Sweden and views mortgage debt accumulation as a dimension of financialization. The econometric findings are that mortgage debt accumulation has been reducing labour shares in France and Sweden. He draws out implications that "finance has been historically a key determinant of the capital-labour conflict" (*ibid.*: 19), although industrial relations and welfare expenditures play the dominant roles.

Frost, Gambacorta and Gambacorta (2020) find evidence of what they term a Matthew effect – a biblical reference that "for unto everyone that hath shall be given, and he shall have abundance: but from him that hath not shall be taken away even that which he hath" (Matthew 25:29). This is viewed in terms of wealth households being able to achieve higher returns than other households. Using Bank of Italy data for the period 1991–2016, they find that households of all wealth deciles benefit from the effects of financial development (measured by number of bank branches) and financial technology (use of remote banking) and that these benefits are larger at the top of the wealth distribution. The economic significance of this gap did, though, decline towards the end of the sample period, as remote banking became more widespread.

Szymborska (2021: 1) argues that the transformations of the financial sector contribute to inequality "by making household balance sheets more complex in the process of financial deregulation, financial innovation, securitization, and broader liberalization and privatization policies in the US economy, over the past five decades". She seeks to show that "heterogeneity of household wealth structures across the distribution of income is an independent distributional channel in financialized economies".

De Vita and Luo (2021: 1934) use data for 33 countries over the period 1996–2015, investigating three dimensions of financialization relating to the financial, non-financial and household sectors, the latter consistently recording a statistically significant, positive effect on income inequality. Their findings "highlight that despite the multi-facets manifestations and pervasiveness of financialization, it is ordinary people, particularly households on low-income that end up bearing the brunt of the costs of financialization, through self-reinforcing spiral of increasing inequality, causing further debt, which in turn, augments the disparity between the 'Haves' and 'Have-nots'".

Alexiou, Trachanas and Vogiazas (2022: 14) undertake an empirical investigation on the relationship between financialization and income inequality for a panel of 19 OECD countries during the period 2000–17. Inequality is measured by the Gini coefficient on different income specifications, and the control variables include banking crises, credit market regulation, globalization and trade union power. Their measures of financialization involve percentage of deposit money bank assets to those assets plus central bank assets, and private credit by deposit money banks, bank deposits and domestic credit to private sector, each expressed as a percentage of GDP. They point to "a growing body of research [which] has shown that financialization has increased inequality. Nonetheless, our results suggest that the subject relationship is not so straightforward and merits further research on the actors and processes at play". Fagereng *et al.* (2020) report in the case of Norway that financial returns are positively correlated with wealth and that individual wealth returns exhibit persistence over time.

Özdemir (2019) writes in the context of a Kaleckian model, whereby factors such as financialization, globalization and trade union power have effects on the mark-up of prices over costs and thereby the shares of profits and wages in national income. He uses a panel of 52 developed and developing countries over the period 1992–2012. Financialization is measured in terms of stock market capitalization to GDP, stock market total value traded to GDP and stock market turnover ratio. With these variables, he finds that each of the financialization variables has a significant and negative effect on the labour share of national income.

Hyde (2020) examines the long-run effects of financialization in 16 affluent nations from 1981 to 2010 and finds that financial crises do not have a statistically significant effect on upper-tail (ratio of income of 90th percentile to income of 50th percentile) and lower-tail (ratio of 50th percentile to 10th percentile). He finds much less support for the effects of credit expansion on inequality and that financial crises do not have a significant effect on inequality.

Financialization and the functional distribution of income

Kohler, Guschanski and Stockhammer (2019: 939) identify four channels through which financialization can affect the wage share: (1) enhanced exit options of firms, based on models of bargaining in which exit options impact on bargaining power; (2) increased financial payments for non-financial businesses as a result of pursuit of shareholder value, based on mark-up pricing, with mark-ups sensitive to financial costs; (3) increased competition on capital markets; and (4) the role of household debt in increasing workers' financial vulnerabilities and undermining their class consciousness. The authors list (in their Table 1) previous econometric studies on financialization and functional income distribution. They use a panel data analysis of 14 OECD countries for the period 1992–2014 and construct "four financialisation variables that capture the exit options of capital, the financial payments of non-financial businesses, the competition in capital markets and household debt", and also include a set of control variables. Their main finding "is that there are strong negative effects of financial liberalisation and financial payments of non-financial corporations on the wage share. Rising household debt also reduces wage shares, albeit only in countries with a high share of mortgage debt among low-income earners combined with weak bargaining institutions."

Davis and Kim (2015: 203), in their sociological review of papers on financialization, focus on the impacts of the pursuit of shareholder value on corporate strategies and on earnings of top management, and on the ways in which financialization shapes the patterns of inequality in society. They conclude that "financialization has shaped patterns of inequality, culture and social change in the broader society".

Darcillon (2015: 477) focuses on the impact of financialization on workers' bargaining power and employment protection legislation in 16 OECD countries over the period 1970–2009. He argues that financialization pushes labour markets in the decentralised bargaining direction and more flexible employment relations. Using panel data models, the results indicate "that financialization is clearly associated with a reduction in workers' bargaining power and in the strictness of employment protection". Financialization is viewed in terms of a finance-led regime of accumulation and of the pursuit of shareholder value measured by share of value added in finance and share of employment of finance.

Hein *et al.* (2017) view financialization as potentially affecting wage and profits shares through three channels of the sectoral composition of the economy, the financial overhead costs and profit claims of the rentiers and the bargaining power of workers. They examine indicators for each of these channels for six OECD economies before and after the GFCs. They conclude that the relationship between financialization and income distribution differs between those countries, which they identify as "debt-led private demand boom" (the USA, UK and Spain in their sample), the "export-led mercantilist" countries (Germany and Sweden in their sample) and the "domestic demand-led" economy of France. In their sample, all countries except the UK saw a decline in the wage share in the period from the early 1990s until the crises. However, the forces behind the general decline in the wage share differed. In the "debt-led private demand" group, the sectoral shifts towards the financial sector with its higher profit share and the declines in the bargaining power of trade unions and workers were seen as the key forces. In the case of the USA, higher financial overheads and rentiers' claims on profits were factors contributing to the lower wage share. In the "export-led mercantilist" group, the changes in the sectoral composition of the economy did not help to explain the falling wage share. There was a general, although not universal, significance of the deterioration of workers' and trade unions' bargaining power for the falling wage share. These differences between the country groups have largely carried through to the post-crisis period.

Stockhammer (2017) investigates the relative impacts of financialization, globalization, welfare state retrenchment and technological change on the functional income distribution, using a dataset covering 28 advanced and 43 DEEs over the period 1970–2007. Financialization is measured in terms of financial globalization, which is the logarithm of external assets plus external liabilities (relative to GDP). An index of financial reforms is also included. Stockhammer (2017) finds that financialization had the largest contribution to the decline of the wage share, with globalization also having a substantial effect.

IILS (2008: 44) argues that "the current dynamics of financial globalization have prevented a further convergence of wealth both across and within countries, with income inequality in low-income countries remaining unaffected by financial openness". It is found that financial globalization (measured by the sum of foreign assets and liabilities, expressed as a percentage of GDP) depresses the share of wages in GDP even after allowing for the decline in wage share, which can be attributed to trade openness (increasing elasticities of labour demand) and changes in labour market regulations and institutions. It is estimated that an increase of financial openness by 1 percentage point reduces the labour income share by 0.3 of a percentage point.

Lin and Tomaskovic-Devey (2013) use cross-section time-series American data at the industry level. They find a long-run relationship, which indicates that a higher ratio of financial income to profits is associated with a reduced labour share of income, an increase in top executives' share of employee compensations and increase in the dispersion of earnings. After allowing for the effects of decline in unionization, the effects of globalization, technical change and capital investment, they find the effects of financialization on inequality to be substantial. "Our counterfactual analysis suggests that financialization could account for more than half of the decline in labor's share of income, 9.6% of the growth in officers' share of compensation, and 10.2% of the growth in earnings dispersion between 1970 and 2008" (Lin & Tomaskovic-Devey 2013: 1284).

Alvarez (2015) investigates the connections between the financialization of French corporations and the functional distribution of income in the non-financial sector. Firm-level data of 6,980 French non-financial firms over the period 2004–13 are utilised. Financialization is measured in terms of the increasing dependence of earnings through financial channels. Increased dependence on financial profits and technological change are found to be the most important determinants of functional income distribution and more important than trade openness or labour market institutions.

Dünhaupt (2017) explores the relationship between financialization (viewed in terms of shareholder value orientation proxied by net interest and net dividend payments of non-financial corporation relative to the capital stock of the business sector) and labour income share for a dataset of 13 countries over the period 1986–2007. Globalization (trade openness, foreign direct investment and prices of raw materials and semi-finished products), worker power (unemployment rate, union density and strike intensity) and government activity are also included in the regression analysis. It is found that net dividend payments have a negative effect on wage share in all specifications. The net interest payment variable is not significant in some specifications but in the absence of the dividend payments variable it has a negative sign. The combined shareholder value variables with both dividends and net interest payment shows a significant and negative effect on the labour share.

Das and Mohapatra (2003) present evidence of a strong statistical association between the event of liberalization and income shares, using panel data for 11 countries that underwent capital account liberalization between 1986 and 1995, and eight countries that did not during that period. Specifically, they find a positive coefficient between financial liberalization and the top quintile's share of mean income, a negative coefficient between liberalization and the income share of the middle-income groups, but no evidence of statistical association between liberalization and the lowest income quintile is found.

The general conclusion from these contributions has been that financialization, along with a range of other factors, such as trade union and collective bargaining power, does impact on the distribution of income, particularly the shares of income between labour and capital. The findings are in line with the expectations of the financialization literature that financialization raises the profit share and diminishes the labour share of income

Financial deepening and inequality

Demirgüç-Kunt and Levine (2009) discuss the range of theories relating financial deepening and the evolution of inequality and poverty. They outline the various routes through which financial deepening can impact on inequality and argue that the theory on this matter is not unambiguous, and that while the theoretical analysis provides indications of a range of possible mechanisms linking inequality with the operation of the financial system, "many of the core questions about the nature of the relationship between inequality and finance are empirical" (*ibid.*: 45). Although they find that the accumulating body of empirical evidence is far from conclusive, they do argue that the findings of "cross-country, firm-level, and industry-level studies, policy experiments, as well as general equilibrium model estimations all suggest that there is a strong beneficial effect of financial development on the poor and that poor households and smaller firms benefit more from this development compared with rich individuals and larger firms" (*ibid.*: 46).

Kim and Lin (2011) argue that most theoretical studies point in the direction that financial deepening and development can be an instrument for improving the distribution of income. They conclude that whether or not that is the case depends on the stages of financial development in a country, with the benefits of financial deepening only occurring beyond a threshold level of financial development. Financial development tends to raise inequality below a critical value of financial development. Their policy implication is that a minimum level of financial development is needed for it to reduce help reduce income inequality.

Beck, Levine and Demirgüç-Kunt (2007) found that financial deepening helped the poor, with their incomes growing faster than average per capita income. Their results indicate that around three-fifths of the effects of financial development on the poorest quintile come through aggregate growth and two-fifths through reduction in income inequality.

Nikoloski (2013) uses a dynamic multivariate panel, data analysis on 161 developed and developing countries over the period 1962–2006. Financial deepening is measured by the ratio of credit to the private sector by financial intermediaries to GDP and inequality is measured by the Gini coefficient. In the regression analysis of the relationship between inequality and the measure of financial deepening, a range of control variables are included, among them GDP per capita and its square, inflation rate, institutional development and government spending as a percentage of GDP. Nikoloski (2013) reports empirical evidence for an inverted U-shaped relationship between financial sector development and income inequality, and hence financial development is associated with higher inequality at lower levels of financial development and with lower inequality at higher levels.

Inequality and financial crisis

The sharp rise in inequality in the USA in the decade prior to the American sub-prime crisis has often been viewed as at least a contributory factor to the generation of that crisis. However, a banking and financial crisis also occurred in the UK, where inequality had in general not risen in the previous decade except with regard to the share of the top 1 per cent. Financial crises have generally been preceded by some combination of rapid credit expansion and rising asset prices, which both foster expansion of aggregate demand and of output and employment. Both are also inherently unsustainable. The links of inequality with financial crisis would then run through credit expansion and rising asset prices. This section delves into the linkages between inequality, particularly rising inequality, and the occurrence of financial crisis. A route often suggested is that rising inequality pushes people who have lost out from rising inequality towards debt to maintain consumption levels, and the burst of debt accumulation proves unsustainable. This leads to an examination of inequality and household debt.

The general set of arguments has been summarized in Stockhammer (2015), where he postulates four channels through which rising inequality contributed to the financial crisis of 2007–09, with the crisis to be viewed as the interaction of the deregulation of the financial sector (a component of financialization) with the effects of rising inequality. The first of the channels identified is the demand-depressing effects of rising inequality as income shifts from poorer income groups with high propensity to spend to richer income groups with lower propensity to spend. This, as numerous authors have argued, may well have slowed economic recovery.

For the third channel, Stockhammer draws on the debt-led versus export-led models, to suggest a channel in debt-led economies where "higher inequality has led to higher household debt as working-class families have tried to keep up with social consumption norms despite stagnating or falling real wages" (*ibid.*: 936). This appears to particularly apply to the USA (often identified as a debt-led economy), whereas the UK, which is also generally identified as debt-led, experienced a credit boom with rising debt and house prices in the decade prior to the GFCs but real wages had generally been rising (at least until 2005), and the sharp rise in inequality having occurred in the 1980s and flattened off since then.

A further channel comes from "rising inequality [increasing] the propensity to speculate as richer households tend to hold riskier assets than other groups. The rise of hedge funds and subprime derivative in particular has been linked to rise of the super-rich" (*ibid*.). This appears to suggest that the overall degree of risk rises as the rich move into riskier assets, but no mechanisms are proposed by which overall risk would rise. However, we can point to the ways in which securitisation in effect raised risk. The remaining channel (numbered two) is seen as financial liberalization of the capital accounts allowed large current account imbalances.

Gezici (2010: 379) studies the distributional consequence of the financial crises of Argentina (2001), Brazil (1999), Korea (1997–98), Mexico (1994) and Turkey (1994). Two distinct distributive outcomes of the crises are found. First, the "redistribution of income from labor to capital is felt mostly by the low-income groups, also leading to an increase in poverty rates in the wake of the crisis". The second takes the form of an increase in financial rents that favour the rich.

In the context of the American financial sub-prime crisis of 2007–09, many have argued for the role of rising inequality in the generation of the crisis. Rajan (2010) argued that the political response to rising inequality in the USA had been the expansion of lending to households, particularly low-income ones. The political response may have been planned or an unpremeditated reaction to constituent demands. There were the stimulating effects through aggregate demand, but with an unsustainable credit boom.

Van Treeck and Sturn (2012) summarize the argument in terms of the rising incomes in recent decades in the USA being confined to a relatively small group of households at the top of the income distribution. Increasing consumer expenditure of the lower- and middle-income groups became mainly financed through rising debt rather than rising incomes. This was aided by government actions of deregulation of the financial sector, which facilitated increased lending to households and through credit promotion policies. The debt-financed, consumer-led demand expansion came to an end as the downturn in the USA housing market and the sub-prime mortgage crisis took their toll and highlighted the over-indebtedness of American households. They conclude with specific reference to the USA that the changes in the functional distribution of income between wages and profits did not play an important part in explaining the increase in the consumer expenditure to output ratio and the decline in the savings ratio. However, they find substantial evidence that rising income inequality between households did make an important contribution to rising personal debt and falling household savings rate. Lower- and middle-income households sought to keep up with the higher consumption levels of top income households, facilitated by readily available credit.

Van Treeck (2014: 421) asks whether inequality caused the USA financial crisis (of August 2007). He concludes that "there is substantial evidence that the rising inter-household inequality in the United States has importantly contributed to the fall in the personal saving rate and the rise in personal debt (and a higher labour supply)". This may be seen as a "demand-side" argument, which Van Treeck relates to a "relative income hypothesis" under which households seek to maintain consumption levels when their relative income declines through borrowing. In order for that to take place, there has to be a willingness of banks and financial institutions to lend.

Goda and Lysandrou (2014) focus on the toxic securities of CDOs, which were central to the financial crises of 2007–09. They argue that low incomes can help explain the demand for mortgage loans, but it remains to be explained why financial institutions were prepared and able to meet the demand and why the mortgage loans were securitised and resecuritised into CDOs. They argue that wealth concentration among the world's richest individuals was a "demand-pull factor" with a "search for yield" as yields on bonds declined and CDOs appeared to offer high returns.

Considering the more general case of the links between inequality and financial crisis, drawing on 25 countries over 100 years, Atkinson and Morelli (2011: 49) find no hard and fast pattern as to whether or not economic crises (in their Table A.1 the term systemic banking shocks is used) are preceded by rising inequality. They find "more evidence that financial crises are followed by rising inequality". Morelli and Atkinson (2015) extend the previous study by adding further data and investigating both the hypothesis that growth of inequality contributes to financial crisis and that the level of inequality does so. They find that the empirical evidence does not provide any convincing support for either of the hypotheses.

Bellettini and Delbono (2013) find that a large majority of banking crises in the last three decades took place in countries where income inequality before the crisis had been persistently higher than the average level in OECD countries. However, the banking crises did not appear to change the relative position of income inequality of the countries experiencing crisis as compared with average OECD levels. They finally conclude that "only in the 2000s relatively low-income inequality seems associated to the lack of banking crises, whereas in the previous decades we do not detect any clear association" (*ibid.*: 12).

UNCTAD (2017) recognised that financial crises have multiple causes and rising inequality may not always be one of the causes, particularly in smaller countries that are vulnerable to changes in external conditions. In their Figure 5.5, they correlate changes in private debt and changes in inequality in developed countries and developing countries prior to financial crisis (using the Laeven and Valencia 2012 data on crises). This shows a generally positive correlation between debt and inequality prior to financial crisis. However, as they argue, the financial institutions and regulation have to provide the credit in the creation of credit bubbles leading to financial crisis. There is a general increase in the Palma ratio, with the income gap rising in 80 per cent of cases in the run-up to financial crisis, and also rising in 66 per cent of cases after a financial crisis (UNCTAD 2017: 101).

Van Treeck and Sturn (2012) followed their study of the USA mentioned above by considering the cases of China and Germany. For China, they note that there is limited access to personal credit. A high level of savings by households is seen as stimulated by high income dispersion and a weak social safety net and, to that degree, income inequality may push towards high savings rather than debt. Higher income inequality is viewed as contributing to higher intensity of status seeking, which appears to result in a higher personal propensity to save as households are precluded from the easy use of credit to support conspicuous consumption.

The authors note that domestic demand in Germany stopped growing in the first decade of the twenty-first century and growth became heavily dependent on rising net exports. The stagnation of German unit nominal labour costs in the fixed exchange rate regime of the eurozone stimulated German exports. Further, the shift towards increased profit margins and lower labour income share weakened consumer expenditure. Rising income inequality and uncertainty of private households, which can be attributed in part to labour market and welfare state reforms, contributed to higher savings rather than to consumer borrowing.

Cardaci and Saraceno (2015) seek to analyse the impact of rising income inequality on the possibilities of a crisis in different institutional settings employing a macroeconomic model and using agent-based modelling in a stock-flow consistent framework. They find that when inequality rises, low credit availability would mean a drop in aggregate demand, whereas relaxed credit constraints result in greater financial instability.

Bordo and Meissner (2012) use data from 14 advanced countries between 1920 and 2000 and their results do not indicate any general relationships between inequality and crisis. They note the role of credit booms in increasing the risks of a banking crisis but they did not find any evidence that a rise in the shares of the top income groups led to credit booms.

Michell (2015) views rising inequality and falling wage share as driven by globalization, deregulation and financialization, with a common theme being the weakening of the bargaining power of workers. He notes that there are two different and mutually reinforcing mechanisms for maintaining growth rates in the face of falling demand in response to a declining wage share, namely credit expansion to a household sector faced with stagnant or falling real income, and an increasing reliance on exports. The credit expansion will likely prove to be unsustainable and may lead to at least a slowdown in economic activity if not to a banking crisis. He argues that for the 2007–09 financial crises, the proximate trigger was the non-performing mortgage debt and the mortgage-backed securities collapse, with the resulting contagion effects on those financial institutions that held the now toxic assets.

Inequality and household debt

The effects of inequality on household debt have been examined by several authors. Klein (2015) investigates long-run relationships between income inequality and household debt in nine industrialized countries (Australia, Canada, France, UK, Italy, Japan, Norway, Sweden and the USA). Two measures of household debt (private household credit and total bank loans) and four measures of inequality (top 1 per cent income share, inverted Pareto-Lorenz coefficient, the Gini coefficient and labour share of income) are used. The results were robust across the four inequality measures and the author finds it reasonable to conclude that in developed economies there is a long-run relationship between income inequality and leverage. A 1 percentage point increase in inequality is found to be associated with a 2 to 6 per cent increase in household credit (varying across measures of inequality used).

Malinen (2016) finds a long-run steady-state relationship between income inequality and bank credit for a sample of eight countries (those in Klein's study except Italy) and for the period 1980 to 2009. Income inequality was found to have one-way Granger causality relationship to bank credit.

With particular reference to the USA, Barba and Pivetti (2009) argue that rising household indebtedness should be seen mainly as a response to stagnating real wages and the cutting back of the welfare state. As others have, they raise concerns over the sustainability of rising indebtedness, where debt has a stimulating effect in the short-term, which cannot be sustained in the longer term.

Kim (2013) examines the relationship between output and household debt in the USA over the period 1951 to 2009, with a structural change in the fourth quarter of 1982 to allow for financial liberalization measures at that time. He finds that in the pre-1982 period household debt levels had no significant effects on output, although new borrowing did boost output. In the post-1982 period, household debt levels had negative effects on output, while new borrowing continued to boost output. In a related study, Kim (2016) remarks that an additional economic stimulus comes in the short-term from debt-financed household spending, but after a while the accumulation of debt becomes excessive and unsustainable. The resulting crisis generates negative impacts on output in the long run. A system operating with high and often rising levels of household debt can become vulnerable to negative shocks and the possibility of a severe economic downturn.

The general conclusion to be drawn from the material reviewed above is that under certain conditions a rise in inequality may contribute to the generation of financial crisis. The key condition would be that the rise in inequality fosters an unsustainable rise in household debt, then when the bubble of debt bursts, it feeds into a financial crisis. That key condition clearly requires that people respond to declining income shares by borrowing to maintain consumption levels and that banks and other financial institutions are keen to extend loans.

The situation in the USA in the early 2000s supported that key condition being met. In other situations that key condition has not held and inequality and financial crisis have not been correlated. As Bazillier and Hericourt (2017: 489) conclude: "the links between inequalities and leverage are likely to be a mixture of direct and indirect causal relations, as well as coincidental factors". They also argue that "the effects of financial development and financial deregulation on income distribution are not necessarily identical and are conditioned strongly on the quality of institutions preventing rent-capturing behaviours".

Conclusions

The general conclusions drawn from this chapter in respect of financialization and inequality in western industrialized economies are fourfold. First, in a general sense, higher levels of inequality and declining labour share of income have accompanied financialization in the present era from the late 1970s onwards. Second, the financial sector itself tends to display high levels of inequality of earnings and income, and inequality in the financial sector has directly had an impact on overall inequality, particularly in respect of the share of the top 1 per cent. Third, there is evidence to support the view that financialization has aided a shift in income distribution from wages to profits but the difficulties of measuring financialization in econometric exercises have been noted. Fourth, rising inequality looks to have been a contributory factor in the generation of the USA sub-prime crisis, although other factors, such as deregulation, banks' and financial institutions' increased willingness to provide credit, have to be involved. However, doubts have been raised as to whether that finding is of universal application to financial crises in general.

9
FINANCIALIZATION OF THE EVERYDAY

The processes of financialization have spread financial motivations and calculations of the financial sector into people's everyday life. The financial system's growth has meant that increasing numbers of ordinary people have dealings with the financial sector and are even more deeply involved in many ways. Personal expenditure is increasingly financed through debit and credit cards and online payments (and of declining importance cheques) rather than by the use of bank notes and cash. There have been generally higher and rising levels of household debt and borrowing from financial institutions (as illustrated in Chapter 4). There are much higher levels of financial assets and liabilities (relative to income) than hitherto held directly or indirectly by households, which has involved increased financial risk-taking by people. The promotion of owning your own home means mortgage borrowing for house purchase and later borrowing against the value of the home in the form of equity release.

Insurance is taken against a range of risks and, as more insurance is required, whether on one's life, car, home, etc., the insurance sector expands. Financialization has often involved the growth of private pension provision in place of state pension provision, and the consequent growth of pension funds with large accumulation of ownership of financial assets. Each individual has, in a sense, become financialized – that is, more closely engaged with and dependent on the financial system than previous generations – and it is relevant to investigate the gains and losses for people, individually and collectively, to become more financialized. It is also relevant to consider the economic and social effects of the growth of private provision over social provision, particularly in the area of pensions. Financialization also has effects on provisions of social and public services indirectly, as a result of the financial sector's involvement in such provision. In this chapter I mention the effects of private equity (as an element of financialization) on social care provision and PPP and PFI on public services.

Financial inclusion and exclusion

Financial inclusion and financial exclusion are important aspects of financialization. In a complex financial system, daily monetary transactions are difficult without access to payments technology, and coping with fluctuations in economic circumstances is difficult without good access to savings accounts and to credit and loans. In that sense, financial inclusion could be viewed as necessary to function in the society and generally beneficial for individuals and societies, at least in contrast with financial exclusion.

Joan Robinson once wrote: "The misery of being exploited by capitalists is nothing compared to the misery of not being exploited at all" (Robinson 1962: 45). I interpret "being exploited" as involving being employed and thereby exploited by the employer whereas "not being exploited" is to be unemployed.

In a society dominated by finance, participation in society is, by necessity, going to involve participation and engagement with the financial sector, and exclusion from the financial sector involves lower participation in society more generally. An illustration of the conflicting views on financial inclusion and financial exclusion comes from the experience of home mortgages in the USA and minorities. Dymski, Hernandez and Mohanty (2013: 124) ask why "minority applicants, who had been excluded from equal access to mortgage credit prior to the spread of subprime loans, superincluded in subprime mortgage lending? And why didn't the flood of mortgage credit in the 2000s housing boom – an oversupply of credit suggesting supercompetition – reduce the proportion of minority and women borrowers burdened with unpayable subprime mortgages?" The exclusion from mortgages severely discriminated against minority groups and then the terms of which those groups were included brought severe problems to the individuals involved and to the stability of the financial system.

A report by the House of Lords (2017: 12) indicates that "an individual might experience financial inclusion if they have the ability to: manage day-to-day financial transactions; meet expenses (both predictable and unpredictable); manage a loss of earned income; and avoid or reduce problem debt".

However, it is necessary to consider how the system as a whole operates and the terms on which individuals are included. For example, if financial inclusion comes at a high cost, involves complexity of products and mis-selling (as discussed in the next chapter), then what is termed financial inclusion may be deemed lacking in benefits.

What are the effects of financial inclusion on the individual? This operates at several levels and two are to be examined in this chapter. There have been considerable concerns expressed at the general rise in household debt observed in the past decades. Some of those concerns relate to the macroeconomic level and the effects of credit booms on macroeconomic stability. Other concerns have come from people being sucked into a debt trap and burdened by high interest payments (cf. the rates of interest charged on payday loans).

In a financially complex society, financial exclusion is closely related with the broader exclusion of individuals from society. "Financial exclusion has come to describe the inability, difficulty or reluctance to access mainstream financial services which, without intervention, can stimulate social exclusion, poverty and inequality" (House of Lords 2017: 12). Exclusion can range from the inability to have a bank account – in North America 94 per cent of individuals held bank accounts (either in a single or joint account) and in the euro area the figure was 95 per cent.[1] The figures for developing countries are much lower at 63 per cent in 2017, although this was an increase of one-half over the figure for 2011 at 42 per cent. Exclusion from access to credit at a reasonable cost without resorting to payday lenders is typical. Partial exclusion comes from tendencies to charge the poor more (e.g. for credit).

The simplest form of financial exclusion is exclusion from bank services as a payments system. This can to some degree be measured by the extent to which people are able to open a bank account. Financial Inclusion Commission (2015) summarizes financial exclusion (in the UK) in numbers. Nearly two million adults (around 4 per cent) do not have a bank account and those they term "financially excluded people" pay a poverty premium of £1,300 a year. It is estimated that two million people took out a high-cost loan in 2012 as the only form of credit they could access. Also, 13 million people do not have sufficient savings to support themselves for a month if they experience a quarter reduction in income; and 50 per cent of the households in the bottom half of the income distribution do not have home contents insurance and hence runs risks of considerable losses.

The House of Lords (2017: 22) drew the contrast between the UK being "the forefront of the global finance industry and is a leader in the fields of financial services, technology and innovation" with "a sizeable number of UK citizens lack access to even the most basic financial services, while still more are forced to rely on high-cost and suboptimal products which can prove damaging to their long-term financial health". The financial system frequently operates to benefit the wealthy at the expense of the poor and financial exclusion comes at considerable cost to the individual – the high-cost and suboptimal products damaging to "financial health". Not having a bank account can limit the most basic of engagement in society. Access to a bank account is also usually a prerequisite for gaining employment, paying bills and receiving social security benefits.

Access to savings accounts and affordable credit is significant in allowing people to meet fluctuations in their economic circumstances. As House of Lords (2017: 9) and many others note: "for a sizeable minority access to these products is lacking". It forces them to use more expensive informal options for loans that are frequently far more expensive or exploitative. Financial exclusion generally goes hand in hand with other forms of social exclusion vulnerability due to old age, disability, poverty or a lack of digital skills, which financial exclusion in turn compounds or reinforces. Leaving the market to

---

1. Figures refer to 2017 and source is Demirgüç-Kunt *et al.* (2018).

regulate financial inclusion has not worked effectively and large swathes of the population are the victims of poor access to fair financial services. In something of an understatement, House of Lords (2017: 9) remarks that "free markets do not always serve the financial needs of these customers effectively".

It is instructive that Financial Inclusion Commission (2015) was supported by MasterCard. Financial inclusion naturally means that the financial industry will extend its markets and the crucial question is whether the additional profits that the financial industry is thereby able to generate through an active government policy reflects additional social benefits. It is not to be forgotten that connecting everyone to the banking system may extend the "horizon" of individuals at the same time as being profitable for the banking industry (as bank accounts on which they profit replace the use of cash).

Financial inclusion can be regarded as an example of the beneficial effects of financial development on economic and social development. Put simply, if financial development brings social and economic gains, then inclusion of more people into the financial system could be reasonably expected to benefit them. The World Bank claims on its website that financial inclusion is a key mechanism for the reduction of poverty and boosts prosperity by bringing financial products and services within the reach of all. "Financial inclusion is a critical enabler for poverty reduction and inclusive growth. Access to transaction accounts opens up a pathway to broader financial inclusion, whereby people and firms can make financial transactions more efficiently and safely, access funds (whether payments, credit, savings, or other) invest in the future, and cope with economic shocks. Access to transaction accounts also enables participation in the digital economy, and is a critical building block for digital development too".[2]

Financial Inclusion Commission (2015: 2) envisaged financial inclusion (for the UK) to be every adult connected to the banking system, with access – when necessary and appropriate – to affordable credit from responsible lenders; encouragement of savings; access to the right insurance cover for his or her needs, at a fair price. The Commission also includes access to "objective and understandable advice on credit, debt, savings and pensions, delivered via the channel most suited to that individual" in addition to financial education.

The Alliance for Financial Inclusion is an "alliance owned and led by member central banks and financial regulatory institutions with the common objective of advancing financial inclusion at the country, regional and international levels". Its "Maya declaration", formulated in 2011 and updated in 2015, argues for "the critical importance of financial inclusion to empowering and transforming the lives of all our people, especially the poor, its role in improving national and global stability and integrity and its essential contribution to strong and inclusive growth" (AFI 2015: 1).

---

2. See World Bank, www.worldbank.org/en/topic/financialinclusion/brief/figi

As Mader (2018) argues, those who have advocated financial inclusion have assumed that the causation runs from financial inclusion to economic growth and development, whereas the causal connection is unclear (and of course similar arguments apply to the relationship between financial development and economic growth). It could well be that growth and development actually drive financial inclusion. Mader argues that "the *assumption* of poor people benefiting directly from financial inclusion is weak; the impact literature cannot show transformative or even clearly positive effects (unless improved money management, a diffuse sense of inclusion, and expanded financial choices are the desired effects)". He further argues "that the business case for financial inclusion – the promise that for-profit actors will deliver comprehensive services at decent quality and affordable prices – is far weaker than normally presumed" (Mader 2018: 478).

Santos (2017: 410) relates the retrenchment of the welfare state as a relevant factor, explaining the ways in which finance has penetrated into even more areas of economic and social life, and social reproduction has become more and more dependent on the financial sector. This growing involvement of individuals with the financial sector requires greater financial knowledge and understanding by the public as financial products have become more complex and hard to understand. Many products that we buy are complex and, as individuals, we do not understand how they work. We may not know the inner workings of the television but we do need to know and understand how to turn it on, change channels and make other adjustments. This, of course, does not stop mis-selling – claims made for the product that turn out to be incorrect. The returns to financial products inevitably relate to an uncertain future – it is not possible for the returns to financial assets to be guaranteed. The extent of mis-selling is explored in the next chapter.

The key question should be the terms on which financial inclusion occurs and the extent to which not being financially included means not being socially included. Financial inclusion can be considered at the individual level – that is, the degree to which any individual is included or excluded from the operations of the financial system. And it can be considered at a society level – for example, private pension provision is a form of financialization that benefits the financial sector in providing business and profits, and when private pension provision is dominant it would in general be in the interests of any individual to be included rather than excluded from such provision. Yet private pension provision involves risks of default, fraud and poor financial performance, all of which have adverse consequences for the individual. Government regulations and oversight may help to limit the risks involved. Yet the social provision of pensions in contrast involves low costs (e.g. administration) and lower risks.

Forms of credit rationing are pervasive when credit, loans, mortgages, etc. are involved. Credit rationing by financial institutions involves them in making decisions on how much is lent to an individual and on what terms, and on whom to lend to. Decisions on credit involve assessment of the ability and intentions of the recipient of the credit to repay and assessment of any collateral. The assessments of default risk may well involve discriminatory practices through favouring some groups over others in their credit rating assessments. The discrimination can be along ethnic lines, gender, area of residence, etc. As Block (2014: 14) argues:

> If a financial system needs gatekeepers, everything hangs on the decision rules that those gatekeepers employ to evaluate creditworthiness. In the past, gatekeeping positions in the United States were filled largely with upper-class individuals who had gone to the right schools and knew all the right people. It was simply common sense for these gatekeepers to define creditworthiness in class terms; the closer an individual came to the manners and styles of upper-class men, the more creditworthy they were seen to be. If they were female, from a minority group, or working class in origin, then they were obviously less creditworthy.

Household debt

A significant feature of the financialization era has been the growth of household assets and liabilities (cf. Chapter 4). Household debt reveals something of the double-edged nature of financial inclusion. On the one side, the availability of debt (on "fair terms") may enable individuals to cope with fluctuations in income (although a time of low or no income does not provide the highest credit ratings!) and can enable some smoothing of consumption over time with borrowing at times of low income and high consumption needs. On the other side, households may be sucked into debt traps with high rates of interest and then the need to borrow more and more as outstanding debt spirals.

While the growth of household debt has been a widespread feature in industrialized economies, it has proceeded at different speeds and there are significant differences between countries. Household debt has a tendency to be unstable and is a contributory factor of macroeconomic instability. Why has there been such a growth of household debt? The focus is often placed on households' desires to maintain and expand consumption ("keeping up with the Joneses"), particularly in a period where growth of wages has been slow, which can be aided by taking on debt.

It is, though, also useful to look at the other side, which is to ask why have financial institutions become keener to lend to households? The high rates of interest often charged on consumer loans (particularly those associated with credit cards and payday loans) are one attraction. There is also the effect of faltering rates of investment and higher rates of savings, which opens up a gap between potential savings and investment. This would have deflationary consequences unless offset by government borrowing, lending overseas or lending to households. The lending to households represented dis-savings by those households. The pushing of loans by financial institutions and by non-financial institutions (notably car companies) then becomes one route for maintaining aggregate demand.

Sparkes and Wood (2021: 598) argue that "household debt levels [in the UK] did not rise exclusively under neoliberalism. Empirical evidence demonstrates that there was a significant increase in outstanding real household debt volumes in Britain between the early 1950s and late 1970s." During that period, there were relaxations of the government controls over credit and restraints on banks' lending to households, and the Competition and Credit Control policies that fit in with the deregulation and liberalization of the financial system.

The growth of consumer spending has in many countries become an important driver of demand and its growth. Particularly where this has taken place against a background of slow growth of real wages and personal disposable income, then the growth of consumption spending relies on household debt to finance it. In the context of the Canadian and US economies over last half century, Costantini and Seccareccia (2020: 444) argue that expansion has relied on household consumption as the key contributor to economic growth, despite weak growth in real wages and personal disposable income. "This growth in consumption spending is highly fragile not only because it is debt-led growth that has relied on an unsustainable expansion of household indebtedness largely dependent on credit bubbles in the housing market, but also because of the perverse form of this indebtedness. … it is the poorest and most vulnerable households who have been building up unsustainable debt, thereby presaging increasing financial fragility and crises."

Dagdeviren et al. (2020: 169) report that a large number of studies have recognised the role of financialization and rising inequality for the dynamics of household indebtedness. The authors find that "while growth of household indebtedness prior to the crisis may have reflected a desire to accumulate wealth or maintain socially acceptable lifestyles, a different phase of indebtedness has emerged under austerity. The evidence from surveys, debt advice organisations and interview data shows that the LIHs [low-income households] have been incurring debt for basic necessities such as food, shelter and key services."

Second, while household debt and liabilities have risen, so have household financial assets. The distributional aspects of that need to be examined; for example, is this the rich getting richer (more financial assets) and poor getting poorer (more financial liabilities)?

Microfinance: a case study

Microfinance involves the provision of small loans, often to groups, which had been hitherto excluded from credit. Microfinance institutions (MFIs) have grown rapidly. Very poor families with a microloan grew from 7.6 million in 1997 to 137.5 million in 2010 (reported in Banerjee et al. 2015).

Cull, Demirgüç-Kunt and Morduch (2009: 169) describe the movement from socially oriented not-for-profit microfinance institutions to for-profit microfinance institutions. They argue that the evidence suggests that investors seeking pure profits would have little interest in most of the institutions we see that are now serving poorer customers. "Commercial investment is necessary to fund the continued expansion of microfinance, but institutions with strong social missions, many taking advantage of subsidies, remain best placed to reach and serve the poorest customers, and some are doing so at a massive scale."

Microcredit is a form of credit offered to the poor generally excluded from credit and loans intended to generate income from microenterprises and to reduce poverty among those most disenfranchised. "Although initially tied to state subsidies or philanthropic funding, since the 1990s microcredit has increasingly been delivered through commercialized vehicles" (Aitken 2013: 474). For the poorer groups in society, and more generally those previously excluded from the financial system, the expansion of microfinance is an element of financialization.

Cull, Demirgüç-Kunt and Morduch (2009: 169–70) argue that:

> the greatest triumph of microfinance is the demonstration that poor households can be reliable bank customers. ... Beginning in the 1980s, microfinance pioneers started shifting the focus. Instead of farmers, they turned to people in village and towns running "nonfarm enterprises" – like making handicrafts, livestock-raising, and running small stores. ... The high loan repayment rates for microfinance institutions were credited to new lending practices, especially "group lending". ... In the original models, customers were typically formed into small groups and required to guarantee each others' loan repayments, aligning their incentives to those of the bank. Today a broader set of mechanisms is recognized as also contributing to microfinance successes – especially the credible threat to deny defaulters' access to future loans, with or without group contracts.

Morduch (1999) reviewed several studies on the impacts of microfinance on poverty and finds that the evidence is mixed, particularly with regard to microcredit (but is more positive regarding savings programmes).

Banerjee *et al.* (2015) report on randomized evaluation of a group-lending microcredit programme in Hyderabad, India. At the end of the three-year study period, 33 per cent of households had borrowed from a microfinance institution, and that is among households selected for their relatively high propensity to take up microcredit. They report this in line with some other studies: "perhaps despite evidence of high marginal rates of return among microbusinesss ... most households either do not have a project with a rate of return of at least 24 per cent – the APR on a Spandana [a MFI studied] loan – or simply prefer to borrow from friends, relatives, or money lenders due to the greater flexibility those sources provide" (*ibid.*: 51). While microcredit enables some to expand their businesses, "it does not appear to fuel an escape from poverty based on those small businesses. Monthly consumption ... does not increase for those who had early access to microfinance" (*ibid.*) either in the short run or the long run.

Critics of microfinance, for example, Bateman, Blankenburg and Kozul-Wright (2019), have doubted its contribution to development and transformation. Microfinance, by definition, provides small loans to individuals. Such loans can provide sufficient funds to acquire (or lease) goods for sale, materials or agricultural inputs. It is self-employment, which is thereby enabled rather than the establishment of a small business.

According to Barrowclough (2018: 12):

> It should be obvious that lending very small amounts of money (usually less than $100) to individual entrepreneurs-to-be is unlikely to be able to generate jobs and create a dynamic market on the scale needed to fundamentally change the economic environment, even at a very local level. Indeed, the fact the level is local is part of the problem – many microfinance loans were financing small-scale trading and could even be displacing other traders or provoking a shift towards informal employment. Lending to the poor can only ever be one aspect of a broader and deeper approach, whereby government tackle directly the issue of job creation, skills development, trade and development rather than imagining that anyone or everyone can be an entrepreneur.

Mader (2018: 463) notes that, over recent years, "microfinance institutions have come under fire for their high interest rates (around 35 per cent on average, according to *The Economist* 2014), their fixation on credit over other financial services, the lack of demonstrable poverty import, their questionable record on women's employment, and for driving over-indebtedness".

Bateman, Blankenburg and Kozul-Wright (2019: 45) point to two specific demand-related outcomes that worked to counter any meaningfully positive impact from micro-credit. The first of these is displacement. This is the situation where a new microenterprise helped into operation by microcredit is able to survive and create some new jobs but it only manages to do so by eating into the local demand that had been supporting an incumbent microenterprise, which is forced to contract its own level of employment and low revenue to a roughly similar degree. The second negative factor here is exit (or enterprise closure). This is the situation where a new or incumbent microenterprise is forced to close outright because of the increased local competition caused by additional new entry.

A global survey by Gomez (2008) has shown that, in general, 75 per cent of new microenterprises do not survive beyond two years. The degree to which small loans to individuals are, or can operate in effect as, household debt and which places individuals into a cycle of debt have also been highlighted.

Aitken (2013: 493–94) speaks of micro/financialization as "the conversion of microcredit networks and the micro-borrowers who populate those networks into investable assets". These processes of micro/financialization bring "micro-credit into close connections with global finance". As such "poor borrowers from the global South [are inevitably brought] into contact with the most dubious risks associated with global finance: speculative instability, over-extended (and oversold) credit, unpredictable chains of financial fragility at both micro and macro levels".

Private pensions

The financial sector has become involved in activities that had previously been the preserve of the state and/or mutual sectors. The most notable example is that of pension provision. Private pension arrangements provide a major growth area for financial institutions and a major source of profits. Private (funded) pension schemes vary from those operated by state-related institutions through occupational pension schemes and (increasingly) individual pension arrangements, such as individual retirement accounts in the USA.

Pension arrangements can be viewed as ways in which spending power is transferred between a person's working life and their retirement. State pension arrangements have generally (but not universally) been on a "pay-as-you-go" basis – that is, taxes are levied (often labelled social security contributions) and benefits paid on a year-by-year basis. Pensions organized on a funded basis have been promoted on the grounds that contributions to pension funds represent savings. It has been (wrongly in my view) argued that a funded pension scheme (as compared with an unfunded pay-as-you-go one) would raise the overall level of savings and thereby the stock of capital as it is assumed that savings readily flow into capital formation (Feldstein 1974). This is in some respects a variant on the argument that financial development promotes more savings and thereby faster growth. It can be noted that this is an application of the line of argument that more savings leads to more investment, whereas the Keynesian perspective is that investment is the driver of savings. The Keynesian perspective of the "savings paradox", whereby intentions to save more are deflationary in consequence and may lead to lower economic activity and no increase in total savings. The key element here, though, is that funded pension arrangements increase the activities of the financial institutions and their profits.

The report by the World Bank in 1994 represented a major push by global institutions in favour of the effective privatization of pension provision. It argued for a public pension provision with the limited object of alleviating old age poverty and co-insuring against a multitude of risks (long spells of low investment returns, recession, inflation and private market failures). It advocated what it termed a "second mandatory pillar", which was fully funded and privately managed and that would link benefits actuarially to costs and carry out the income-smoothing or saving function for all income groups within the population. Significantly it argued that "full funding should *boost capital accumulation and financial market development*" (World Bank 1994: 19, emphasis added) and erroneously argued that the additional economic growth "should make it easier to finance the public pillar."

As Bonizzi and Churchill (2017: 74) note, around 2000 "the European Commission began a concerted effort to encourage member states to set up or enhance the role of private funded pension schemes as one step towards managing the predicted rising costs of state-managed Pay As You Go (PAYG) pension schemes", and the growth pf private pension funds would aid the growth of the financial sector. They note the influence of the World Bank and the theoretical support from the idea that financial deepening coming from the expansion of pension funds aids growth.

Bonizzi, Churchill and Guevara (2021: 810) indicate how the rise of pension funds in Colombia and Peru played an important role of the form of financialization in those countries. They report that the evolution of demand for financial assets from pensions has been a key force behind the financial liberalization and the development of new financial asset classes. They conclude that pension privatization has produced only limited beneficial economic effects and that the promises of increased funds and capital accumulation have not been fulfilled. "Funded pensions were supposed to accelerate financial development, savings and capital formation, However, savings rates in many EEs [emerging economies] have not increased, and in Latin America, where the pension privatization was most intense, savings rates ... and capital formation remain lower than in other development economies."

In Table 9.1 statistics are presented for the G7 countries plus a sample of other industrialized economies relating to the assets of pension funds relative to GDP. These statistics illustrate the growth of assets under management by pension funds, as well the large differences between countries.

Table 9.1 Pension funds' assets as percentage of GDP

	2000	2005	2010	2015	2019
Australia	n/a	78.0	89.0	118.2	134.5
Canada	55.6	56.3	62.9	83.1	90.5
Denmark	n/a	32.9	47.9	43.7	48.9
Finland	n/a	65.5	78.7	48.9	51.9
France	n/a	0.0	0.2	0.6	0.8
Germany	3.9	4.2	5.5	6.7	7.5
Italy	n/a	2.7	4.4	6.8	8.4
Japan	n/a	6.3	n/a	n/a	20.6
Korea	n/a	1.6	3.5	7.7	11.6
Netherlands	113.1	112.5	118.9	168.6	194.4
Spain	n/a	7.1	7.8	9.6	9.3
Sweden	0.0	8.5	8.8	8.7	4.2
Switzerland	112.0	106.6	102.0	120.5	143.7
United Kingdom	n/a	71.3	80.5	96.5	108.7
United States	81.4	74.1	73.8	77.7	85.8

Source: OECD Funded Pension Statistics

Braun (2021: 1) notes that "the upswing in financialization since the 1970s has coincided with the steady accumulation of long-term retirement savings and their consolidation in institutional capital pools. Pension fund demand for high-yield, long-term financial claims has acted as a catalyst for financialization, understood as the reorganization of ownership relations and economic activity in ways that serve the needs of institutional capital pools." Pension fund assets have "fueled the growth of the asset management sector, which in many countries has actively lobbied for pension privatization. When pension fund activism brought corporate governance reform, corporations' quest for shareholder value brought workplace fissuring and wage stagnation. When pension funds pushed into real estate for better returns, private equity firms delivered by raising rents and evicting those that could not pay."

Pension fund arrangements provide inflow of funds into pension funds, and those funds are used to acquire financial assets. In turn, those financial assets have to provide for future pension payments. Hassel, Naczyk and Wiss (2019: 484) comment on the changing relationship between pension systems and types of capitalism through financialization. "The lifting of capital controls, the steep increase in profits from financial activities, the rise of shareholder value – a doctrine that has sometimes been pushed by pension funds – have all characterised the shift from industrial to financial capitalism. At the same time, public pensions have been targeted for partial privatisation, thereby opening up new business opportunities for financial firms, such as insurance companies, mutual funds and banks."

Ebbinghaus (2015: 56) indicates the general moves in Europe towards privatization and marketization of pensions. It also involves a shift from a defined benefits approach to a defined contributions approach. He also notes the "short-term problems and long-term uncertainties about the social and political sustainability of these privatized and marketized multi-pillar strategies".

The growth of private pension funds also involves a dependence of pensioners' livelihoods on the performance of financial markets and the growing role of pension funds as providers of capital (e.g. Hassel, Naczyk & Wiss 2019). It also has to be backed up by regulation and oversight of the pension funds to safeguard individuals pensions. There is also "undoubtedly a positive association between the rise of pre-funded pensions and the growth of the financial sector. The size of assets of non-sovereign pension funds – of the defined-contribution and defined-benefit type – is relatively strongly correlated with the market capitalisation of domestic listed companies" (*ibid.*: 49) with a correlation coefficient of 0.624 reported for the 2001–08 period.

State provision via social security is (usually) unfunded pay as you go. The administrative costs are relatively small compared to those of private funded schemes. Although a social security system often has the appearance of being an insurance scheme (as in the UK where it is called "national insurance") – for an individual there is some relationship between their contributions and their pension, although the length of time for which pensions are received is on an insurance basis. Public pensions can build in elements of redistribution, noting that the relatively wealthy make relatively higher contributions than the poorer and may or may not receive higher pensions, although they are likely to be paid for a longer time (given life expectancy). Private (individual) pensions may have the "benefit" that the individual can choose the level of savings to be made and thereby the expected pensions.

Housing

The construction and purchase of a house (in a market economy) requires financing; it has to be paid for and represents a large outlay (relative to income). There is then a sense in which finance will be involved with housing. The terms and conditions under which finance is provided is a significant factor in the amount of construction and its location. There are of course many other factors involved. Housing has always been dependent on the provision of finance, whether purchased on an individual basis for owner-occupation or purchased for renting out as part of a property portfolio. In many countries, housing finance had been provided through specialist institutions whose main or sole focus was the provision of mortgages, including building societies, savings and loans institutions. These institutions have often been in mutual ownership and the processes of financialization have often involved the decline of such institutions. Indeed, it can be said that "the mortgage finance channel is now integrated with other financial channels and therefore other financial markets" (Aalbers 2017: 542). A major development during financialization that had major effects on mortgage provision was that of securitization. In the housing market case, this was the development of mortgage-backed securities, a development that was closely associated with the GFCs.

Kohl (2021: 413) argues that the rapid growth of mortgage finance did not lead to a corresponding expansion of the supply of houses in a study of 17 countries over the period 1913–2016. The paper examines the co-movements of construction, house prices and mortgage credit, and finds "a decoupling of house-price mortgage spirals from the underlying stagnating or declining construction activity since the 1980s. Mortgage debt is nonlinearly associated with new construction: positive up to a threshold, negative thereafter." In a manner similar to other findings on growth and capital formation (see Chapter 10), "beyond a certain threshold, there is a curse of too much finance".

Health and social care

Social care, as with education and health provision, can be provided in many different ways, ranging from family and friends through state provision, not-for-profit organizations and profit organizations. In many countries, families and friends had and still have a major role to play; similarly, not-for-profit organizations, charities, etc. have major roles to play.

A not-for-profit organization can be described as having two bottom lines – there are the objectives for which they were established and the requirement to break even with a balance between income and expenditure. In the case of for-profit organizations, there are the requirements to raise capital and to make profits (or at least ensure that income exceeds expenditure). Profit-seeking organizations have some financial involvements, and large ones become quoted companies and engage in stock market activities. There are important considerations on the differences in performance between not-for-profit and profit organizations in areas such as social care. However, the specific focus here is the involvement of the financial sector. A profit organization seeks to make profits from the difference between its revenues and its costs and, although financial calculations are involved, the emphasis is on production and sales.

Hunter and Murray (2020: 1264) outline the ways in which institutions, instrument and ideas have facilitated the involvement and penetration of private capital into the healthcare sector. The authors argue that this financialization represents a basic shift in the organizing principles for healthcare systems, with negative implications for health and equity. They show "the transformation of healthcare into a set of saleable and tradeable assets has built on four decades of healthcare commercialization that has deregulated activities to enable profitable investment and provision." Healthcare companies are focused on financial engineering and extraction of dividends rather than on the provision of good quality healthcare.

Burns *et al.* (2016: 2) show how the techniques of debt -based financial engineering have been applied completely inappropriately to an "activity like adult care which is low risk and should be low return". They argue that chains of care homes have target rates of return of up to 12 per cent and seek to achieve that through "cash extraction tied to the opportunistic loading of subsidiaries with debt; and tax avoidance through complex multi-level corporate structures which undermine any kind of accountability for public funding".

PFI and PPP provide further examples of privatization-cum-financialization. They are often used for infrastructure of hospitals, schools, etc., although are not limited to those. What has often been described as "traditional" public investment would often be constructed by private companies but directly funded by government, whether through tax revenues or through borrowing. The financial sector would be involved insofar as borrowing was involved and interest paid on the borrowing.

Under PFI, the investment comes as a "package" under which the company (often a special investment vehicle) builds the infrastructure with funds that it has raised itself and then leases the infrastructure to the government, in general, along with the provision of some services. For example, a school may be funded and constructed and then the maintenance and cleaning of the school are also provided on a long-term contract. This type of contract builds in inflexibilities in, for example, the use and internal design of buildings built under PFI.

I argued in Sawyer (2009: 39) that the costs of finance is higher under PFI than under "conventional" public investment. "PFI is one element of privatization that has been a high-cost way of undertaking public investment." Shaoul (2009: 1) points to the UK government's case for PFI as providing "additional finance and deliver[ing] value for money through the greater efficiency of and transfer of risk and costs to the private sector. The evidence rebuts the UK government's case for private finance." Of particular significance here is her conclusion that the PFI "policy, never popular, was introduced, developed and controlled by financial consultants. The policy benefits the financial elite not the broad mass of the population."

The financial sector has long been involved in the funding of government in terms of the difference between government expenditure and tax revenues. Some have argued for a "golden rule" of public finance whereby the average amount of borrowing is equal to the average amount of public investment, with the current budget (that is current government expenditure minus tax revenues) being in balance. The adoption of a PPP/PFI approach has meant the greater involvement of the financial sector broadly defined, particularly in the design stages and in the operation of the public investment. It has attempted to put the funding of public investment "off balance sheet", such that the debt associated with public borrowing does not appear on the government's balance sheet. It has often involved development of new financial instruments and special investment vehicles. The PFI approach has often led to public investment being more expensive and less flexible and, in effect, raising the cost of finance for government.

Conclusions

A very notable feature of the present era of financialization, as compared with previous eras, has been the rapid growth of the involvement of people with the financial system and financial decisions. The financialization of the everyday has been to the benefit of the financial sector as it means the growth of that sector, the services it provides and its profits. As the financial system grows, those who are, in effect (wholly or partially), excluded are disadvantaged (as compared with others), and financial exclusion is added to economic and social exclusion. Financial inclusion brings, though, its own drawbacks for those now included.

10

HAS THE FINANCIAL SECTOR BECOME TOO BIG AND DYSFUNCTIONAL?

The GFCs and the following "great recession" brought sharply to the fore the scale and nature of the workings of the financial sector and its inherent fragilities and instabilities. It served as a sharp reminder that the financial sectors and the non-financial ("real") sectors were closely intertwined and could not be viewed through the spectrum of the "classical dichotomy" of mainstream macroeconomics that separates monetary factors from real ones.

Financialization has involved the growth of the financial sector and changes in its structure, and the changing relationships between finance and the non-financial "real" economy. The financial sector uses resources that could be deployed elsewhere and financial institutions and some of their employees benefit handsomely (as indicated in Chapter 7). The processes of financialization have involved a substantial increase in the resources, both capital and labour, deployed in the financial sector. The question then can be asked as to whether the use of those additional resources has improved the *quality* of financial activity (see Kay 2015: 5). Also, has the financial sector become "too big" (see Epstein & Crotty 2013) and has it become dysfunctional for the economy and society?

It can also be asked whether the ways in which the financial system has evolved during financialization (such as a shift to activities undertaken through financial markets rather than by financial institutions, developments of a wide range of financial instruments) have adverse impacts. Asking the question of whether the financial sector is in some senses "too big" is (at least implicitly) to acknowledge that the financial sector can make positive contributions to society and the economy but that it can also have negative effects (the GFCs being a notable example).

It is helpful to begin by considering the perceived functions of the financial sector that would aid the performance of the real economy. Kay (2015), for example, lists four: the provision of a payments systems; matching lenders with borrowers and directing saving; aiding management of personal finances over our lifetime and between generations; and aiding the management of risk. Minsky (1993) identified six functions of a banking and financial system in which, by comparison with those given by Kay, splits down the provision of finance into housing finance, consumer credit and investment banking, and also adds provision of portfolio advice and asset management for households. In a similar vein, Epstein and Crotty (2013) view a healthy and well-functioning financial sector in terms of channelling finance to investment, enabling households to save, reducing risk through provision of insurance, provision of stable and flexible liquidity, an efficient payments mechanism and financial innovation.

In respect of the payments mechanism and the provision of safe and secure outlets for transaction balances and household savings (and indeed provision of loans), the financial sector may be too small in the sense that many are excluded from engaging in the system – the financially excluded (as discussed in Chapter 9).

The financial sector (broadly defined) does offer insurance services and, as such, could be said to aid the transfer and pooling of risk from the insured individual to the insurance company. It became apparent in the years preceding the financial crises that in some areas the operations of the financial sector were risk-creating through the processes of securitization (as for example illustrated in Kay 2015).

Judged by the costs of financial intermediation, the larger scale of the financial sector does not appear to have led to that sector becoming more effective. Philippon (2015: 1434) concluded that in the case of the USA "the unit cost of financial intermediation appears to be as high today as it was around 1900" (despite advances in information technology). "Trading costs have indeed decreased ... but trading volumes have increased even more, and active fund management is expensive." The unit cost of financial intermediation is estimated to represent an annual spread of 1.87 per cent on average. Bazot (2018) covers 20 mainly industrialized countries over the period 1970–2015. Among his results are that unit costs of financial intermediation decreased over that period in most countries, although in large financial countries such as the UK and USA there was no downward trend. He also finds that the ratio of banks' distributed profits to banks' intermediated assets and liabilities tends to rise, indicating that most of the decrease in unit costs comes from reduced input costs, suggesting higher economic rents and mark-ups.

The general idea that the financial sector has become, in some sense, too large and does not focus on its key roles is not a new one, although it was not widely acknowledged before the GFCs. The growth of financial markets and in the volumes of trade, the frequency of trades and the complexity of financial products have featured heavily in the critiques. Tobin (1984: 14) doubted the value of "throwing more and more of our resources, including the cream of our youth, into financial activities remote from the production of goods and services, into activities that generate high private rewards disproportionate to the social productivity". The idea that the rewards in the financial sector (or indeed any other) run ahead of productivity and the value of the contributions of the resources deployed leads into the receipt of economic rents, which is elaborated below.

Stiglitz (1994) argued that financial innovations often contribute little to the achievement of economic efficiency and may well be welfare-decreasing. Financial innovations often appear profitable to the financial institutions making the innovation, yet do not yield economic and social benefits. This is an important argument that what is privately profitable is not always socially beneficial, rather than the presumption that profit-seeking behaviour leads to socially efficient outcomes. Stiglitz's example was technology that permitted faster transactions and may do little for economic efficiency but absorbs resources that could have been used elsewhere.

A relatively recent example enabled by technical development is that of "high frequency trading" (HFT), which relies on computer algorithms in the context of trading strategies carried out by computers to move in and out of positions in seconds or fractions of a second. HFT exacerbates the issues raised by Keynes in the 1930s when he wrote that "speculators may do no harm as bubbles on a steady stream of enterprise. But the position is serious when enterprise becomes the bubble on a whirlpool of speculation. When the capital development of a country becomes a by-product of the activities of a casino, the job is likely to be ill-done" (Keynes 1936: 159). As Tobin (1984) was later to advocate in what has often been called a Tobin tax, particularly on foreign exchange transactions, Keynes then argued for the introduction of a transfer tax on all financial transactions "with a view to mitigating the predominance of speculation over enterprise in the United States" (Keynes 1936: 160).

Electronic trading has reduced the role of human market-makers, replaced by electronic intermediaries. HFT involves algorithmic financial trading at very high speed and with high rates of turnover. It involves the use of trading strategies with movement in and out of positions in fractions of a second. The casino analogy used by Keynes serves as a reminder that risks can be generated through gambling rather than reduced through insurance. It also can be viewed in terms of who profits from HFT – in the case of the casino we know it is the house as the expected pay-outs based on the known probabilities are less than the placed bets; for HFT, those operating the system appear to find it highly profitable but at whose expense?

HFT may be profitable to the participants, although that leaves the question of profiting at whose expense in what is in effect a zero-sum game. Further, HFT appears to be socially pointless – the trading depends on small price discrepancies, and by "buying low" and "selling high" is said to aid the elimination of those price differences. But do such price differences have to be eliminated in a nanosecond, and what are the gains from doing so? There are further costs of operating the trading system, including the employment of highly skilled computer programmers. And that pointlessness adds up. Lewis (2014) describes the scheme of spread networks to lay fibre optic cable between Chicago and New York in as straight a line as possible and at great cost to have the fastest possible links (measured in nanoseconds), which would enable advantages to be taken of price differences on the stock exchanges.

The growth of HFT raises issues of corporate governance; someone who is the (proud) owner of equity in a company for a second cannot exercise much influence on the corporate governance of that company. Further, when price movements are in effect following a random walk, then HFT is akin to playing the casino.

Stiglitz (1994: 22), in something of an understatement, postulated that "improvements in secondary markets do not necessarily enhance the ability of the economy either to mobilize savings or to allocate capital". The secondary markets are trading in existing financial assets, and such trading, whether on a high frequency or a low frequency basis, does not mobilize savings or aid the allocation of capital, which are often considered to be the key functions of the financial sector. Further, the rapid expansion of trading in financial assets and the ways in which financial innovations have created rather than diminished risks and the likelihood of financial crises have strongly reinforced the arguments that Tobin and Stiglitz made many years ago.

Zingales (2015) poses the question in the title of his paper based on his presidential address to the American Finance Association of "whether finance benefits society?" and then comments that for an academic economist the answer would appear to be obvious. It is obvious in the sense that the answer would be yes, and by appeal to notions of efficient markets and the benefits of competitive markets (as discussed in Chapter 5). But he argues that there is a need to acknowledge that academic economists and finance experts have inflated the perception of the benefits of the scale and growth of finance. After acknowledging that an economy has need of a well-developed financial system, he argues that "at the current state of knowledge there is no theoretical reason or empirical evidence to support the notion that all the growth of the financial sector in the last forty years has been beneficial to society" (*ibid.*: 1328). He continues by arguing that there is both theory and empirical evidence that a component of that growth has been pure rent-seeking and that a task of academics is to use research and teaching to reduce the rent-seeking dimension of finance, an issue that is returned to below.

The route to finding an answer to the question of whether the financial sector has become "too big" and dysfunctional is divided into five steps. In the next section the contribution of the financial sector in terms of the sector's measured output is examined, specifically the question of whether measured output overstates the contribution of the sector. The relationships between the scale of the financial sector and economic growth are investigated in the following section. A key function of the financial sector would be the provision of loans for investment purposes, facilitating savings and monitoring fund allocation, and along those lines a larger financial sector with higher levels of savings and investment would be associated with higher growth. Financial crises have many causes but those involving banks, credit and asset price booms centrally involved in the generation of such crises and their costs are considered. The following section then moves on to misdeeds and mis-selling in the financial sector and their costs for the rest of society. The notion of a "financial curse" is outlined and considered specifically in connection with "rent extraction" by the financial sector.

Measuring the contribution of the financial sector to economic activity

In earlier chapters, the output of the financial sector has been reported and, in general, the sector appears to make a significant contribution to output and national income, and also to be more productive (as measured by output per person employed) than the rest of the economy. But the way in which output of the financial sector is measured can be questioned and whether the measured output is indeed a reflection of the contribution of the financial sector.

Christophers (2011: 115) considers how the measurement of financial activities has come to make finance appear productive in the sense of making a positive contribution to the level of production. He notes that what is defined and measured as economic activity is that which is "deemed to sit inside a designated 'production boundary'". It is well known that work and production inside the household (and not sold through the market) is not included in the estimation of GDP and hence not included in the national accounts and not regarded as "productive". He then argues that "the positioning of certain fundamental services *vis-á-vis* the production boundary has long been a locus of bewilderment, debate and even open conflict". The treatment of financial services in the national accounts has changed over time, with successive editions of the Standardised National Accounts, with (as detailed by Christophers 2011 and Assa 2017) the changes having the effect of making banking and finance appear more productive.

A starting point can be seen as what was labelled by Haig (1986) as "the banking problem", which is that if financial services were treated like other industries, the banking sector would be depicted as making a negligible or negative contribution to output. National income accounts had treated the receipts and the payments of interest as transfer between economic agents, which do not result in current productive activity. This means that the net receipts of interest were not counted in national income and expenditure nor in the contribution of industries or sectors to total national product. "The expenditure, and profit, of banks are financed chiefly through receipts, less payments of interest. If net interest is deducted from the recorded profits, the result is a small or zero contribution of banks to national product and to a negative profit" (Haig 1973: 624).

Basu, Inklaar and Wang (2011: 227) note that the measurement of bank output is challenging, since much of bank service output is not explicitly priced. They argue that "the implicit revenue from screening and monitoring services should equal the spread of the gross loan interest rate over the yield on an equally risky fixed-income security, *not* a risk-free security such as a Treasury bill or bond". They provide new estimates that seek to use the risky interest rate rather than the risk-free one, and since the former is greater than the latter, the spread will be less. In their estimates for the USA, bank output is reduced by 21 per cent and GDP by 0.3 per cent.

Money is not directly consumed or used in production, although the use of money facilitates demand (in the sense that in a monetary economy possession of money is required to enable expenditure to take place). Assa (2017: §4.3) argues that the financial sector should be regarded as a cost of producing the rest of GDP. The " 'output' of finance should be deducted, not merely excluded, from GDP as it is the ultimate and ubiquitous intermediate input (albeit an intermediate cost rather than an input for intermediate consumption) to all industries producing a use-value output of either goods or services".

Assa (2017) identifies three major types of financial services and that the types are treated in the national accounts in different ways. Revenues from changes in asset prices (capital gains) are excluded from production accounts. Interest flows generated by financial intermediation are treated as intermediate input to other industries and, as such, deducted from GDP. The third type, fee-based financial services, are considered productive and are imputed as value-added based on net revenue. Assa (2017: 54) argues that the System of National Accounts (SNA 93) measure of GDP "gives finance a special treatment even though it has no final use-value. Instead of netting it out as it does with other intermediate inputs, GDP counts it as output". To some extent an analogy may be drawn with people's travel to work, which would be regarded as final consumption and hence part of GDP in the national accounts, whereas travel to work is a cost of production.

Assa (2017) provides a measure, which he labels final value added (FVA), as it applies the value-added formula to all sectors producing output that has a final use-value, while deducting the "output" of finance (which only transfers exchange value) as a cost (or intermediate input) to the total economy. He provides estimates for each of these concepts for the USA over the period 1987–2011. One significant aspect of his estimates and calculations is that the contribution of the financial sector to output is much reduced and indeed may be negative. Over that period, the conventional measure of GDP had a mean annual growth rate of 2.6 per cent with standard deviation of 1.8 per cent (Assa 2016: table 4.7). A measure, labelled FGDP, is Final GDP: FVA plus taxes minus subsidies is then calculated, for which mean growth rate was 2.3 per cent (standard deviation 2 per cent). He also calculates NFVA (non-financial value added) with a mean growth rate of 2.8 per cent, standard deviation 2.6 per cent). Also calculated is "narrow measured value added" (NMVA), which excludes all industries where output is imputed (based on net income) rather than directly measured. The sectors omitted in constructing NMVA are the government, FIRE, other services and the rest of the world. Here the mean growth rate is 1.3 per cent (standard deviation 2.8 per cent). It is perhaps not surprising in an era of financialization that growth rate of FGDP is half of that of GDP. The significance of this is that FGDP is much more closely attuned to what is available for consumption and for investment, and more a reflection of rising consumption levels. Further, the volatility (as reflected in the standard deviation) of the "real" economy is higher than the financial sector.

Financialization and growth

There have been ongoing debates over the role of the financial sector in economic growth. Some have argued that growth and economic development themselves lead to growth of the financial sector. In the words of Joan Robinson (1952: 86): "where enterprise leads finance follows"; economic growth raises the demand for a range of services provided by the financial sector. Lucas (1988: 6) dismisses finance as an "over-stressed" determinant of economic growth. However, many others – ranging from Bagehot (1873), Schumpeter (1912), Gurley and Shaw (1955), Goldsmith (1969) and McKinnon (1973) – have argued that finance and the growth of the financial sector are a stimulus for economic development and growth.

A particularly significant set of functions of the financial sector can be seen in terms of facilitating and encouraging savings and allocating and monitoring funds for investment. From those functions, it would be argued, faster economic growth flows. There has been an extensive literature on the relationship between what is termed financial deepening or financial development and economic growth. The growth of banks in the context of financial development can be interpreted in terms of banks providing the main vehicle for savings (in the form of bank deposits), which are then allocated for investment purposes. Commercial banks provide loans and thereby create bank deposits and money. Banks then are rather more than passive accepters of deposits, which are then recycled as loans, and rather provide and create loans, whereby deposits are also created. This involves the credit creation process and links with the endogenous view of money. It is the ability of banks to create spending power through loans that is a feature of growth and expansion.

The significant element here is, of course, that a well-functioning financial sector is postulated to raise the rate of growth (through increased and higher quality investment). The empirical difficulty is measuring the performance of those functions, whereas what is often measured is some dimension of the size of the financial sector (e.g. bank deposits relative to GDP). The question may be also asked as to whether the manner in which the financial sector has grown in the past three decades, through securitization and in the ratio of assets and liabilities to GDP, has improved those functions and aided economic growth.

In his extensive review of the empirical literature, Levine (2005: 921) concluded that "[a] growing body of empirical analyses, including firm-level studies, industry-level studies, individual country-studies, time-series studies, panel-investigations, and broad cross-country comparisons, demonstrate a strong positive link between the functioning of the financial system and long-run economic growth".

Arestis, Chortareas and Magkonis (2015: 557–9) conducted a meta-analysis of the empirical evidence on the effects of financial development on growth. They conclude that in terms of the correlations between financial development and growth, the usage of market-based proxies of financial development appear to lead to lower correlations than the use of either liquid liabilities or market-based variables. However, "the estimated coefficients of bank-based measures and complex indices are found [to be] statistically insignificant in all specifications". Overall, "the results suggest the existence of a statistically significant and economically meaningful positive genuine effect from financial development to economic growth".

The relationship between financial development and economic growth in the past three decades or so in the industrialized world is of particular interest. Casual observation may suggest that the general growth of the financial sector and the enhanced size of that sector have not obviously been associated with any faster growth. Indeed, it is often argued that growth in the western industrialized economies has been somewhat slower over the past three decades of financialization (see Chapter 11). Further, the literature on financialization has indeed suggested a variety of ways in which the processes of financialization may have diminished investment.

There has been a spate of papers in recent years that have widened the ways in which financial deepening and development have been measured and that have tended to find that there is a negative (or no) relationship between financial deepening and economic growth, at least at higher levels of financial deepening. This is often based on econometric evidence and the regressions are estimated to span many years. In Sawyer (2014b, 2016, 2018, 2019), I have surveyed much of this literature, and here provide a flavour of the results.

Rousseau and Wachtel (2011: 276) show that the finance-growth relationship is "not as strong in more recent data as it was in the original studies with data for the period from 1960 to 1989". They regard the increased incidence of financial crises, which are often followed by recession and lost output that is never recovered, as a possible explanation for the weakening of the relationship.

Sahay *et al.* (2015) use a new, broad, measure of financial development and find that the effect of financial development on growth is bell-shaped; it weakens at higher levels of financial development, although remains positive for emerging markets. They find that, primarily, the impact of financial deepening is on total factor productivity growth, rather than on capital accumulation. And that when financial development proceeds too fast, deepening financial institutions can lead to economic and financial instability.

Bucci, Marsiglio and Prettner (2020: 106) suggest that "the most recent empirical evidence [on the nature of the growth-finance nexus] suggests that this relationship may be nonmonotonic and in particular bell-shaped". In their paper the authors present a theoretical model on the endogenous growth tradition as well as empirical investigation that supports that bell-shaped relationship.

Alexiou, Vogiazas and Nellis (2018: 12) argue that their evidence suggests that the potential benefits of the financial sector may have been reversed in the past few decades resulting in "un-creative destruction". Hence, "the degradation of finance eventually rendered its function of intermediation as ineffective, causing more harm than good to economic growth". The results for subsamples of countries exhibit significant variation, although "in the case of developing market economies, the financial intermediation proxies are not significant in explaining economic growth".

Bezemer, Grydaki and Zhang (2016: 667) analyse data from 46 countries over the period from 1990 to 2011, observing that financial deepening supports investments and the reallocation of factors of production between sectors. However, they find that a large credit-to-GDP ratio can be a drag on growth, with rising credit-to-GDP ratios coinciding with shifts in the composition of credit toward real estate and other asset markets and hence away from investment in productive assets. They "find that the growth coefficient of different credit stocks scaled by GDP is insignificant or negative, especially credit stocks supporting asset markets. We observe insignificant or negative correlations of credit stocks with output growth. ... The positive effect of credit flows diminishes at higher levels of financial development. ... Bank credit has shifted away from non-financial business toward asset markets, where it has no or small growth effects."

Bezemer *et al.* (2021) talk of a "debt shift", with the majority of bank credit allocated towards the purchase of existing real estate and financial assets rather than funding non-financial firms' investment. This "debt shift" has negative consequences for income growth, income inequality and macroeconomic stability. Based on empirical analysis of 178 advanced economies over the 1973–2005 period, the gradual removal of credit policies (including credit quotas, credit controls and ceiling, restrictions on interest rates, subsidies for specified industrial sectors) and the privatization of state investment banks are significantly correlated with a decline in the business credit share.

Arcand, Berkes and Panizza (2012: 1) state that their empirical results suggest that finance starts having a negative effect on output growth when credit to the private sector reaches 100 per cent of GDP and that their results "are consistent with the 'vanishing effect' of financial development and that they are not driven by output volatility, banking crises, low institutional quality, or by differences in bank regulation and supervision".

This leads to a consideration of why the relationship may have changed. Four particular features stand out. First, the lending activities of the financial sector have shifted from lending to firms for investment purposes towards lending to households (mortgages, consumer credit), which have less growth potential. Consumer credit may help to boost spending in the short term but does not directly aid investment and, indeed, higher levels of consumer debt are often a factor in financial crisis. Second, financial fragility and instability may come along with higher rates of financial deepening and, in turn, financial fragility increases the risks of financial crisis, which has depressing consequences for economic activity.

Third, resources are deployed in the financial sector that could otherwise have been deployed in the rest of the economy. It is also the case that the financial sector employs often highly skilled labour, which is thereby not available employment in the real sector of the economy; financial engineering replaces engineering. More generally, the "financial system costs the economy on a daily basis by attracting too many talented workers, distorting incentives to engage in long-term investments, making poor strategic decisions in managing firms it controls, and other problems associated with allocation of credit, capital and talent" (Epstein & Montecino 2016: 3). Misallocation costs come from speculative finance, which "harms the economy on a daily basis ... by growing too large, utilizing too many skilled and productive workers, imposing short-term orientations on businesses, and starving some businesses and households of needed credit. We estimate that the cost of misallocating human and financial resources amounted to $2.6 trillion–$3.9 trillion between 1990 and 2005" (*ibid.*).

Malkiel (2013: 97) argues that the data does not support the argument that the increase in fees reflected increasing returns for investors from active management, nor whether it was necessary to improve the efficiency of the market for investors who availed themselves of low-cost passive (index) funds. "Thus, the increase in fees is likely to represent a deadweight loss for investors. Indeed, perhaps the greatest inefficiency in the stock market is in 'the market' for investment advice."

Fourth, much of the growth of the financial sector has been in the extensive trading of financial assets with the growth of securitization and derivatives, which do not themselves facilitate savings and investment. As the financial sector has shifted towards the generation of and then to high-volume trading in derivatives and securitization, it has shifted away from the facilitation of savings and the financing of investment. It is perhaps not surprising that the growth of the financial sector (relative to GDP) is not linked with economic growth, as the growth of the capital stock is no longer being facilitated by the operations of the financial sector.

Epstein and Montecino (2016) use the work of Cecchetti and Kharroubi (2012) and Arcand, Berkes and Panizza (2012) to estimate the reduction in annual growth in the USA over the period 1990–2005, which could be attributed to the high private credit-to-GDP ratio (a 130 per cent ratio as compared to a 90 per cent ratio identified by Cecchetti and Kharroubi (2012) as corresponding with maximum economic growth). Epstein and Montecino (2016) then estimate that GDP in 2005 was lower by between $2.6 trillion and $4 trillion as a result of the high credit-to-GDP ratio.

Costs of financial crises

The GFCs had two immediately apparent economic and social costs – the fiscal costs of the bail-out of banks and the subsequent recession, higher unemployment and diminished output. The GFCs are one in a long line of financial crises that have occurred in the era of financialization, with over 400 recorded since 1970. These crises (particularly banking crises) are a clear cost of financialization.

In the present era of financialization there has been a burst of financial crises, and their occurrence can be linked with financial liberalization and the ways in which the financial system has developed. Laeven and Valencia (2020) identify 151 banking crises over the period 1970–2017. The years 2007–08 saw 21, although there have been only four since 2011. Two basic criteria for a banking crisis are used. First, significant signs of financial distress in the banking system (e.g. bank runs). Second, significant policy interventions in response to losses in the banking system, such as bank holidays, bank nationalizations).

A further 236 currency crises and 79 sovereign debt crises are identified. A currency crisis is defined in terms of a sharp nominal depreciation of the currency vis-à-vis the US dollar. Sovereign debt crisis involves sovereign debt default and restructuring. Particularly large financial crises include Mexico/Latin America 1994 and the East Asian crisis 1997. Laeven and Valencia (2020) note that before the 2007–08 GFCs, the vast majority of banking crises occurred in low- and middle-income countries. As Eichacker (2017: 58) notes, there are strong indications of markedly increased trends in financial crises since the early 1980s. Financial crises impose severe costs on the economy, reducing output and employment, and are part of the general costs of financialization.

Fiscal costs

Banks and other financial institutions (as indeed other corporations) run into difficulties in terms of illiquidity and insolvency. The illiquidity comes in effect from the "borrow short, lend long" aspects of their operations and can in general be addressed through provision of liquidity by the state, notably through the central bank acting as "lender of last resort". Insolvency with liabilities exceeding assets necessarily imposes losses and the key issue is who will bear those losses.

The essential component, in my view, of the "too big to fail" idea, as far as banks are concerned, emanates from their role in the payments system with their liabilities (deposits) being accepted as money, and through the provision and support of credit and debit cards. Recent IT failures in banks illustrate some of the difficulties. But those arguments do not mean that failing banks should be "bailed out", rather systems need to be in place to enable the payments system to continue under new management (and to the degree to which they are unprofitable to enable an orderly run-down with the passage of business to others). This has similarities with the ways in which the FDIC (Federal Insurance Deposit Corporation) operates in that (admittedly small) banks in difficulty are taken over by others.

The range of support provided by the UK government during the GFCs included the recapitalization of Lloyds Banking Group and RBS, lending money to the Financial Services Compensation Scheme, lending directly to insolvent banks, nationalizing Northern Rock and Bradford & Bingley, a Special Liquidity Scheme, Credit Guarantee Scheme and an Asset Protection Scheme. At its peak, the support given by the UK government amounted to £1,162 billion (equivalent to around two-thirds of UK GDP), of which £133 billion was a "cash outlay" and £1,029 billion guarantee commitments. As the support schemes were withdrawn, guaranteed debts and assets matured and repaid, and some shareholdings sold loans to banks repaid, the support declined. In March 2018 the remaining guarantee commitments were £14 billion and the cash outlay £32 billion.[1]

Table 10.1 illustrates the wide range of countries involved in providing financial support to the financial sector following the GFCs. Among the countries reported in that table, the average support in terms of impact on government debt peaked at 7.4 per cent of GDP and reduced as economies recovered and financial support lessened to 2.5 per cent by 2014. It is notable that the country at the epicentre of the financial crises (USA) had the lowest fiscal costs among the countries included, and that by 2014 the net effect on public debt was positive.

Laeven and Valencia (2020) find that the median fiscal costs for crises in high income countries is 6.7 per cent of GDP, and 10 per cent of GDP for low- and middle-income countries. Allowing for proceeds from sales of financial assets acquired to resolve a banking crisis, revenues from fees on guarantees etc., the net fiscal costs goes to 3.3 per cent for high income countries and 9.6 per cent for low- and middle-income countries.

Table 10.1 Financial sector support in range of advanced economies (percentage of 2014 GDP)

	Impact on gross public debt and other support	Recovery to date (2014)	Impact on gross public debt and other support after recovery
Austria	n/a	n/a	6.2
Belgium	7.2	3.3	4.0
Cyprus	20.0	0.0	20.0
Germany	12.3	4.4	7.9
Greece	34.9	8.1	26.7
Ireland	36.3	6.5	29.9
Netherlands	17.3	13.7	3.7
Slovenia	12.0	1.7	12.0
Spain	7.4	3.2	4.3
UK	11.6	4.7	6.9
USA	4.3	4.8	−0.5
Average	7.4	5.0	2.5
$US billions	2,114	1,391	723

Source: International Monetary Fund (2015).

---

1. Information in this paragraph taken from www.nao.org.uk/highlights/taxpayer-support-for-uk-banks-faqs/

Costs of recession

Laeven and Valencia (2020: fig.13) report on the cumulative loss of national output (relative to trend) following a banking crisis. The median cumulative loss of output for high income countries is 34.95 per cent of GDP, and for low- and middle-income countries 13.83 per cent of GDP. Around the median there is a wide range in the case of high-income countries, 10 per cent of banking crises resulting in losses of output of 10 per cent or less, and a small number where losses of output are well in excess of 100 per cent of annual GDP.

Financial crises, particularly in the banking sector, had major negative impacts on employment and output. The GFCs of 2007–09 had global effects – output in OECD countries declined by 3.6 per cent during 2008 to 2009, unemployment rose by a third (6 to 8.1 per cent) and there was a sharp decline in international trade of over 11 per cent.[2]

Bova *et al.* (2016) construct a database on realizations of contingent liabilities, which documents more than 200 episodes across 80 countries for the period 1990 to 2014. Information is provided in each episode on the size and type of liability and type of fiscal response. Their analysis of the data finds that the costliest contingent liabilities are related to the financial sector. They report that the fiscal costs of contingent liability realization averages 6 per cent of GDP but can go as high as 40 per cent of GDP in the case of major financial sector bailouts.

For the costs of the financial crisis, Epstein and Montecino (2016) use the estimates from the Dallas Federal Reserve (Atkinson, Luttrell and Rosenblum 2013; Luttrell, Atkinson and Rosenblum 2013). They report that the cost of the crisis ranges from 40 per cent to 90 per cent of 2007 output over the period 2008 and 2013, during which output is forecast to remain below long-term trend as a consequence of the financial crisis. These estimates relate to the USA and the recent financial crisis, and indications of the costs of other financial crises are given above.

The IMF (2009: Chapter 4) summarized its findings on the effects of financial crisis on output, growth and employment. The output path in general is substantially and persistently lowered following a banking crisis, and although growth does eventually return to the pre-banking-crisis rate in most countries it does so from the lower base. The depressed output path tends to result from long-lasting reductions of roughly equal proportion in the employment rate, the capital-to-labour ratio and total factor productivity.

A further illustration comes from IMF (2018b: Chapter 2). It estimated deviations from pre 2009 trends for two samples, those involved in banking crises in 2007–08 (24 in number) and all other economies. In the group suffering banking crisis, 85 per cent showed negative deviations from the pre-2009 trend a decade after the GFCs. In

---

2. Figures taken from OECD *Economic Outlook,* June 2013.

the group without a banking crisis in 2007–08, output remained below pre-crisis trends in about 60 per cent of economies.

A significant caveat to these results can be that they relate to the "bust" phase of a boom-and-bust cycle and do not consider whether the boom period was stronger and/ or lasted longer through the rapid expansion of credit, which in the end was unsustainable, leading into the financial crisis. A capitalist economy is inherently cyclical, and the expansion and contraction of loans and credit are key elements in the cycles. Sharp reversals from "boom" to "bust" are often associated with financial crises. Focusing on the downswing, without allowing for the upswing, may overstate the impact of financial crisis; a debt-fuelled expansion prior to the crisis will have lifted output and employment.

It can be concluded that financial crises in general and banking crises in particular can impose substantial costs in terms of lost output and unemployment.

Mis-selling and misdeeds in the financial sector

The mis-selling of products through phoney claims, misrepresentations and the like is no doubt widespread, as is the exploitation of market power and corruption. However, many of the cases that have received publicity in recent years have come from the financial sector and the sale of financial products. Mis-selling, anti-competitive and fraudulent activities in the financial sector impose their costs. Dzimwasha (2015) indicates that the 20 largest global banks paid $235 billion in fines for a range of mis-selling in the seven years following the 2008 financial crisis. Zingales (2015) reports that fines paid by financial institutions to US regulatory agencies amounted to $138.59 billion over 2010–14. Fines imposed in the UK by the Financial Services Authority and its successor, the Financial Conduct Authority, amounted to just over £4 billion during the years 2009–19.[3] Robert Jenkins provides a list of the "misdeeds" of banks.[4] He gives over 140 proven cases, ranging from mis-selling (e.g. of payment protection insurance, interest rate swaps) to manipulation of markets (e.g. precious metals markets, US Treasury Market auction/client sales, energy markets), from aiding and abetting tax evasion and money laundering for violent drug cartels to collusion with the Greek authorities to mislead EU policymakers on meeting Euro criteria.

Fligstein and Roehrkasse (2016: 617) provide a detailed study of fraud in the mortgage-backed securities industry in respect of the financial crises of 2007–09. From around 2003, as supply of mortgages began to decline, "mortgage originators lowered credit standards and engaged in predatory lending to shore up profits. In turn, vertically

---

3. Calculated from www.fsa.gov.uk/about/press/facts/fines www.fca.org.uk/news/news-stories/2015-fines (and subsequent dates).
4. See www.finance-watch.org/hot-topics/blog/1186-jenkins-bank-misdeeds

integrated mortgage-backed securities issuers and underwriters committed securities fraud to conceal this malfeasance and enhance the value of other financial products."

The Trade Union Congress (TUC 2017: 10), in its economic and social audit of the UK financial sector, detail the evidence of poor conduct and mis-selling within the financial sector that has led to significant financial and social losses for individuals and businesses. It estimates "the combined misselling costs for all the major retail misselling scandals over the past 30 years has now reached £45 bn – payment protection insurance (PPI) misselling is the largest cost. UK banks paid out a total of £30 bn between 2009 and 2014 – the same as the amount of capital raised by them to repaid balance sheets. A further £26 bn has been paid to 4.5 m customers of firms that have gone bust since 2001."

The Conduct Costs Project Research Foundation has a definition of conduct costs, which includes all costs borne by a bank in connection with regulatory proceedings, including fines and financial penalties imposed by a regulator; any costs or losses directly related to an event or series of events or conduct or behaviour of the bank or a group of individuals employed by the bank for which any fine or comparable penalty has been imposed; any censure issues by a regulator; and the sum payable as result of any breach of conduct.

The Centre for Banking Research (2020) reports that on aggregate during the 11 years covering 2008–18 inclusive, the 20 international banks included in their analysis paid conduct costs of more than £377 billion. The cumulative total of conduct costs for banks in their sample amounts to £205.25 billion for US banks, £86.09 billion for UK banks, £41.31 billion for Euro area banks, £40.19 billion for Swiss banks and £4.62 billion for Australian banks. Conduct costs peaked in the UK at an equivalent of 0.88 per cent of UK annual GDP and had been above 0.4 per cent since 2012. US conduct costs peaked in 2014 at 0.35 per cent of GDP. The latest Centre for Banking Research report shows that, in 2014–18, UK banks are world-beating in the cost of misconduct fines and redress. RBS tops the chart at £26.6 billion, Lloyds is third at £18.8 billion, Barclays fifth at £15.94 billion, shared with Bank of America at £26.5 billion and Deutsche Bank at £17.6 billion.

The LIBOR (London Inter-bank Offered Rate) scandal was a series of fraudulent actions (see, e.g. Enrich 2017; Stenfors 2017; Vaughan & Finch 2017). The LIBOR is an average interest rate calculated through submissions of interest rates by major banks across the world, and the scandal came from banks falsely inflating or deflating their rates so as to profit from trades or to give the impression that they were more creditworthy than was the case. The banks are supposed to submit the actual interest rates they are paying, or would expect to pay, for borrowing from other banks. Mortgages, student loans, financial derivatives and other financial products often rely on LIBOR as a reference rate, so the manipulation of submissions used to calculate those rates can have significant negative effects on consumers and financial markets worldwide. The wording in the subtitles of some of the books on the LIBOR scandal give a flavour of it: "a gang of backstabbing bankers and one of the greatest scams in financial history" (Enrich 2017);

"how bankers lied, cheated and colluded to rig the world's most important number" (Vaughan & Finch 2017).

In 2012, Barclays Bank was fined $360 million by the US regulators and £59.5 million by the Financial Services Authority for attempted manipulation of the LIBOR and Euribor rates. In December 2012, UBS agreed to pay regulators $1.2 billion to the US Department of Justice and the Commodity Futures Trading Commission, £160m to the UK Financial Services Authority and 59m CHF to the Swiss Financial Market Supervisory Authority for its role in the scandal. RBS, which had been rescued by the UK government at the height of the financial crisis and was largely owned by the UK government, was fined £390 million by regulators. Others fined include Rabobank £660 million in 2013, Lloyds Bank £226 million in 2014 and Deutsche Bank $2.5 billion in 2015. In 2013, ICAP an inter-bank dealer firm was fined £55 million for its involvement and Martin Brokers paid out £630,000 (see Stenfors 2017: ch. 3).

The Bank Fines 2020[5] report includes fines imposed by regulators for, among other things, breaches of anti-money laundering, violation of "Know Your Customer" and operating guidelines and personal data leaks. During 2020, it reports $14.21 billion in total bank fines, with the largest being issued to Goldman Sachs of $3.90 billion, who also was issued with the third largest at $2 billion, and Wells Fargo were fined $3 billion. The European Commission fined five banks (UBS, Barclays, RBS, HSBC and Credit Suisse) €344 million for participating in a foreign exchange spot trading cartel.

The Financial Conduct Authority (2017), in its report on asset management funds, found weak price competition in several areas of the asset management industry and high levels of profitability, with average profit margins of 36 per cent in the firms sampled. The evidence indicates that, on average, both actively managed and passively managed funds did not outperform their own benchmarks after fees, and that active funds investors paying higher prices for funds, on average, achieve worse performance.

A report from EU Tax Observatory (reported in *The Guardian*, 6 September 2021) found that leading European banks booked around €20 billion a year in tax havens, equivalent to 14 per cent of their total profits. Some of the banks then paid an effective tax rate on their profits of less than 15 per cent.

Finance curse and rent extraction

The ideas of a "resource curse" has been developed in respect of a country with discovery and development of a natural resource (such as oil, minerals), which appears as additional wealth for the country but that may turn out to be something of a curse. Christensen, Shaxson and Wigan (2016) (see also Shaxson & Christensen 2013) develop the idea of a

---

5. See https://finbold.com/bank-fines-2020/.

"finance curse" along the same lines, with particular reference to the UK. In this section I draw on and elaborate their comparison between "finance curse" and "resource curse".

A first line of comparison comes from what has become known as "Dutch disease", labelled after the perceived effects of the discovery of natural gas in the waters of the Netherlands in the late 1950s. The natural resource provides export potential for the country concerned and a higher exchange rate results. This benefits domestic households in that imports become cheaper and their real incomes are thereby higher. But it comes at the cost for industries producing tradeable goods for exports, which are significantly more expensive as far as foreign countries are concerned. The natural resource sector can often be a capital-intensive economic enclave, with a relatively smaller number of jobs created (for a given output) and with few production linkages with the rest of the economy. The capture and use of the large economic rents, which can flow from the natural resources, fosters political corruption.

A second comes from the high wages paid in the financial sector (as indicated in Chapter 8), which serves to draw workers into the financial sector from other sectors. If the higher wages in the financial sector were a reflection of higher beneficial output, it could be deemed acceptable reward. It has been questioned earlier in this chapter whether the reported higher output in the financial sector is indeed a good measure of its social benefits. Further, the rewards paid in the financial sector are more akin to economic rent.

The third comes from the economic instability, with the economic cycle based on financial booms and busts and the concomitant effects on output and growth.

The fourth relates to the economic rents that are gained by the financial sector. Epstein and Montecino (2016: 14) regard financial rents as "the excess incomes that operators and investors in the financial sector receive over and above the incomes they would need to induce them to supply their financial products or services in an efficient, competitive, capitalist economy". This is an application of the general notion of economic rent in terms of the payments received in excess of those necessary to deploy resources in a specific activity. The comparison is made between an actual set of circumstances and a hypothetical alternative (an efficient competitive economy); and an alternative that does not exist and may well be infeasible. Epstein and Montecino (2016) view rents gained by the financial sector as coming from two sources, namely excess payments made to highly paid employees of banks and other financial institutions' bankers, and excess profits, namely returns over and above the long-run sustainable returns that accrue to shareholders of financial corporations.

In Chapter 8, I considered research that had been undertaken on wages and earnings in the financial sector. A general indication there was that earnings in the financial sector had risen relative to earnings in the rest of the economy. Further, in general, the higher earnings in the financial sector could not be justified or explained by an appeal to higher skills and education. A substantial part of earnings in the financial sector could be considered as "economic rent" and, as such, represented extraction of income from the rest of the income without compensating economic gains.

Epstein (2018) estimates the costs of the financial sector over a quarter of a century (1990–2015) for the USA. His estimate of "excess wages" (on a similar basis to the discussion above) comes to just under $1,400 billion (in 2014 prices), and "excess profits" to $2,283 billion. The lower growth rate arising from an inflated financial sector is estimated to have a cumulative effect on output over the period of between $2,658 billion and $3,981 billion. And the cost of recession associated with financial crisis of between $6,566 billion and $14,550 billion.

Conclusions

Epstein (2010: 293) summarized the devastating flaws [of "financier" dominated finance]: "it creates major externalities that contribute to financial and real economic instability; it promotes short-term investment strategies; it contributes to inequality; and it undermines economic efficiency and the achievement of social goal in the real economy".

The processes of financialization and the growth of the financial sector have often been supported in terms of the employment in the financial sector, its output and contributions to tax revenue. In this chapter, it has first been suggested that the measure of the contribution of the financial sector in terms of GDP is overstated. The operations of the financial sector also detract from the real economy through its propensities to lead to financial crisis and the costs of such crises. The financial sector further gains through the extraction of economic rent from the rest of the economy.

A key role of the financial sector has often been viewed in terms of facilitating savings, allocating and monitoring loans and enabling investment in productive capacity, thereby underpinning economic growth and development. The recent evidence has suggested that the growth and size of the financial sector detracts from investment and growth rather than stimulating it. However, as environmental and climate change concerns mount, the future will need to be slower and environmentally sustainable growth. The financial sector should be contributing to that through the ways in which funds are allocated; that is, towards "green investment" and away from carbon-intensive activities.

11

THE FUTURE OF (DE)FINANCIALIZATION

Financialization, along with the growth of the financial sector in scale and power, and the increasing involvement of people with finance has been a central feature of industrialized economies since at least the late nineteenth century. In the era since circa 1980, rapid financialization has encompassed most if not all countries of the world, taking different forms and proceeding at different paces. Variegated financialization serves as a useful moniker for pervasive, yet differentiated, financialization. The GFCs of 2007–09 brought to public attention the scale of the national and international financial systems and the ways in which those systems had not only grown but also evolved with the complexities of financial instruments. Financial crises have become frequent, imposing economic and social costs, and the GFCs brought into sharp focus the instabilities of the financial system and their global effects. The ways in which the financial sector had penetrated our lives through credit, debt and private pension provision were to some degree apparent. The GFCs and the aftermath raised questions about the scale and role of the financial sector in society, and a less relaxed attitude to the regulation of the financial system followed.

In this concluding chapter, I start by briefly reviewing the question as to whether, and to what extent, financialization has continued since the GFCs. In Chapter 4 I have briefly indicated some quantitative measures of financialization with comparisons between the post-GFC period with the preceding times. This discussion of any slowdown of financialization now is linked with issues as to whether the pace of globalization and of economic growth has continued in that period of time.

In earlier chapters, the relationship between financial development and economic growth have been explored, with the general observation that the growth of the financial sector often appears to be associated with a slowdown of economic growth. Advocates of the financial sector have often portrayed it as facilitating savings, funding and monitoring investment, and thereby promoting wider economic growth. From the perspective of growth promotion, the financial system has become dysfunctional. The climate emergency may well have to be addressed through slower economic growth, particularly in the industrialized nations but, in any case, with different structures of growth that are less carbon-intensive and environmentally damaging. A financial system that serves the public good would be one that allocates funds towards environmentally friendly "green" investment and away from environmentally damaging investments.

In the previous chapter, I discussed the degree to which the financial system has become too large and dysfunctional. In what sense is it dysfunctional? And does "dysfunctional" mean that there will be forces that will "repair" the financial sector? Here I describe the ways in which the financial system could function in the general social interest and it can be against such functioning that the financial system (or at least parts of it) could be said to have become dysfunctional. My main focus is a consideration of policy measures to scale back the financial sector and financialization more generally – in effect policies designed to confront its dysfunction. These measures include the use of taxation to reduce the scale of financial transactions and to level up the taxation of the financial sector with other sectors of the economy. The central part of this section is, though, how the financial sector could be restructured, particularly in terms of the types of financial institutions.

I will also discuss the relationships between financialization and the major challenges of our time, namely climate change and environmental degradation. In confronting its dysfunction, the restructuring of the sector could be used to deal with climate change.

The final section tackles the question of whether the policies designed to scale back the financial sector and to have "definancialized" it are economically and political feasible. The forces propelling the expansion of finance into areas and activities that were previously outside the purview of the financial sector are strong, as evidenced by the past 150 years. The political strength of the financial sector is immense and the recent experiences of seeking to reform the financial system do not offer hope that the major restructuring that is required can be accomplished.

The slowdown of financialization?

The current era of financialization, viewed as emerging around 1980, is broadly coincident with the onset of neoliberalism and globalization. The GFCs brought a global recession and, when recovery returned, it was at lower rates of GDP growth. A significant question is whether the GFCs marked a notable shift in the global economy and whether there has been any change in the processes of financialization.

The financial sector has always been closely involved in the expansion of the capitalist mode of production. The processes of accumulation have to be financed, and the financial system facilitates that. The financial sector gathers savings and channels them to firms for investment, although, of course, much investment is internally funded. Banks provide loans, which create money (in the form of bank deposits), which enables the expansion of investment ahead of prior savings. Insofar as the future is one of slower and more sustainable growth and hence lower savings and investment, the funding functions of the financial sector will be required to a lesser extent in the future and the role for the financial sector diminished.

In Chapter 4, a wide range of those dimensions of financialization that can be readily quantified were displayed. The rapid financialization of the 2000s up to the GFCs was apparent in those figures (employment in the financial sector being something of an exception). In several of those dimensions, particularly relating to the size of the banking sector, there has been a slackening in the pace of financialization, and in some it has reversed, in the industrialized countries. There have been shifts of direction with regard to regulation of the financial sector, including changes in the capital requirements for banks and other financial institutions seeking to reduce instabilities. In other dimensions – and this includes "shadow banking" – the financial sector has continued to grow. The general scale of financialization could be described as being at or above the levels of the mid-2000s before the GFCs. Financialization, understood as a process of growth of the financial sector, may well have slackened since the GFCs.

The measures of the dimensions of financialization outlined in Chapters 4 and 5 were quantitative in nature and relate to the scale of the financial sector. These measures have not incorporated the broader questions of the economic and political impacts of finance. In subsequent chapters, some of those impacts of finance have been explored. These have included the interrelationships between financialization and the distribution of income, and the pursuit of shareholder value (as a dimension of financialization) with pervasive effects on investment, innovation and employees.

The processes of financialization have often been viewed as routes through which growth and accumulation are maintained and stimulated. As Streeck (2016: 62) notes, "'financialization' … seemed the last way to restore growth and profitability to the overextended hegemon of global capitalism". The paradox is that, as indicated above and supported by a great deal of evidence, a larger financial sector has itself been a drag on accumulation and growth. The term finance-led capitalism has been used as an alternative to the term financialization; however, a more appropriate term would be finance-retarded capitalism. Financialization and a large financial sector are not conducive to the attainment of environmentally sustainable growth. The development of and then trading in financial assets, such as derivatives and securitization, does not stimulate investment and accumulation, rather it diverts resources away from real investment. The financial sector in private hands allocates funds on the basis of private profit and will not be particularly concerned with environmental sustainability.

Superficially, it did seem that the growth of the financial sector in the 1990s and 2000s was underpinning growth. The expansion of credit, particularly household credit, enabled consumer demand to expand. Asset prices, and notably house prices, often rose rapidly, creating feelings of rising wealth and boosting the apparent returns on financial investments. The expansion of credit was often encouraged by the deregulation of the

Table 11.1 Average annual growth rates of GDP and GDP per capita

Average annual growth rate of GDP (%)

	1971–79	1980–89	1990–99	2000–09	2010–19
Canada	4.20	2.86	2.38	2.09	1.32
France	3.87	2.36	2.00	1.47	0.29
Germany	n/a	n/a	1.35	0.36	0.67
Italy	3.66	2.57	1.47	0.55	−0.81
Japan	4.65	4.37	1.63	0.53	0.33
UK	2.64	2.66	2.34	1.76	0.48
USA	3.57	3.12	3.22	1.91	1.67
OECD	3.76	3.02	2.71	1.85	1.30
world	3.75	3.11	3.57	3.70	2.61
euroarea	n/a	n/a	1.92	1.37	0.43

Average annual growth rate of GDP per capita (%)

	1971–79	1980–89	1990–99	2000–09	2010–19
Canada	2.89	1.73	1.28	1.06	0.79
France	3.23	1.89	1.57	0.79	0.81
Germany		n/a	1.13	0.90	1.01
Italy	3.14	2.42	1.43	0.09	−0.04
Japan	3.36	3.95	1.35	0.41	1.26
UK	2.51	3.04	2.05	1.17	1.16
USA	2.51	2.55	1.98	0.94	1.69
OECD	3.08	2.53	2.10	1.34	1.53
euroarea	n/a	n/a	1.78	1.06	0.93

Source: calculated from OECD Economic Outlook database

financial sector, which in turn brought unstable credit booms. These ways of boosting expansion are unsustainable.

Rising asset prices are themselves unsustainable and yet formed the basis of consumer borrowing and of the financial institutions selling loans and mortgages. Financial institutions and others can readily profit through buying and selling financial assets in a rising market but cannot collectively do so in a falling market. There are limits to how long rising consumer debt can be sustained.

Table 11.1 illustrates the tendency for growth in the industrialized countries to slow down. The figures show this in general for each of the G7 countries, as well as the OECD as a whole. Figures 11.1a and b map out the growth rate of GDP and of GDP per capita at the world level since 1960. The overall picture for the world is one of relative stable growth of GDP and of GDP per capita over the past three decades though lower than in the earlier decades.

The findings of Li and Mendieta-Muñoz (2020) indicate a significant decline in long-run growth rates, which is not associated with the detrimental effects of the Great Recession, and it is the rate of growth of technical progress that appears to be behind

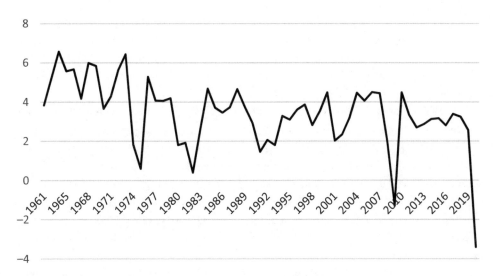

Figure 11.1a Summary growth statistics (world GDP growth rate)
Source: calculated from World Bank database

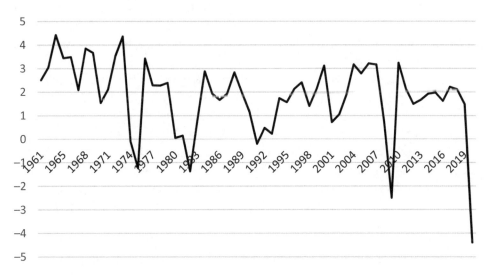

Figure 11.1b Summary growth statistics (growth rate of GDP per capita)
Source: calculated from World Bank database

the slowdown in long-run GDP growth. In the past decade, recession and austerity have been the order of the day and growth across western Europe and North America has been sluggish. With much talk of secular stagnation, taking heed of the environmental concerns and the possible longer-term effects of the Covid-19 pandemic, continuing slower growth in the western European and North American economies looks to be a plausible scenario. The IMF (2018b), for example, projects continuing slow growth into the future. Others have hypothesised a secular stagnation, which can be viewed as a combination of the prospect of slow economic growth through slowing technological change and productivity growth, and a tendency for investment requirements to fall short of savings (Gordon 2012, 2014; Summers 2016).

The performance of international trade in goods, considered in Chapter 3, has tended to decline (relative to global GDP), with a small rise in trade in services, which has led some to talk of "peak trade". The flow of FDI (relative to global GDP) shows a remarkable increase during the 1990s, with over a fourfold rise in FDI. In the decade since the GFCs, FDI relative to GDP has been around 2 per cent. The stock of FDI continues to rise, which is not surprising since there are significant additional flows each year. Dollar (2019) notes the rapid growth of GVCs, especially complex ones, at a faster rate than GDP in the years 2000–07. The GFCs brought some retrenchment of GVCs, followed by quick recovery and then slow growth.

A future in which growth of output, of international trade and of cross-border capital flows are lower than in recent decades would indicate the need for a smaller financial sector. Simply put, there would be less requirement for its services in terms of funding investment and financing trade. In recent decades, the growth of the financial sector has not come from such funding and financing but from development of and trading in financial assets and, in general, these activities have not contributed to economic and social well-being.

In brief, I take this as indicative that from the perspective of providing a payments system (national and international) and in channelling funds, there is little requirement for the financial system to expand. It is, though, well known that financialization and the expansion of the financial system have not predominantly taken the form of banking. It is rather the expansion of financial markets in trading in complex financial assets and the expansion of financial companies into new areas such as private pension provision.

The capitalist system has historically expanded into areas where non-capitalist modes of production had predominated – whether geographically or sectorally. Financialization in the past few decades has involved geographic expansion as countries around the world were drawn into the processes of financialization. In most European and North American economies, much of the expansion of the financial sector has been through its involvement with the rest of the economy and society. It has involved the replacement of not-for-profit financial institutions as well as its geographical expansion.

The financial sector continues to expand into areas of social provision previously dominated by mutual cooperation and the state. Pension provision is the notable example here – often organized through implicit intergenerational contracts, mutual organizations (e.g. friendly societies) and state welfare state provision. The interests of the financial sector are served by the privatization of pension arrangements, and pension funds and others are able to extract substantial fees, thereby significantly reducing the value of pensions payable.

The development of schemes such as the PFIs and PPPs represent greater involvement of financial interests. This extends the role of the financial sector beyond the arms-length supply of finance (through the purchase of government bonds), with finance in effect now supplied at a higher rate of interest; it involves the financial sector involvement in the design and management of infrastructure and the like.

Definancialization?

In the previous chapter, the arguments were put that financialization has become dysfunctional for the real economy and for society more generally. There were clearly ways in which the financial sector had become "too large", and that the contributions the sector made to society were not commensurate with the resources it was using.

The interests of the financial sector will, though, continue to push towards its further expansion into areas of social provision through privatization, and in ways that would be generally detrimental to social well-being. In an era of slower growth, the functional requirements would be for a smaller financial sector that concentrated on its role as intermediary between savers and investors. The push by the financial sector to expand would on balance be detrimental for the overall growth and profitability, and financialization does little to underpin environmentally sustainable investment and development. Continuing financialization would again involve creation of credit booms and asset price bubbles, which in turn would be unsustainable and prone to crisis.

If the argument that the financial sector has become dysfunctional and/or imposes a range of economic and social costs is broadly right, then are there in effect market mechanisms through which the financial sector would be constrained and restructured to become less economically inefficient and more socially beneficial? By market mechanisms I mean ways in which private financial institutions would make changes in their operating practices, introduce new financial products and withdraw some existing products, for example.

The approach here is that there is a need for a collection of policies to facilitate the restructuring of the financial sector. The arguments, theoretical and empirical, have been laid out above to the effect that the financial sectors have become dysfunctional and operate on a scale that has become too large; the financial sector has become a drag on, rather than a facilitator of economic growth. Yet the future of capitalist economies will have to be one of, if not slower growth, then growth that is different to the past in being much less environmentally damaging, and focused on growth of economic and social welfare that is not captured by growth of GDP.

The secular stagnation view suggests slower growth, at least among the industrialized economies. Many would argue that avoiding the climate emergency and catastrophe will require growth (of GDP) rates close to zero (e.g. Hickel 2020; Kallis *et al.* 2020). Others would advocate major shifts in the composition of demand and of output towards low or zero-carbon activities, towards renewable energy sources, for example, and there are those promoting some form of a "green new deal" (e.g. Green New Deal Group 2008; European Commission 2019; Sanders 2019; Pianta & Lucchese 2020). There are major implications for the future of the financial system. A zero-growth scenario (or even one that involves significantly lower growth than in the past few decades) would generally mean that the productive capital stock was not growing and hence net investment would be close to zero. Gross investment would cover depreciation of the existing capital stock, leaving net investment close to zero. A green new deal requires major shifts in the structure of the economy. Of particular relevance here is that investment flows into the low-carbon forms of production and away from the high-carbon ones and those investment flows have to be funded. Financial institutions determine the direction of the flow of funds. And, as argued above, financial institutions operate on a "credit rationing" basis, evaluating perceived credit worthiness of potential borrowers and potential investment projects.

Epstein (2018: 348) set out one part of a set of policies to restructure the financial sector in socially beneficial ways. His agenda included reducing the size of "too big to fail" banks, the use of financial transaction taxes and the establishment of what he terms "green banks"; that is, financial institutions dedicated to the funding of environmentally sustainable projects ("green investment"). He indicates that these policies would be an "example of how restructuring finance can be a much better alternative to roaring banking and bubble finance for job creation and socially useful investment". In earlier work, Epstein (2010) had put forward arguments for longer-term social ownership and control of banks. In his view, the main arguments for bank nationalization were twofold, namely their usefulness in helping achieve important public economic goals, and equity (and fairness) concerns. He considers numerous models: large and multi-purpose; smaller, more specialized public banks; and public utility banks.

As the financial sector has shifted towards the generation of high-volume trading in derivatives and securitization, it has shifted away from the facilitation of savings and the financing of investment. It is then perhaps not surprising that the growth of the financial sector (relative to GDP) is not linked with economic growth as the growth of the capital stock is no longer being facilitated by the operations of the financial sector.

It is relevant to ask what roles and functions would be performed by a socially useful financial system? In a market economy, it can be easy to slip from observing that a sector is profitable (and hence as far as its owners are concerned privately useful) to arguing that the sector is socially beneficial. Indeed, in neoclassical economics under conditions of perfect competition, there is an alignment between private costs and benefits with social costs and benefits. The maximization of profits, being the difference between private benefits (revenue) and private costs, aligns with the difference between social benefits and social costs.

These types of functions for a well-operating financial sector stand in some contrast to the developments of the financial sector in the last four decades of financialization. In several respects, it can be said that the financial sector has become too large in economic, social and political terms. The policies for a smaller and more focused role for finance could be thought of in terms of definancialization. The focus of attention here is structural changes to diminish the scale of the financial system and put the resources deployed in the financial sector to more socially beneficial uses. Definancialization would also include reversal of the dominance of financial calculations, etc.

The tax system would be a ready tool to be deployed in reducing some of the activities of the financial sector and to address the undertaxation of the financial system.

Downsizing the financial sector by tax

There has long been advocacy for a form of financial transactions tax to discourage transactions in financial assets.[1] An early proponent was Keynes (1936: 101–2), who called for a financial transaction tax that "might prove the most serviceable reform available, with a view to mitigating the predominance of speculation over enterprise in the United States". Keynes saw the changing balance between what he termed enterprise and speculation as disadvantageous. "When the capital development of a country becomes a by-product of the activities of a casino, the job is likely to be ill-done".

Kay (2015: 297–98) argues that "volumes of trading in financial markets have reached absurd levels – levels that have impeded rather than enhanced the quality of intermediation and increased rather than diversified the amount of risk to which the global economy is exposed. The capital resources needed to reconcile these trading volumes with stability have not been available; nor will they ever be." The complexity of financial products feeds into financial instability, with resulting damage on the non-financial economy.

The underlying rationale for financial activity taxes (FATs) can be viewed in terms of the relative undertaxation of the financial sector since indirect taxes, such as VAT, are often not applied to the financial sector (see Sawyer 2018). There are, of course, examples where forms of indirect taxation (other than financial transactions tax) are applied to parts of the financial sector. This can be complemented by the use of FATs to seek to reduce the size of the financial sector. The argument can be put that levying taxes on

---

1. See, for example, Arestis and Sawyer (2013) for recent discussion on financial transactions taxes and the references cited there. Pollin, Heintz and Herndon (2018) provide evidence on the revenue potential of a financial transaction tax in the case of the USA.

a sector will have effects on the demands for the goods and services of that sector. The tendency to undertax the financial sector would imply that other sectors are relatively overtaxed and those sectors are perhaps relatively smaller than they would have been and the financial sector relatively larger. A FAT is essentially a tax on the sum of profits and remunerations of the financial sector and, as such, has features of being close to a variant for a value-added tax on the sector since sum of profits and remunerations is a good proxy for value-added.

Alternative financial institutions

Financial institutions are the channels through which funds flow from surplus units to deficit units, and the direction in which the funds are channelled is heavily dependent on the credit allocation decisions made by the financial institutions. In the next sub-section, I will return to questions of credit allocation by financial institutions on the grounds that different types of financial institutions will make different credit allocation decisions and the suitability of a diversity of financial institutions arises from the diversity of decision-making. In this respect, the line of argument advanced by Groenveld (2015: 6) is followed, when he writes that "diversity in ownership and business orientation leads to diversity in risk appetite, management, incentive structures, policies and practices as well as behaviours and outcomes. It offers greater choice for customers and society through enhanced competition that derives in part from the juxtaposition of different business models".

The nature of the relationships between financial institutions and customers becomes highly relevant for the ways in which finance and credit are provided, on what terms and to whom, and the monitoring and other efforts of financial institutions to ensure the repayment of loans. It is then in the nature of credit that there will be what may be termed credit rating and pricing of credit, which reflects assessment of likelihood of default (partial or total). Informational problems give rise to equity rationing as well as to credit rationing and firms will be limited in their ability to raise equity capital. And it is often observed that a rather small proportion of new funds are raised through issue of new equity (Stiglitz & Greenwald 2003: 34), and indeed, through share buy-backs and mergers, the contribution of equity markets to additional funding can be negative.

The pervasiveness of credit rationing extends across all types of financial systems but how credit rationing is dealt with will differ, as will how it impacts on those who receive credit and at what price. Financial systems develop what appear to be discriminatory practices through favouring some groups over others in their credit rating assessments. The discrimination can be along ethnic lines, gender or area of residence, for example.

Two major aspects stand out in thinking about the role of different types of financial institutions. The first is whether these institutions are focused on what should be the key roles of the financial sector, namely providing vehicles for savings and funding investment (as well as providing a payments system), and the effectiveness of their operations. The second is the ways in which loans are allocated, to whom and under what conditions. This second aspect is particularly important as different forms of financial institutions will take different decisions about the allocation of funds.

Financial banking institutions cover a range of different forms – clearing or commercial banks, savings banks, investment banks and universal banks. Banks differ substantially in terms of their ownership structures – whether private, public (state), mutual or cooperative. Depending on ownership and management structures, the objectives pursued by banks differ. The objectives of privately owned banks would generally be that of profits – although a range of objectives may be stated (providing employment, for example), and the effective decision-makers in a bank may pursue other objectives such as growth and size (as postulated in the managerial theories of the firm). The objectives of public and mutual ownership are often more difficult to state (at least on any universal principles) but would often include the provision of finance for stated aims – for example, to support industrial development, to provide housing finance, to facilitate savings and provide housing finance. As the question arises for privately owned banks about whether their managers will seek to maximize profits, so the question arises for public and mutual organizations as to whether their managers will maintain the objectives set for them or whether their interests will lie elsewhere.

Herndon and Paul (2020) argue that household financial services are an essential infrastructure and, as such (writing in the context of the USA), the federal government should ensure universal access to banking services. This is a reflection of the costs (to individuals) of financial exclusion, although there are costs for individuals from involvement with the financial sector over, for example, debt and mis-selling.

Ayadi et al. (2010: 7) and others have drawn the distinction between stakeholder value (STV) banks and shareholder value (SHV) banks. They "conceptualise SHV banks as those whose primary (and almost exclusive) business focus is maximizing shareholder interests, while STV banks in general (and cooperative banks in particular) have a broader focus on the interests of a wider group of stakeholders (notably customer-members in the case of cooperative banks, the regional economy and the society in the case of savings and public banks)". Another way of expressing a similar idea is to draw on the notion of "double bottom lines"; for financial institutions (in this context but can be extended to others) there is the bottom line of profits – at least the requirement to earn sufficient profits to survive and grow – and the second bottom line of other objectives, which can include serving the local community or providing finance for specific groups. There are important differences between SHV institutions and STV institutions. Two mentioned by Ayadi et al. (2010, 9) are the potential intermediation margin and how value-added is distributed between the stakeholders.

Block (2014: 16) suggests a good way forward is the introduction of:

> significant competition from financial intermediaries who are not seeking to generate profits. These could take the form of credit unions, community banks, non-profit loan funds, or banks that are owned by government entities; but the key is that their mission is defined as facilitating economic development in a particular geographical area. With this mission, they have a reason to employ loan officers who develop the skill set needed to provide credit to individuals and firms who fall outside the parameters of the standard lending algorithms.

He advocates "a combination of governmental supports and grassroots entrepreneurialism to create an expanding network of non-profit financial institutions that would redirect household savings to finance clean energy, growth of small and medium-sized enterprises, and infrastructure" (*ibid.*: 3). This would be an illustration of the general idea that local and mutual financial organization would make different lending decisions as compared with the large profit-making financial institutions.

The development of more localised banking can come from regional banking. Klagge and Martin (2005: 414) put a case for regional banking in terms of three advantages:

> First, the presence of a local critical mass of financial institutions and agents – that is of a regionally identifiable, coherent and functioning market – enables local institutions, SMEs, and local investors to exploit the benefits of being in close spatial proximity. ... Second, the existence of regional capital markets specialising in local firms may help to keep capital within the regions, as local investors direct their funds into local companies – and hence into local economic development – rather than investing on the central market. ... Third, in a nationally integrated financial system, the case can be made for a regionally decentralized structure on the grounds that it increases the efficiency of allocation of investment between the centre and the regions.

However, they acknowledge limitations. Regional financial institutions may raise most of their funds locally as well as providing funds and credit to local firms, and their ability to raise funds is dependent on the economic prosperity and development of the region.

Minsky (1993) advocated the establishment of and support for community development banks (CDBs), which would have characteristics of providing "narrow banking". The characteristics of CDBs would be the operation of a payments system, providing a secure depository for savings, providing commercial banking services, funding housing and consumer debt, providing investment banking services and asset management services and advice.

State development and investment banks have often been viewed in terms of their role in economic development through their abilities to channel funds into industrialization. There are now a range of state development and investment banks around the world; some notably examples are the German KfW, Brazilian development bank, and recently proposals such as the BRICs Development Bank (Griffith-Jones 2014), and European Investment Bank; and recently established but relatively small-scale ones such as the UK Green Investment Bank. The United Nations Department of Economic and Social Affairs (2005) provides a history of national development banks. That report also illustrates the different institutional forms that development banks can take and different objectives that have been assigned to development banks.

The roles of state development banks (with names such as Green Investment Bank) are of particular importance. As Griffith-Jones and Cozzi (2016: 138) argue, "the existence of development banks is justified by the existence of sectors and investment projects that require funding for the future development of the economy, but have high uncertainty as to their future success". These projects may find difficulty in securing private funding because of the uncertainties involved. The long-time horizons, the fundamental uncertainty of investment projects and the path dependence involved are often particularly important with the climate emergency.

Development banks "have a double mandate. They mainly aim to maximise sustainable and inclusive development impact (including economic, environmental and social impacts), while maintaining some financial profits or avoiding financial losses" (Griffith Jones *et al.* 2022: 1), contrasted with commercial banks "whose main (and usually only) aim … is to maximize risk adjusted expected returns, often short-term ones. … While commercial banks need to manage the range of economic, environmental and social risks, they generally only do so to the extent that these risks impact financial returns" (*ibid.*: 2). They argue that public development banks should support long-term productive investments, including those that emphasize low-carbon projects, as well as those benefiting poorer regions and populations, and base their selection on criteria that put development impact first, with financial returns an important but secondary objective.

Griffith-Jones (2015) argues that:

> Well run development banks can provide the vision – and part of the resources, to do those things that at present are not done at all. This requires good development banks with the expertise and the strategic vision to fund new sectors and technologies. The fact that development banks can provide long-term loans, have a long-term development perspective, as well as require lower returns further facilitates this financing.

She postulates four functions that are important for development banks to play. These are provision of counter-cyclical finance, "funding a dynamic vision and strategy of growth and structural transformation", the mobilization of financial resources and the funding of public goods. Development banks, as with the other types of financial institutions reviewed in this section, provide benefits of diversity with a more diversified financial system leading to less systemic risk and different types of financial institutions having different strengths (and weaknesses).

Financial institutions operating along these lines at least offer the potential that savers can express their social values through the provision of funds to such institutions. They also offer possibilities for the channelling of funds in specific directions, in line with the social objectives of the institution. The specific issues that arise are (as with microfinance) whether such institutions suffer from "mission creep", and whether the pressures push them towards profits. Much may then depend on whether the activities into which these alternative financial institutions put funds are ones that yield an acceptable rate of profit and, hence, although the social returns to such investments may be high, are the private returns similarly so. But, if the private returns are indeed relatively high, then profit-seeking financial institutions would themselves be willing to lend. Thus, it can be argued that alternative financial institutions would, in effect, require subsidies, which can come in the form of direct government subsidy or through savers' willingness to accept a lower rate of interest.

Financialization and the climate emergency

The processes of financialization raise many issues with respect to environmental degradation, and two are highlighted here. First, are the changing structures of the financial sector conducive to the channelling of funds into "green investment" and away from "brown investment"? Second, financialization has involved financial calculations and motives being applied to a widening range of human activities, notably to the environment.

Sullivan (2013: 199) shows "how business and finance sectors, in collaboration with conservation organisation, conservation biologists and environmental economists, are engaging in an intensified financialization of discourses and endeavours associated with financialization more generally. This tendency permits capital accumulation to be generated through the movement of interest-bearing capital into new areas of social and economic (re)production, even as other areas of production are stagnating". The financialization of the everyday "extends into discourses of environmental conservation and sustainability and atmospheric change".

Gabbi and Ticci (2013: 38) point out that "financialization is conducive to an agenda attempting to save nature through a commodification of its resources, services, perceived values, but the complexity of ecosystems cannot be narrowed down, compressed and summarised in a single metric or in a single service." A major part of the responses to the climate emergency has to involve decommodification of some resources and activities, and that means that the financial system, seeking profits, has to be removed from those resources and activities. Finance Watch (2020) argues for the role of what it terms public finance as being "especially useful for projects that provide public value without being financially bankable themselves" (p.5), in particular with regard to protection of nature and biodiversity. It points out that "the nature of private investment is to focus on financial risks and returns and revenue streams, but *many nature-related projects have no revenue source.* Indeed, nature tends to benefit when there is less economic activity. Conversely, it can be easier to finance businesses that keep their costs low by harming nature" (p.4 – emphasis in original). It argues that "*Nature projects are often too small for institutional investors to invest in directly.* They are complex to understand, illiquid and take a long time to mature … the [finance] industry's reliance on CAPM and other structural factors mean that fund managers have little appetite for alternative or long-term investments" (p.4).

The transition to a low-carbon sustainable economy would involve a shift of resources, including capital equipment from carbon-intensive industries into low-carbon industries. Lewney (2020: 211) argues that "because the net zero technologies are more capital-intensive, the overall scale of investment in the energy system would be higher, especially in the period to 2050 when the entire new system needs to be put in place".

It is well recognized that climate change itself impacts on the financial system through two main channels of risks that serve to reduce asset values. One can be described in terms of the physical risks from damage to property, infrastructure and land. The other set of risks comes from changes in climate policy, technology, consumer behaviour, etc. during the adjustment to a low-carbon economy. Concerns over financial stability can arise through rapid changes in asset prices, reflecting realizations of transition physical risks. Risks can materialize, especially if the shift to a low-carbon economy is abrupt (as a consequence of prior inaction), poorly designed or uncoordinated globally.

There are issues of financial instability arising from the challenge of climate change. There is recognition of potential "transition risks" arising from the revaluation of carbon-intensive assets arising from shifts to a low-carbon economy (e.g. Dafermos, Nikolaidi andGalanis 2018; Breeden 2019). The change in asset values (assumed to be downwards, although the valuation of carbon unintensive assets could well rise) has implications for the range of financial institutions and households who own the corresponding assets. This may well be another example of financial markets mis-pricing financial assets – why have the risks involved not been incorporated into the financial asset prices? While it may be relevant for the central banks and others to warn about the likely shifts in asset prices, it is far from clear what actions would follow for monetary policy.

Reduced global demand for fossil fuels is likely to lead to "stranded assets", with loss of profits on the underlying assets and falls in market valuation of the assets. Mercure *et al.* (2018) analyse the macroeconomic impact of stranded fossil fuel assets. "Our analysis suggests that part of the SAFA [stranded fossil fuel assets] would occur as a result of an already ongoing trajectory, irrespective of whether or not new climate policies are adopted; the loss would be amplified if new climate policies to reach the 2° target of the Paris Agreement are adopted and/or if low-cost producers ... maintain their level of production ... despite declining demand; the magnitude of the loss from SFFA may amount to a discounted global wealth loss of US$1–4 trillion."

The clear dangers here are that financial institutions and others continue to own financial assets of carbon-intensive companies and the value of those financial assets will decline as the underlying assets become stranded. The financial institutions and the owners of the stranded assets then seek bailouts for their mistaken investment decisions.

As Epstein (2018: 348) argues, restructuring finance (e.g. reducing the size of "too big to fail" banks, use of financial transactions taxes, implementing asset-based reserve requirements, establishing "green banks") "could help to make the green transition and generate jobs and sustainable growth as well".

Shareholder value maximization, a dimension of financialization, has been viewed in terms of a focus on short-term profits at the expense of investment – and here investment in the long-term sustainability of the planet (Brett, Buller & Lawrence 2020).

Any hope of definancialization?

The material in this book and in many other places demonstrates the powers of financialization and the financial sector. Financialization has involved that growth of financial institutions (banks, stock markets) and their importance in the operations of national and global economies. This has been well documented and, in its quantitative form, is easy to do. Our modest proposals above would aim to correct some of that growth on the grounds that the scale of the financial sector has become too large. Financialization also involves the increasing role of financial motives and calculations, and the involvement of society with the financial industry. As illustrated in Chapter 9, financial inclusion enables people to participate in a financialized society but at a cost of mis-selling, complex financial calculations and debt traps. Financialization has involved markets and market activity spreading into areas previously largely outside of the market ("commodification"), and pension arrangements have been a key area where this has occurred in many countries.

The political power of the financial sectors and the difficulties of securing any meaningful reforms of the financial sector are well known. The pressures from the financial sectors to avoid serious regulatory restrictions on their activities, even where the purpose is to address financial instability and the sustainability of the financial system are likewise well known. Two case studies here would be the defeat of proposals within the European Union on financial transactions taxes and the watering down of measures of banking regulation such as the Dodd-Frank Act in the USA.

The statistics given above provide some indication of a slowing down in the pace of financialization but in general not what may be termed definancialization or any significant moves to the functions of the financial sector suggested above. But those statistics refer to the quantitative aspects of financial institutions and tell us little about the qualitative aspects of such institutions and, more significantly, nothing on some of the broader dimensions of financialization.

Financialization has been an integral part of capitalism. Yet, the arguments above have suggested that financialization has in some sense become "too large" and has become dysfunctional in the sense of not fulfilling the functions that could be ascribed to a financial sector. Definancialization could viewed (as with Keynesian economic policies) in terms of rescuing capitalism from itself – that is, correct a major fault with it in order for it to continue. In the case of Keynesian economics, to address unemployment and instability.

This did not mean that capitalists welcomed the application of Keynesian policies – particularly those that involved fiscal policy and budget deficits. Kalecki (1943) cast doubts on the acceptability of budget deficits and noted the resistance to full employment. In retrospect, the resistance was more to the forms of public expenditure rather than budget deficits *per se*. In a similar vein, the financial sector and its supporters will put up strong resistance to any attempts to scale its size back, even though a smaller and more diverse financial sector would be economically and socially beneficial. Kalecki (1943: 356) also argued that "'Full employment capitalism' will, of course, have to develop new social and political institutions which will reflect the increased power of the working class. If capitalism can adjust itself to full employment, a fundamental reform will have been incorporated in it. If not, it will show itself an outmoded system which much be scrapped." In the postwar world there were "fundamental reforms" in terms of the development of the welfare state, extension of public ownership and some incorporation of trade unions.

The "golden age" of capitalism of a postwar quarter century did enable low levels of unemployment and substantial economic growth. But, as King (2013: 32) argues, "by 1971 the crucial reform was already beginning to unravel". King lists five aspects: collapse of the Bretton Woods system of fixed exchange rates, leading to increased financial instability; financialization; unwinding of the first five principles of social democracy (government commitment to full employment, unionized and tightly regulated labour market, highly progressive taxation, comprehensive welfare state, public ownership of public utilities); tendency for the various "varieties of capitalism" to approach the Anglo-Saxon model; and "the so-called 'Great Moderation' after 1992 appears to demonstrate the advantages of neoliberal capitalism and to confirm the case against the 'crucial reform'". The end of the "golden era" ushered in the eras of neoliberalism, globalization and financialization, which have been accompanied by rising inequality and generally slower economic growth.

Definancialization, including the scaling back on the size and range of the financial sector and its restructuring, is the "fundamental reform" required to restore a stable and prosperous economy and, more importantly, an economy that can address issues of inequalities in all their forms and the climate emergency.

Conclusions

Before the GFCs, many scholars had been documenting and analysing the many dimensions of the growth of the financial sector – that is, "financialization" – and enquiring into the economic and social effects of financialization. The GFCs multiplied the study of financialization and a realization of its multiple dimensions and its economic and social effects. In this book I have sought to document the many dimensions of financialization over the past four decades and to evaluate its effects on inequalities, growth and corporate power. The growth of the financial sector, especially banking, may well at one time have facilitated savings and investment, and thereby growth, but now the evidence points in the opposite direction. The challenge today is not to restructure finance so that it facilitates growth, but rather to ensure that "it is the right sort of growth" – that is, growth of economic and social well-being (rather than GDP), which is environmentally sustainable. The financial system has to be restructured to support such aims.

REFERENCES

Aalbers, M. (2017). "The variegated financialization of housing". *International Journal of Urban and Regional Research* 41(4), 542–54.

Abiad, A., E. Detragiache & T. Tressel (2008). "A new database of financial reforms". IMF Working Paper WP/08/266, December.

Aglietta, M. and R. Breton (2001). "Financial systems, corporate control and capital accumulation". *Economy and Society*, 30(4), 433–66.

Aitken, R. (2013). "The financialization of micro-credit". *Development and Change* 44(3), 473–99.

Akyüz, Y. (2017). *Playing with Fire: Deepening Financial Integration and Changing Vulnerabilities of the Global South.* Oxford: Oxford University Press.

Alexiou, C., E. Trachanas & S. Vogiazas (2022). "Income inequality and financialization: a not so straight-forward relationship". *Journal of Economic Studies*, in process.

Alexiou, C., S. Vogiazas & J. Nellis (2018). "Reassessing the relationship between the financial sector and economic growth: dynamic panel evidence". *International Journal of Finance and Economics*, 1–19.

Alliance for Financial Inclusion (AFI) (2015). "Maya declaration".

Alvarez, I. (2015). "Financialization, non-financial corporations and income inequality: the case of France". *Socio-Economic Review* 13(3), 449–75.

Appelbaum, E., R. Batt & I. Clark (2013). "Implications of financial capitalism for employment relations research: evidence from breach of trust and implicit contracts in private equity buyouts". *British Journal of Industrial Relations* 51(3), 498–518.

Arcand, J.-L., E. Berkes & U. Panizza (2012). "Too much finance?" IMF Working Paper WP/12/161.

Arestis, P. (2004). "Washington Consensus and financial liberalisation". *Journal of Post Keynesian Economics* 27(2), 251–71.

Arestis, P. (2016). "Financial liberalization, the finance-growth nexus, financial crises and policy implications". In P. Arestis & M. Sawyer (eds), *Financial Liberalisation: Past, Present and Future.* Basingstoke: Palgrave Macmillan.

Arestis, P. & A. Caner (2005). "Financial liberalization and poverty: channels of influence". In P. Arestis & M. Sawyer (eds), *Financial Liberalization: Beyond Orthodox Concerns.* Basingstoke: Palgrave Macmillan.

Arestis, P., A. Charles & G. Fontana (2013). "Financialization, the Great Recession, and the stratification of the US labor market". *Feminist Economics* 19(3), 152–80.

Arestis, P., A. Charles & G. Fontana (2014). "Identity economics meets financialisation: gender, race and occupational stratification in the US labour market". *Cambridge Journal of Economics* 38(6), 1471–91.

Arestis, P., G. Chortareas & G. Magkonis (2015), "The financial development and growth nexus: a meta-analysis". *Journal of Economic Surveys* 29(3), 549–65.

Arestis, P. & M. Glickman (2002). "Financial crisis in South East Asia: dispelling illusion the Minskyan way". *Cambridge Journal of Economics* 26(2), 237–60.

Arestis, P. & M. Sawyer (eds) (2009), *Critical Essays on the Privatization Experience.* Basingstoke: Palgrave Macmillan.

REFERENCES

Arestis, P. & M. Sawyer (2013). "The potential of financial transactions taxes". In P. Arestis & M. Sawyer (eds), *Economic Policies, Governance and the New Economics*, 87–121. Basingstoke: Palgrave Macmillan.

Arestis, P. & M. Sawyer (eds) (2016). *Financial Liberalisation: Past, Present and Future*. Basingstoke: Palgrave Macmillan.

Arestis, P. & H. Stein (2005). "An institutional perspective to finance and development as an alternative to financial liberalisation". *International Review of Applied Economics* 19(4).

Arrighi, G. (1994). *The Long Twentieth Century*. London: Verso.

Ashman, S. & B. Fine (2013). "Neo-liberalism, varieties of capitalism, and the shifting contours of Africa's financial system". *Transformation: Critical Perspectives on Southern Africa* 81/82, 144–78.

Asker, J., J. Farre-Mensa & A. Ljungqvist (2015). "Corporate investment and stock market listing: a puzzle?" *Review of Financial Studies* 28(1), 342–90.

Aslı Demirgüç-Kunt, A. *et al.* (2019). Financial Development and Structure Dataset. www.worldbank.org/en/publication/gfdr/data/financial-structure-database

Assa, J. (2012). "Financialization and its consequences: the OECD experience". *Finance Research* 1(1) January.

Assa, J. (2017). *The Financialization of GDP: Implications for Economic Theory and Policy*. London: Routledge.

Atkinson, T., D. Luttrell & H. Rosenblum (2013). "How bad was it? The costs and consequences of the 2007–09 financial crisis". Federal Reserve Bank of Dallas, Staff Papers No. 20.

Atkinson, A. & S. Morelli (2011). "Economic crises and inequality". Human Development Research Paper, 2011/06.

Ayadi, R. *et al.* (2010). "Investigating diversity in the banking sector in Europe: key developments, performance and role of co-operative banks". Centre for European Policy Studies, Brussels; http://ssrn.com/abstract=1677335

Baddeley, M. & J. McCombie (2001). "An historical perspective on speculative bubbles and financial crises: tulipmainia and the South Sea bubble". In P. Arestis, M. Baddeley & J. McCombie (eds), *What Global Economic Crisis?* Basingstoke: Palgrave Macmillan.

Bagehot, W. (1962) [1873]. *Lombard Street*. Homewood: Irwin.

Bakija, J., A. Cole & B. Heim (2012). "Jobs and income growth of top earners and the causes of changing income inequality: evidence from US tax returns data". Williams College, US Department of Treasury and Indiana University.

Banerjee, A. *et al.* (2015). "The miracle of microfinance? Evidence from a randomized evaluation". *American Economic Journal: Applied Economics* 7(1), 22–53.

Barba, A. & M. Pivetti (2009). "Rising household debt: its causes and macroeconomic implications – a long period analysis". *Cambridge Journal of Economics* 33(1), 113–37.

Barradas, R. (2017). "Financialisation and real investment in the European Union: beneficial or prejudicial effects?" *Review of Political Economy* 29(3), 376–413.

Barradas, R. & S. Lagoa (2017). "Financialization and Portuguese real investment: a supportive or disruptive relationship?" *Journal of Post Keynesian Economics* 40(3), 413–39.

Barrowclough, D. (2018). "Starting with the poor". In D. Barrowclough (ed.), *The Ins and Outs of Inclusive Finance: Some Lessons from Microfinance and Basic Income*, 10–19. Geneva: UNCTAD.

Basu, S., R. Inklaar & J. Wang (2011). "The value of risk: measuring the service output of the US commercial banks". *Economic Inquiry* 49(1), 226–45.

Bateman, M., S. Blankenburg & R. Kozul-Wright (eds) (2019). *The Rise and Fall of Global Microcredit: Development, Debt and Disillusion*. Abingdon: Routledge.

Batt, R. & E. Appelbaum (2013). "The impact of financialization on management and employment outcomes". W. E. Upjohn Institute Working Paper No. 13–191.

Batt, R. & J. Morgan (2020). "Private equity and public problems in a financialized world: an interview with Rosemary Batt". *Real World Economics Review* 94, 83–108.

Baumol, W. (1959). *Business Behaviour, Value and Growth*. London: Macmillan.

Bazillier, R. & J. Hericourt (2017). "The circular relationship between inequality, leverage, and financial crises". *Journal of Economic Surveys* 31(2), 463–96.

Bazot, G. (2018). "Financial intermediation costs, rents, and productivity: an international comparison". European Historical Economics Society, Working Paper No. 141.

Beck, T., R. Levine & A. Demirgüç-Kunt (2007). "Finance, inequality and the poor". *Journal of Economic Growth* 12(1), 27–49.

Beck, T. *et al.* (2011). *Financing Africa: Through the Crisis and Beyond.* Washington, DC: World Bank.

Becker, J. & P. Cetkovic (2015). "Patterns of financialisation in Southeast European and Visegrád countries". In D. Radošević & V. Cvijanović (eds), *Financialisation and Financial Crisis in South-Eastern European Countries*, 71–91. Frankfurt: Peter Lang.

Bell, B. & J. Van Reenen (2014). "Bankers and their bonuses". *Economic Journal* 124(574), F1–21.

Bellettini, G. & F. Delbono (2013). "Persistence of high-income inequality and banking crises: 1980–2010". CESifo Working Paper, No. 4293.

Berle, A. & G. Means (1932). *The Modern Corporation and Private Property.* New York: Macmillan.

Bernanke, B. (2004). "The Great Moderation". Remarks at the Meetings of the Eastern Economic Association, Washington DC www.federalreserve.gov/BOARDDOCS/SPEECHES/2004/20040220/default.htm

Bezemer, D., M. Grydaki & L. Zhang (2016). "More mortgages, lower growth?" *Economic Inquiry* 54(1), 652–74.

Bezemer, D. *et al.* (2021). "Credit policy and the 'debt shift' in advanced economies". *Socio-Economic Review*, in process.

Bivens, J. & L. Mishel (2013). "The pay of corporate executives and financial professionals as evidence of rents in Top 1 percent incomes". *Journal of Economic Perspectives* 27(3), 57–78.

Block, F. (2014). "Democratizing finance". *Politics & Society* 42(1), 3–28.

Boehmer, E., R. Nash & J. Netter (2005). "Bank privatization in developing and developed countries: cross-sectional evidence on the impact of economic and political factors". *Journal of Banking and Finance*, 29(8–9), 1981–2013.

Bonizzi, B. (2013). "Financialization in developing and emerging countries: a survey". *International Journal of Political Economy* 42(4), 83–107.

Bonizzi, B. (2017). "International financialisation, developing countries and the contradictions of privatised Keynesianism". *Economic and Political Studies* 5(1), 21–40.

Bonizzi, B. & J. Churchill (2017). "Pension funds and financialisation in the European Union". *Revista de Economia Mundial* 46, 71–90.

Bonizzi, B., J. Churchill & D. Guevara (2021). "Variegated financialization and pension fund asset demand: the case of Colombia and Peru". *Socio-Economic Review* 19(2), 789–815.

Bordo, M. & C. Meissner (2012). "Does inequality lead to a financial crisis?" *Journal of International Money and Finance*, 2147–61.

Bortz, P. & A. Kaltenbrunner (2018). "The international dimension of financialization in developing and emerging economies". *Development and Change* 49(2), 375–93.

Bova, E. *et al.* (2016). "The fiscal costs of contingent liabilities: a new dataset". IMF Working Paper, WP/16/14.

Boyer, R. (2000). "Is a finance-led growth regime a viable alternative to Fordism? A preliminary analysis". *Economy and Society* 29(1), 111–45.

Boyer, R. (2013). "The Global Financial Crisis in historical perspective: an economic analysis combining Minsky, Hayek, Fisher, Keynes and the regulation approach". *AEL: A Convivium* 3(3), 93–139.

Braun, B. (2021). "Fueling financialization: the economic consequences of funded pensions". *New Labor Forum*, 1–9.

Breeden, S. (2019). "Avoiding the storm: climate change and the financial system". Speech given at Official Monetary & Financial Institutions Forum, London, 15 April.

Brett, M., A. Buller & M. Lawrence (2020). "A blueprint for a Green New Deal". Common Wealth.

Brown, A., D. Spencer & M. Veronese Passarella (2017). "The extent and variegation of financialisation in Europe: a preliminary analysis". *Revista de Economia Mundial/Journal of World Economy* 46, 49–69.

Bucci, A., S. Marsiglio & C. Prettner (2020). "On the (non-monotonic) relation between economic growth and finance". *Macroeconomic Dynamics* 24, 93–112.

Bumann, S., N. Hermes & R. Lensink (2012). "Financial liberalisation and economic growth: a meta-analysis". *Journal of International Money and Finance* 33, 255–81.

Burns, D. *et al.* (2016). "Where does the money go? Financialised chains and the crisis in residential care". CRESC Public Interest Report, March.

Caner, A. (2010). "Does financial liberalization help the poor?" In G. Fontana, J. McCombie & M. Sawyer (eds), Macroeconomics, Finance and Money, Essays in Honour of Philip Arestis. Basingstoke: Palgrave.

Cardaci, A. & F. Saraceno (2015). "Inequality, financialisation and economic crises: an agent based macro model". Working Paper 2015–21, Dipartimento di Economia, Universita degli di Milano.

Carney, M. (2015). "Building real markets for the good of the people". Speech given at Lord Mayor's Banquet for Bankers and Merchants of the City of London at the Mansion House, London.

Carvalho, M. & J. Cerejeira (2019). "Financialization, corporate governance and employee pay: a firm level analysis". Núcleo de Investigação em Politicase Económicas e Empresariais, Working Paper 08.

Castree, N., R. Kitchin & A. Rogers (2013). "Regime of accumulation". In *A Dictionary of Human Geography*. Oxford: Oxford University Press.

Cecchetti, S. & E. Kharroubi (2012). "Reassessing the impact of finance on growth". BIS Working Papers No 381.

Centre for Banking Research (2020). *The CBR Conduct Costs Project.* City University.

Christensen, J., N. Shaxson & D. Wigan (2016). "The finance curse: Britain and the world economy". *British Journal of Politics and International Relations* 18(1), 255–69.

Christophers, B. (2011). "Making finance productive". *Economy and Society* 40(1), 112–40.

Christophers, B. (2018). "Financialisation as monopoly profit: the case of US banking". *Antipode* 50(4), 864–90.

Chwieroth, J. (2014). "Controlling capital: the International Monetary Fund and transformative incremental change from within international organizations". *New Political Economy* 19(3), 445–69.

Clark, I. (2009). "Owners and managers: disconnecting managerial capitalism? Understanding the private-equity business model". *Work, Employment and Society* 23(4), 775–86.

Cordonnier, L. *et al.* (2019). "The (over)cost of capital: financialization and nonfinancial corporations in France (1961–2011)". *Review of Political Economy* 31(3), 407–29.

Correa, E., G. Vidal & W. Marshall (2012). "Financialization in Mexico: trajectory and limits". *Journal of Post Keynesian Economics* 35(2), 255–75.

Costantini, O. & M. Seccareccia (2020). "Income distribution, household debt and growth in modern financialized economies". *Journal of Economic Issues* 54(2), 444–53.

Creel, J., P. Hubert & F. Labondance (2015). "Financial stability and economic performance". *Economic Modelling* 468, 25–40.

Cull, R., A. Demirgüç-Kunt & J. Morduch (2009). "Microfinance meets the market". *Journal of Economic Perspectives* 23(1), 167–92.

Cushen, J. (2013). "Financialisation in the workplace: hegemonic narratives, performative interventions and the angry knowledge worker". *Accounting, Organizations and Society* 38, 314–31.

Dafermos, Y., M. Nikolaidi & G. Galanis (2018). "Climate change, financial stability and monetary policy". *Ecological Economics* 152, 219–34.

Dagdeviren, H. *et al.* (2020). "Financialisation, welfare retrenchment and subsistence debt in Britain", *New Political Economy* 25(2), 159–73.

Dallery, T. (2009). "Post-Keynesian theories of the firm under financialisation". *Review of Radical Political Economics* 41(4), 492–515.

Darcillon, T. (2015). "How does finance affect labor market institutions? An empirical analysis in 16 OECD countries". *Socio-Economic Review* 13(3), 477–504.

Das, M. & S. Mohapatra (2003). "Income inequality: the aftermath of stock market liberalization in emerging markets". *Journal of Empirical Finance* 10(1), 217–48.

Dávila-Fernández, M. & L. Punzo (2021). "Some new insights on financialization and income inequality: evidence for the US economy, 1947–2013". *International Review of Applied Economics* 35(3/4), 520–39.

Davis, A. & C. Walsh (2016). "The role of the state in the financialisation of the UK economy". *Political Studies* 64, 666–82.

Davis, G. & S. Kim (2015). "Financialization of the economy". *Annual Review of Sociology* 41, 203–21.

Davis, L. (2016). "Identifying the 'financialization' of the nonfinancial corporation in the US economy: a decomposition of firm-level balance sheets". *Journal of Post Keynesian Economics* 39(1), 115–41.

Davis, L. (2017). "Financialization and investment: a survey of the empirical literature". *Journal of Economic Surveys* 31(5), 1332–58.

Davis, L. (2018). "Financialization, shareholder orientation and the cash holdings of US corporations". *Review of Political Economy* 30(1), 1–27.

Davis, S. *et al.* (2014). "Private equity, jobs and productivity". *American Economic Review* 104(12), 3956–90.

De Bernis, G. (1988). *El Capitalismo Contemporáneo*. México: Editorial Nuestro Tiempo.

De Vita, G. & Y. Luo (2021). "Financialization, household debt and income inequality: empirical evidence". *International Journal of Finance and Economics* 26, 1917–37.

Demirgüç-Kunt, A. & E. Detragiache (1998). "Financial liberalization and financial fragility". IMF Working Papers WP/98/83.

Demirgüç-Kunt, A. & R. Levine (2009). "Finance and inequality: theory and evidence". NBER Working Paper 15275.

Demirgüç-Kunt, A. *et al.* (2018). *The Global Findex Database 2017: Measuring Financial Inclusion and the Fintech Revolution*. Washington, DC: World Bank.

Denk, O. (2015). "Financial sector pay and labour income inequality: evidence from Europe". OECD Economics Department Working Papers, No. 1225.

Denk, O. & B. Cournède (2015). "Finance and income inequality in OECD countries". OECD Economics Department Working Papers, No. 1224.

Detzer, D. *et al.* (2013). "The German financial system". FESSUD Studies in Financial Systems No. 3.

Diaz-Alejandro, C. (1985). "Good-bye financial repression, hello financial crash". *Journal of Development Economics* 19(1/2), 24.

Do Carmo, M., M. Sacomano Neto & J. Donadone (2019). "Financialization in the automotive industry: shareholders, managers and salaries". *Journal of Economic Issues* 53(3), 841–62.

Dollar, D. (2019). Executive summary in WTO, Technological innovation, supply chain trade, and workers in a globalized world. Geneva: WTO.

Dos Santos, P. (2013). "A cause for policy concern: the expansion of household credit in middle-income countries". *International Review of Applied Economics* 27(3), 316–38.

Duffie, D. (2019). "Prone to fail: the pre-crisis financial system". *Journal of Economic Perspectives* 33(1), 81–106.

Dumenil, G. & D. Levy (2005). "Costs and benefits of neoliberalism". In G. Epstein (ed.), *Financialization and the World Economy*. Cheltenham: Elgar.

Dünhaupt, P. (2012). "Financialisation and the rentier income share – evidence from the USA and Germany". *International Review of Applied Economics* 26(4), 465–87.

Dünhaupt, P. (2017). "Determinants of labour income share in the era of financialisation". *Cambridge Journal of Economics* 41(1), 283–306.

Dupuis, M., J. Peters & P. Scrimger (2020). "Financialization and union decline in Canada: the influence on sectors and core industries". *Competition and Change* 24(3/4), 268–90.

Durand, C. & M. Gueuder (2018). "The profit-investment nexus in an era of financialisation, globalisation and monopolisation: a profit-centred perspective". *Review of Political Economy* 30(2), 126–53.

Dymski, G., L. Hernandez & L. Mohanty (2013). "Race, gender, power, and the US subprime mortgage and foreclosure crisis: a meso analysis". *Feminist Economics* 19(3), 124–51.

Dzimwasha, T. (2015). "20 global banks have paid $235bn in fines since the 2008 financial crisis". *International Business Times*, 24 May.

Ebbinghaus, N. (2015). "The privatization and marketization of pensions in Europe: a double transformation facing the crisis". *European Policy Analysis* 1(1), 56–73.

Ederer, S., C. Heumesser & C. Staaritz (2016). "Financialization and commodity prices – an empirical analysis for coffee, cotton, wheat and oil". *International Review of Applied Economics* 30(4), 462–87.

Eichacker, N. (2015). "Financial liberalization and the onset of financial crisis in Western European states between 1983 and 2011". *North American Journal of Economics and Finance* 34, 323–43.

Eichacker, N. (2017). *Financial Underpinnings of Europe's Financial Crisis: Liberalization, Integration and Asymmetric State Power*. Cheltenham: Elgar.

Engelen, E. (2008). "The case for financialization". *Competition and Change* 12(2), 111–19.

Enrich, D. (2017). *The Spider Network: The Wild Story of a Math Genius, and One of the Greatest Scams in Financial History*. London: W H Allen.

Epstein, G. (2005). "Introduction: financialization and the world economy". In G. Epstein (ed.), *Financialization and the World Economy*, 3–16. Cheltenham: Elgar.

Epstein, G. (ed.) (2005b). *Financialization and the World Economy*. Cheltenham: Elgar.

Epstein, G. (2006). "Central banks as agents of economic development". UNU-Wider and PERI.

Epstein, G. (2010). "David Gordon memorial lecture: finance without financiers: prospects for radical change in financial governance". *Review of Radical Political Economy* 42(3), 293–306.

Epstein, G. (2018). "On the social efficiency of finance". *Development and Change* 49(2), 330–54.

Epstein, G. & J. Crotty (2013). "How big is too big? On the social efficiency of the financial sector in the United States". In J. Wicks-Lim & R. Pollin (eds), *Capitalism on Trial: Explorations in the Tradition of Thomas E. Weisskopf*, 293–310. Cheltenham: Elgar.

Epstein, G. & A. Jayadev (2005). "The rise of rentier income in OECD countries: financialization, central bank policy and labor solidarity". In G. Epstein (ed.), *Financialization and the World Economy*. Cheltenham: Elgar.

Epstein, G. & J. Montecino (2016). "Overcharged: the high cost of high finance". Roosevelt Institute. www.peri.umass.edu/236/hash/fd100f263f6805db4562d7816b225e5f/publication/711/

Ertürk, I. & S. Solari (2007). "Banks as continuous reinvention". *New Political Economy* 12(3), 369–88.

European Central Bank (ECB) (2017). *Financial Integration in Europe*, May 2017.

European Commission (2019). "The European Green Deal". Brussels 11.12.2019, COM (2019) 640 final.

Evans, T. (2014). "The impact of financial liberalization on income inequality". *International Journal of Labour Research* 6(1), 129–42.

Fagereng, A. *et al.* (2020). "Heterogeneity and persistence in returns to wealth". *Econometrica* 88(1), 115–70.

Fama, E. (1970). "Efficient capital markets: a review of theory and empirical work". *Journal of Finance* 25(2): 383–417.

Fasianos, A., D. Guevara & C. Pierros (2018). "Have we been here before? Phases of financialization within the twentieth century in the US". *Review of Keynesian Economics* 6(1), 34–61.

Feldstein, M. (1974). "Social security, induced retirement, and aggregate capital accumulation". *Journal of Political Economy* 82(5): 905–26.

Ferreiro, J. & C. Gomez (2016). "Financialization and the financial balance sheets of economic sectors in the eurozone". In P. Arestis & M. Sawyer (eds), *Financial Liberalisation: Past Present and Future*. Basingstoke: Palgrave Macmillan.

Fiebiger, M. (2016). "Rethinking the financialisation of non-financial corporations: a reappraisal of US empirical data". *Review of Political Economy* 28(3), 354–79.

Finance Watch (2020). "Nature's return: embedding environmental goals at the heart of economic and financial decision-making".

Financial Conduct Authority (2017). "Asset management market study". Market Study MS15/2.3.

Financial Inclusion Commission (2015). *Financial Inclusion: Improving the Financial Health of the Nation*, March.

Financial Stability Board (FSB) (2018). Global Shadow Banking Monitor Report 2017. London: Financial Stability Board.

Fine, B. (2011). "Financialisation on the rebound?" Mimeo.

Flaherty, E. (2015). "Top incomes under finance-driven capitalism, 1990–2010: power resources and regulatory orders". *Socio-Economic Review* 13(3), 417–47.

Fligstein, N. & L. Markowitz (1993). "Financial reorganization of American corporations in the 1980s". In W. Wilson (ed.), *Sociology and the Public Agenda*, 185–206. London: Sage.

Fligstein, N. & A. Roehrkasse (2016). "The causes of fraud in the financial crisis of 2007 to 2009: evidence from the mortgage-backed securities industry". *American Sociological Review* 81(4), 617–43.

Fligstein, N. & T. Shin (2007). "Shareholder value and the transformation of the US economy, 1984–2000". *Sociological Forum* 22(4), 399–424.

Fonteyne, W. (2007). "Co-operative Banks in Europe – Policy Issues", IMF Working Paper 07/159.

Foster, J. (2007). "The financialization of capitalism". Monthly Review, 1 April. http://monthlyreview.org/2007/04/01/the-financialization-of-capitalism

Frangakis, M. & J. Huffschmid (2009). "Privatisation in Western Europe". In M. Frangakis *et al.* (eds), *Privatisation Against the European Social Model*, 9-29. Basingstoke: Palgrave Macmillan.

Friedman, M. (1970). "The social responsibility of business is to enhance its profits". *New York Times*, 13 September.

Frost, J., L. Gambacorta & R. Gambacorta (2020). "The Matthew effect and modern finance: on the nexus between wealth inequality, financial development and financial technology". BIS Working Papers No. 871.

Froud, J. *et al.* (2006). *Financialisation and Strategy: Narrative and Numbers*. London: Routledge.

Gabbi, G. & E. Ticci (2013). "Implications of financialisation for sustainability". FESSUD Working Paper No. 47.

Gezici, A. (2010). "Distributional consequence of financial crises: evidence from recent crises". *Review of Radical Political Economics* 42(3), 373–80.

Ghosh, J. (2005). "The economic and social effects of financial liberalization: a primer for developing countries". DESA Working Paper No. 4, ST/ESA/2005/DWP/4.

Glyn, A. (2006). *Capitalism Unleashed: Finance, Globalization and Welfare*. Oxford: Oxford University Press.

Goda, T. & P. Lysandrou (2014). "The contribution of wealth concentration to the subprime crisis: a quantitative estimation". *Cambridge Journal of Economics* 38(2), 301–27.

Godard, J. (2004). "A critical assessment of the high-performance paradigm". *British Journal of Industrial Relations* 42(2), 349–78.

Godechot, O. (2012). "Is finance responsible for the rise in wage inequality in France". *Socio-Economic Review* 109, 447–70.

Goldsmith, R. (1969). *Financial Structure and Development*. New Haven, CT: Yale University Press.

Golub, S., A. Kaya & M. Reay (2015). "What were they thinking? The Federal Reserve in the run-up to the 2008 financial crisis". *Review of International Political Economy* 22(4), 657–92.

Gomez, G. (2008). *Do micro-enterprises promote equity or growth?* Gorinchem, The Netherlands: Woord en Daad.

Gordon, R. (2012). "Is US economic growth over? Faltering innovation confronts the six headwinds". NBER Working Paper No. 18315. Cambridge, MA: National Bureau of Economic Research.

Gordon, R. (2014). "The demise of US economic growth: restatement, rebuttal, and reflections". NBER Working Paper, No. 19895. Cambridge, MA: National Bureau of Economic Research.

Gouzoulis, G. (2021). "Finance, discipline, and the labour share in the long-run: France (1911–2010) and Sweden (1891–2000)". *British Journal of Industrial Relations* 59(2), 568–94.

Grabel, I. (1997). "Savings, investment and functional efficiency: a comparative examination of national financial complexes". In R. Pollin (ed.), *The Macroeconomics of Saving, Finance and Investment*, 251–98. Ann Arbor, MI: University of Michigan Press.

Grabel, I. (2016). "Capital controls in a time of crisis". In P. Arestis & M. Sawyer (eds), *Financial Liberalisation: Past, Present and Future*, 177–225. Basingstoke: Palgrave Macmillan.

Green New Deal Group (2008). *A Green New Deal: Joined-up Policies to Solve the Triple Crunch of the Credit Crisis, Climate Change and High Oil Prices*. London: New Economics Foundation. https://neweconomics.org/2008/07/green-new-deal

Griffith-Jones, S. (2014). "A BRICS Development Bank: a dream coming true?" UNCTAD Discussion Paper No. 215, March.

Griffith-Jones, S. (2015). "The positive role of good development banks". www.un.org/esa/ffd/ffd3/blog/positive-role-development-banks.html

Griffith-Jones, S. & G. Cozzi (2016). "The roles of development banks; how they can promote investment, in Europe and globally". In A. Noman & J. Stiglitz (eds), *Efficiency, Finance, and Varieties of Industrial Policy*, 131–55. New York: Columbia University Press.

Griffith-Jones, S. *et al.* (2022). "Matching risks with instruments in development banks". *Review of Political Economy*, 34(2), 197–223.

Groeneveld, H. (2015). "European co-operative banking actual and factual assessment". www.globalcube.net/clients/eacb/content/medias/publications/eacb_studies/TIAS_Coop_Banking_w.pdf

Gurley, J. & E. Shaw (1955). "Financial aspects of economic development". *American Economic Review* 45, 515–38.

Haig, B. (1973). "The treatment of banks in the social accounts". *Economic Record* 49, 624–28.

Haig, B. (1986). "The treatment of interest and financial intermediaries in the national accounts of Australia". *Review of Income and Wealth* 32, 409–24.

Hanieh, A. (2016). "Absent regions: spaces of financialisation in the Arab world". *Antipode* 48(5).

Hanieh, A. (2018). *Money, Markets, and Monarchies: The Gulf Cooperation Council and the Political Economy of the Contemporary Middle East*. Cambridge: Cambridge University Press.

Hanieh, A. (2020). "Variegated finance capital and the political economy of Islamic banking in the Gulf". *New Political Economy* 25(4), 572–89.

Hardie, I. *et al.* (2013). "Banks and the false dichotomy in the comparative political economy of finance". *World Politics* 65, 691–728.

Harvey, D. (2005). *A Brief History of Neoliberalism*. Oxford: Oxford University Press.

Hassel, A., M. Naczyk & T. Wiss (2019). "The political economy of pension financialisation: public policy responses to the crisis". *Journal of European Public Policy* 26(4), 483–500.

Heil, M. (2021). "How does finance influence labour market outcomes? A review of empirical studies". *Journal of Economic Studies* 47(6), 1197–232.

Hein, E. (2012). *The Macroeconomics of Finance-Dominated Capitalism – and Its Crisis*. Cheltenham: Elgar.

Hein, E., D. Detzer & N. Dodig (eds) (2015a). *The Demise of Finance-Dominated Capitalism: Explaining the Financial and Economic Crises*. Cheltenham: Elgar.

Hein, E., D. Detzer & N. Dodig (2015b). "Introduction". In E. Hein, D. Detzer & N. Dodig (eds), *The Demise of Finance-Dominated Capitalism: Explaining the Financial and Economic Crises*, 1–6. Cheltenham: Elgar.

Hein, E. *et al.* (2017). "Financialisation and distribution before and after the crisis: patterns for six OECD countries". In P. Arestis & M. Sawyer (eds), *Economic Policies since the Global Financial Crisis*, 127–72. Basingstoke: Palgrave Macmillan.

Herndon, T. & M. Paul (2020). "A public banking option as a mode of regulation for household financial services in the US". *Journal of Post Keynesian Economics* 43(4), 576–607.

Hickel, J. (2020). *Less is More*. London: Penguin.

Hindmoor, A. & A. McConnell (2015). "Who saw it coming? The UK's great financial crisis". *Journal of Public Policy* 35(1), 63–96.

Hirst, P. & G. Thompson (2019). "The future of globalisation". In J. Michie (ed.), *The Handbook of Globalisation, Third edition*, 16–31. Aldershot: Edward Elgar.

House of Lords (2017). Select Committee on Financial Exclusion Report of Session 2016–17 HL Paper 132 Tackling Financial Exclusion.

Hunter, B. & S. Murray (2020). "Deconstructing the financialization of healthcare". *Development and Change* 50(5), 1263–86.

Hyde, A. (2020). "Left behind?" Financialization and income inequality between the affluent, middle class, and the poor". *Sociological Inquiry* 90(4), 891–99.

Hyde, A., M. Wallace & T. Vachon (2018). "Financialization, income inequality and redistribution in 18 affluent democracies, 1981–2011". *Social Currents* 5, 193–211.

International Institute for Labour Studies (IILS) (2008). *World of Work Report 2008: Income Inequalities in the Age of Financial Globalization*. Geneva: International Labour Organization.

International Monetary Fund (IMF) (2009). *World Economic Outlook 2009*. Washington, DC: IMF.

International Monetary Fund (IMF) (2012). *Liberalizing Capital Flows and Managing Outflows*. Washington, DC: IMF.

International Monetary Fund (IMF) (2015). "Now is the time fiscal policies for sustainable growth". *Fiscal Monitor*, April 2015.

International Monetary Fund (IMF) (2018a). *How Developed and Inclusive are Financial Systems in the GCC?* Washington, DC: IMF.

International Monetary Fund (IMF) (2018b). *World Economic Report 2018*. Washington, DC: IMF.

Jauch, S. & S. Watzka (2011). "Financial development and income inequality". CESifo working paper: Fiscal Policy, Macroeconomics and Growth, No. 3687.

Jensen, M. (1986). "Agency costs of free cash flow, corporate finance and takeovers". *American Economic Review* 76, 323–29.

Jensen, M. & W. Meckling (1976). "Theory of the firm: managerial behaviour, agency costs and ownership structure". *Journal of Financial Economics* 3(4), 305–60.

Jessop, B. (2013). "The North Atlantic financial crisis and varieties of capitalism: a Minsky and/or Marx moment? And perhaps Max Weber too?" In S. Fadda & P. Tridico (eds), *Financial Crisis, Labour Markets and Institutions*, 40–59. London: Routledge.

Jung, J. (2015). "Shareholder value and workforce downsizing, 1981–2006". *Social Forces* 93(4), 1335–68.

Kalecki, M. (1943). "Political aspects of full employment". *Political Quarterly* 14(4), 322–31.

Kallis, G. *et al.* (2020). *The Case for Degrowth*. Cambridge: Polity.

Kaltenbrunner, A. (2015). "Financial integration and exchange rate determination: a Brazilian case study". International Review of Applied Economics. 29(2), 129–149.

Kaltenbrunner, A. & J. Painceira (2018). "Subordinated financial integration and financialisation in emerging capitalist economies: the Brazilian experience". *New Political Economy* 23(3), 290–313.

Kaplan, S. & J. Rauh (2010). "Wall Street and Main Street: what contributes to the rise in the highest income?" *Review of Financial Studies* 23(3), 1004–50.

Karwowski, E. (2019). "Economic development and variegated financialization in emerging economies". Financial Geography Working Paper Series.

Karwowki, E., M. Shabani & E. Stockhammer (2020). "Dimensions and determinants of financialisation: comparing OECD countries since 1997". *New Political Economy* 25(6), 957–77.

Karwowski, E. & E. Stockhammer (2017). "Financialisation in emerging economies: a systematic overview and comparison with Anglo-Saxon economies". *Economic and Political Studies* 5(1), 60–86.

Kay, J. (2015). *Other People's Money: Masters of the Universe or Servants of the People?* London: Profile.

Keynes, J. (1936). *The General Theory of Employment, Interest and Money*. London: Macmillan.

Kim, D. & S. Lin (2011). "Nonlinearity in the financial development-income inequality nexus". *Journal of Comparative Economics* 39(3), 310–25.

Kim, Y. (2013). "Household debt, financialisation, and macroeconomic performance in the United States, 1951–2009". *Journal of Post Keynesian Economics* 35, 675–94.

Kim, Y. (2016). "Macroeconomic effects of household debt: an empirical analysis". *Review of Keynesian Economics* 4, 127–50.

King, J. (2013). "Whatever happened to the crucial reforms?" In R. Bellofiore, E. Karwowski & J. Toporowski (eds), *Economic Crisis and Political Economy, Volume 2 of Essays in Honour of Tadeusz Kowalik*, 29–41. Basingstoke: Palgrave Macmillan.

Klagge, B. & R. Martin (2005). "Decentralized versus centralized financial systems: is there a case for local capital markets?" *Journal of Economic Geography* 5, 387–421.

Klein, M. (2015). "Inequality and household debt: a panel cointegration analysis". *Empirica* 42, 391–412.

Kliman, A. & S. Williams (2015). "Why 'financialisation' hasn't depressed US productive investment". *Cambridge Journal of Economics* 39(1), 67–92.

Kohl, S. (2021). "Too much mortgage debt? The effect of housing financialization on housing supply and residential capital formation". *Socio-Economic Review* 19(2), 413–40.

Kohler, K., A. Guschanski & E. Stockhammer (2019). "The impact of financialisation on the wage share: a theoretical clarification and empirical test". *Cambridge Journal of Economics* 43, 937–74.

Kollmeyer, C. & J. Peters (2019). "Financialization and the decline of organized labor: a study of 18 advanced capitalist countries, 1970–2012". *Social Forces* 98(1), 1–30.

Kotz, D. (2008). "Financialization and neoliberalism". Mimeo available at: http://people.umass.edu/dmkotz/KotzPapers.html

Kregel, J. (2010). "Is deregulation of the financial system an oxymoron?" Levy Economics Institute Working Paper, No. 585.

Krippner, G. (2005). "The financialization of the American economy". *Socio-Economic Review* 3, 173–208.

Kwon, R., A. Roberts & K. Zingula (2017). "Whither the middle class? Financialization, labor institutions, and the gap between top and middle-income earners in advanced industrial societies". *Sociology of Development* 3(4), 377–402.

Laeven, L. & F. Valencia (2012). "Systemic banking crises database: an update". IMF Working Papers, WP/12/163.

Laeven, L. & F. Valencia (2013). "Systemic banking crises database". *IMF Economic Review* 61, 225–70.

Laeven, L. & F. Valencia (2020). "Systemic banking crises database II". *IMF Economic Review* 68, 307–61.

Laffont, J.-J. & D. Martimort (2002). *The Theory of Incentives: The Principal-Agent Model*. Princeton, NJ: Princeton University Press.

Lagarde, C. (2018). "Ten years after Lehman: lessons learned and challenges ahead". IMF blog. https://blogs.imf.org/2018/09/05/ten-years-after-lehman-lessons-learned-and-challenges-ahead/

Lane, P. & G. Milesi-Ferretti (2007). "The external wealth of nations mark II". *Journal of International Economics* 73, 223–50.

Lane, P. & G. Milesi-Ferretti (2018). "The external wealth of nations revisited: international financial integration in the aftermath of the Global Financial Crisis". *IMF Economic Review* 66(1), 189–222.

Lapavitsas, C. (2011). "Theorizing financialization". *Work, Employment and Society* 25(4), 611–26.

Lapavitsas, C. & I. Mendieta-Muñoz (2018). "Financialization at a watershed in the USA". *Competition and Change* 22(5), 488–508.

Lapavitsas, C. & J. Powell (2013). "Financialisation varied: a comparative analysis of advanced economies". *Cambridge Journal of Regions, Economy and Society* 6, 359–79.

Lazonick, W. (2013). "The financialization of the US corporation: what has been lost, and how it can be regained". *Seattle University Law Review* 36(2), 857–909.

Lazonick, W. (2017). "The functions of the stock market and the fallacies of shareholder value". INET Working Paper No. 58, 3 June (revised 30 July).

Lazonick, W. & M. O'Sullivan (2000). "Maximizing shareholder value: a new ideology for corporate governance". *Economy and Society* 29(1), 13–35.

Lee, R. *et al.* (2009). "The remit of financial geography – before and after the crisis". *Journal of Economic Geography* 9(5), 723–47.

Levine, R. (2005). "Finance and growth: theory and evidence". In P. Aghion & S. Durlauf (eds), *Handbook of Economic Growth*, 866–934. Amsterdam: Elsevier.

Levy-Orlik, N. (2012). "Effects of financialization on the structure of production and nonfinancial private enterprises: the case of Mexico". *Journal of Post Keynesian Economics* 35(20), 235–54.

Levy-Orlik, N. (2014), "Financialization and economic growth in developing countries: the case of the Mexican economy". *International Journal of Political Economy*, 42(4), 108–127.

Lewis, M. (2014). *Flash Boys: A Wall Street Revolt*. London: Allen Lane.

Lewney, R. (2020). "Environmental policies to save the planet". In P. Arestis & M. Sawyer (eds), *Economic Policies for a Post Neo-liberal World*, 179–224. London: Palgrave Macmillan.

Leyshom, A. & N. Thrift (2007). "The capitalization of almost everything: the future of finance and capitalism". *Theory Culture Society* 24(7/8), 97–115.

Li, M. & I. Mendieta-Muñoz (2020). "Are long-run output growth rates falling?" *Metroeconomica* 71(1), 204–34.

Lin, K.-H. & D. Tomaskovic-Devey. "Financialisation and US income inequality, 1970–2008". *American Journal of Sociology* 118(5), 1284–329.

Lindley, J. & S. McIntosh (2017). "Finance sector wage growth and the role of human capital". *Oxford Bulletin of Economics and Statistics* 79(4): 570–91.

Lindo, D. (2018). "Why derivatives need models: the political economy of derivative valuation models". *Cambridge Journal of Economics* 42(4), 987–1008.

Lucas, R. (1988). "On the mechanics of economic development". *Journal of Monetary Economics* 22, 3–42.

Luttrell, D., T. Atkinson & H. Rosenblum (2013). "Assessing the costs and consequences of the 2007–2009 financial crisis and its aftermath". *Federal Reserve Bank of Dallas Economic Letter* 8(7).

Mader, P. (2018). "Contesting financial inclusion". *Development and Change* 49(2), 461–83.

Malinen, T. (2016). "Does income inequality contribute to credit cycles". *Journal of Economic Inequality* 14, 309–25.

Malkiel, B. (2003). "The efficient market hypothesis and its critics". *Journal of Economic Perspectives* 17(1), 59–82.

Malkiel, B. (2013). "Asset management fees and the growth of finance". *Journal of Economic Perspectives* 27(2), 97–108.

Manne, H. (1965). "Mergers and the market for corporate control". *Journal of Political Economy* 73(2), 110–20.

Marglin, S. & J. Schor (1992). *The Golden Age of Capitalism: Reinterpreting the Postwar Experience*. Oxford: Clarendon Press.

Marris, R. (1964). *The Economic Theory of "Managerial" Capitalism*. London: Macmillan.

McKinnon, R. (1973). *Money and Capital in Economic Development*. Washington, DC: Brookings Institution.

Meeks, G. (1977). *Disappointing Marriage: A Study of the Gains from Merger*. Cambridge: Cambridge University Press.

Mercure, J-F. *et al.* (2018). "Macroeconomic impact of stranded fossil fuel assets". *Nature Climate Change* 8, 588–593.

Meyer, B. (2019). "Financialization, technological change, and trade union decline". *Socio-Economic Review* 17(3), 477–502.

Michell, J. (2015). "Income distribution and the financial and economic crisis". In E. Hein, D. Detzer & N. Dodig (eds), *The Demise of Finance-Dominated Capitalism: Explaining the Financial and Economic Crises*, 240–64. Cheltenham: Elgar.

Michell, J. & J. Toporowski (2014). "Critical observations on financialization and the financial process". *International Journal of Political Economy* 42(4), 67–82.

Milberg, W. & D. Winkler (2010). "Financialisation and the dynamics of offshoring in the USA". *Cambridge Journal of Economics* 34, 275–93.

Minsky, H. (1988). "Schumpeter: finance and evolution". Hyman P. Minsky Archive Paper 314. https://digitalcommons.bard.edu/hm_archive/314

Minsky, H. (1993). "Community Development Banks: an idea in search of substance". *Challenge*, March/April.

Mishel, L. & J. Wolfe (2019). "CEO compensation has grown 940% since 1978 typical worker compensation has risen only 12% during that time". Economic Policy Institute Report, 14 August.

Morduch, J. (1999). "The microfinance promise". *Journal of Economic Literature* 37(4), 1569–614.

Morelli, S. & A. Atkinson (2015). "Inequality and crises revisited". *Economia Politica* 32(1), 31–51.

Nau, M. (2013). "Economic elites, investments, and income inequality". *Social Forces* 92, 437–61.

Nikoloski, Z. (2013). "Financial sector development and inequality: is there a financial Kuznets curve?" *Journal of International Development* 25(5), 897–911.

Oren, T. & M. Blyth (2019). "From big bang to big crash: the early origins of the UK's finance-led growth model and the persistence of bad policy ideas". *New Political Economy* 24(5), 605–22.

Orhangazi, O. (2008). "Financialisation and capital accumulation in the non-financial corporate sector: a theoretical and empirical investigation on the US economy: 1973–2003". *Cambridge Journal of Economics* 32(3), 863–86.

Orhangazi, O. (2014). "Financial deregulation and the 2007–08 US financial crisis". FESSUD Working Paper Series, No. 49.

Orhangazi, O. (2015). "Financial deregulation and the 2007–08 US financial crisis", in E. Hein, D. Detzer & N. Dodig (eds), *The Demise of Finance-Dominated Capitalism*, 289–307. Cheltenham: Edward Elgar.

Özdemir, P. (2019). "Financialization and the labor share of income". *Review of Economic Perspectives* 19(4), 265–306.

Palladino, L. (2021). "Financialization at work: shareholder primacy and stagnant wages in the United States". *Competition & Change* 25(3/4), 382–400.

Palley, T. (2018). "Three globalizations, not two: rethinking the history and economics of trade and globalization". FMM Working Paper No. 18.

Pariboni, R. & P. Tridico (2019). "Labour share decline, financialisation and structural change". *Cambridge Journal of Economics* 43(4), 1073–102.

Peck, J. & N. Theodore (2007). "Variegated capitalism". *Progress in Human Geography*, 31(6), 731–772.

Peters, J. (2011). "The rise of finance and the decline of organised labour in the advanced capitalist countries". *New Political Economy* 16(1), 73–99.

Philippon, T. (2015). "Has the US financial industry become less efficient? On the theory and measurement of financial intermediation". *American Economic Review* 105(4), 1408–38.

Philippon, T. & A. Reshef (2012). "Wages and human capital in the US financial industry: 1909–2006". *Quarterly Journal of Economics* 127(4): 1551–609.

Philippon, T. & A. Reshef (2013). "An international look at the growth of modern finance". *Journal of Economic Perspectives* 27(2), 73–96.

Phillips, K. (1993). *Boiling Point.* New York: Random House.

Phillips, K. (1994). *Arrogant Capital: Washington, Wall Street, and the Frustration of American Politics.* Boston, MA: Back Bay Books.

Pianta, M. & M. Lucchese (2020). "Rethinking the European Green Deal: an industrial policy for a just transition in Europe". *Review of Radical Political Economics* 52(4), 633–41.

Pickett, K. & R. Wilkinson (2009). *The Spirit Level: Why More Equal Societies Almost Always Do Better.* London: Allen Lane.

Pollin, R., J. Heintz & T. Herndon (2018). "The revenue potential of a financial transaction tax for US financial markets". *International Review of Applied Economics* 32(6), 772–806.

Prates, D. (2017). "Monetary sovereignty, currency hierarchy and policy space: a post-Keynesian approach". Mimeo.

Rajan, R. (2010). *Fault Lines.* Princeton, NJ: Princeton University Press.

Rappaport, A. (1998). *Creating Shareholder Value: A Guide for Managers and Investors.* New York: Simon & Schuster.

Reid, M. (1982). *The Secondary Banking Crisis, 1973–75: Its Causes and Course.* Berlin: Springer.

Roberts, A. & R. Kwon (2017). "Finance, inequality and the varieties of capitalism in post-industrial democracies". *Socio-Economic Review* 15(3), 511–38.

Robinson, J. (1952). "The generalization of the General Theory". In *The Rate of Interest and Other Essays,* 67–142.

Robinson, J. (1962). *Economic Philosophy.* Harmondsworth: Penguin.

Rodrik, D. (2006). "Goodbye Washington Consensus, Hello Washington confusion? A review of the World Bank's economic growth in the 1990: learning from a decade of reform". *Journal of Economic Literature* 44(3), 973–87.

Rousseau, P. & P. Wachtel (2011). "What is happening to the impact of financial deepening on economic growth?" *Economic Inquiry* 49(1), 276–88.

Saad-Filho, A. & D. Johnston (eds) (2005). *Neoliberalism: A Critical Reader.* London: Pluto.

Sahay, R. *et al.* (2015). "Rethinking financial deepening: stability and growth in emerging markets". IMF Staff Discussion Note, SDN15/08.

Sanders, B. (2019). "The Green New Deal". berniesanders.com/issues/green-new-deal/

Santos, A. (2017). "Cultivating the self-reliant and responsible individual: the material culture of financial literacy". *New Political Economy* 22(4), 410–22.

Sawyer, M. (1979). *Theories of the Firm.* London: Weidenfeld & Nicolson.

Sawyer, M. (1985). *Economics of Industries and Firms: Theories, Evidence and Policy.* London: Croom Helm.

Sawyer, M. (2009). "Private Finance Initiative and Public Private Partnerships: the key issues". In P. Arestis & M. Sawyer (eds), 39–74. *Critical Essays on the Privatization Experience.* Basingstoke: Palgrave Macmillan.

Sawyer, M. (2014a). "Bank-based versus market-based financial systems: a critique of the dichotomy". FESSUD Working Papers, No. 19.

Sawyer, M. (2014b). "Financialisation, financial development and economic growth". FESSUD Working Papers, No. 21.

Sawyer, M. (2016). "Confronting financialisation". In P. Arestis & M. Sawyer (eds), *Financial Liberalisation: Past, Present and Future,* 43–86. Basingstoke: Palgrave Macmillan.

Sawyer, M. (2018). "Financialisation and economic and social performance". In K. Opolski & A. Gemzik-Salwach (eds), *Financialisation and the Economy,* 9–25. Abingdon: Routledge.

Sawyer, M. (2019). "Financialisation and the dysfunctional nature of the financial system". In J. Jespersen & F. Olesen (eds), *Progressive Post-Keynesian Economics: Dealing with Reality.* Cheltenham: Elgar.

Schumpeter, J. (1912). *Theorie der wirtschaftlichen Entwicklung,* 2nd ed. München: Duncker & Humblot. [*The Theory of Economic Development.* Oxford: Oxford University Press, 1934].

Shaoul, J. (2009). "The political economy of the Private Finance Initiative". In P. Arestis & M. Sawyer (eds), 1–38. *Critical Essays on the Privatization Experience.* Basingstoke: Palgrave Macmillan.

Shaw, E. (1973). *Financial Deepening in Economic Development.* New York: Oxford University Press.

Shaxson, N. & J. Christensen (2013). *The Finance Curse: How Oversized Financial Sectors Attack Democracy and Corrupt Economics*. London: Commonwealth Publishing.

Shiller, R. (2000). *Irrational Exuberance*. Princeton, NJ: Princeton University Press.

Shiller, R. (2003). "From efficient markets theory to behavioral finance". *Journal of Economic Perspectives* 17(1), 83–104.

Singh, A. (1971). *Takeovers: Their Relevance to the Stock Market and the Theory of the Firm*. Cambridge: Cambridge University Press.

Slater, G. & D. Spencer (2014). "Workplace relations, unemployment and finance-dominated capitalism". *Review of Keynesian Economics* 2(2), 134–46.

Smith, A. (1776). An Inquiry into the Nature and Causes of the Wealth of Nations.

Sparkes, M. & J. Wood (2021). "The political economy of household debt and the Keynesian policy paradigm". *New Political Economy* 26(4), 598–615.

Spillenkothen, R. (2010). "Notes on the performance of prudential supervision on the years preceding the financial crisis by a former director of banking supervision and regulation at the Federal Reserve Board (1991 to 2006)". http://fcic-static.law.stanford.edu/cdn_media/fcic-docs/2010-05-31%20FRB%20Rich ard%20Spillenkothen%20Paper-%20Observations%20on%20the%20Performance%20of%20Prudent ial%20Supervision.pdf

Statista (2019). "Ratio between CEO and average worker pay in 2018, by country", www.statista.com/sta tistics/424159/pay-gap-between-ceos-and-average-workers-in-world-by-country/

Stenfors, A. (2017). *Barometer of Fear: An Insider's Account of Rogue Trading and the Greatest Banking Scandal in History*. London: Zed.

Stigler, G. (1971). "The theory of economic regulation". *Bell Journal of Economics and Management Science* 2(1), 3–21.

Stiglitz, J. (1994). "The role of the state in financial markets". In M. Bruno & B. Pleskovic (eds), *Proceedings of the World Bank Annual Conference on Development Economics 1993*, Supplement to *World Bank Economic Review* and *World Bank Research Observer*, 19–52; http://documents.worldbank.org/cura ted/en/1994/03/9314597/

Stiglitz, J. & B. Greenwald (2003). *Towards a New Paradigm in Monetary Economics*. Cambridge: Cambridge University Press.

Stockhammer, E. (2004). "Financialization and the slowdown of accumulation". *Cambridge Journal of Economics* 28, 719–41.

Stockhammer, E. (2015). "Rising inequality as a root cause of the present crisis". *Cambridge Journal of Economics* 39, 935–58.

Stockhammer, E. (2017). "Determinants of the wage share: a panel analysis of advanced and developing economies". *British Journal of Industrial Relations* 55(1), 3–33.

Stout, L. (2012). *The Shareholder Value Myth*. Oakland, CA: Berrett-Koehler Publishers.

Streeck, W. (2016). *How Will Capitalism End?* London: Verso.

Subramanian, A. & M. Kessler. (2013). "The hyperglobalization of trade and its future", Peterson Institute for International Economics Working Paper 13–6.

Sullivan, S. (2013). "Banking nature? The spectacular financialisation of environmental conservation". *Antipode* 45(1), 198–217.

Sum, A. *et al.* (2008). "The great divergence: real-wage growth of all workers versus finance workers". *Challenge* 51(3), 57–79.

Summers, L. (2016). "The age of secular stagnation". *Foreign Affairs*, 15 February.

Svirydzenka, K. (2016). "Introducing a new broad-based index of financial development". IMF Working Paper, WP/16/5.

Sweezy, P. (1994). "The triumph of financial capital". *Monthly Review* 46(2).

Szymborska, H. (2021). "Rethinking inequality in the 21st century – inequality and household balance sheet composition in financialized economies". *Journal of Post Keynesian Economics*, in process.

Tarullo, D. (2019). "Financial regulation: still unsettled a decade after the crisis". *Journal of Economic Perspectives* 33(1), 61–80.

Thompson, G. (2019). "Financial globalization? History, conditions and prospects". In J. Michie (ed.), *The Handbook of Globalisation, Third edition*, 32–47. Aldershot: Edward Elgar.

Thompson, P. (2011). "The trouble with HRM". *Human Resource Management Journal* 21(4), 355–67.

Tobin, J. (1984). "On the efficiency of the financial system". *Lloyds Bank Review*, July.

Tomaskovic-Devey, D. & K. Lin (2011). "Income dynamics, economic rents, and the financialisation of the US economy". *American Sociological Review* 76, 538–59.

Tonveronachi, M. (2020). "Ages of financial instability". *Journal of Post Keynesian Economics* 43(2), 69–309.

Tori, D. & O. Onaran (2017). "Financialisation and physical investment: a global race to the bottom in accumulation?" UNCTAD Research Paper No. 17.

Tori, D. & O. Onaran (2018). "The effects of financialization on investment: evidence from firm-level data for the UK". *Cambridge Journal of Economics* 42(5), 1393–416.

Tori, D. & O. Onaran (2020). "Financialization, financial development and investment: evidence from European non-financial corporations". *Socio-Economic Review* 18(3), 681–723.

Trade Union Congress (TUC) (2017). *An Economic and Social Audit of the "City"*. A report by Mick McAteer of the Financial Inclusion Centre for the TUC.

Tridico, P. (2018). "The determinants of income inequality in OECD countries". *Cambridge Journal of Economics* 42(4), 1009–42.

Tulum, O. & W. Lazonick (2018). "Financialized corporations in a national innovation system: the US pharmaceutical industry". *International Journal of Political Economy* 47(3/4), 281–316.

UNCTAD (2015). *Trade and Development Report, 2015*. Geneva: UNCTAD.

UNCTAD (2017). *Trade and Development Report: Beyond Austerity Towards a Global New Deal*. Geneva: UNCTAD.

UNCTAD (2020). *World Investment Report: International Production Beyond the Pandemic*. Geneva: UNCTAD.

United Nations (2020). "Inequality – bridging the divide", un.org/UN75

United Nations Department of Economic and Social Affairs (2005). "Rethinking the role of national development banks". Background document for the Ad hoc expert group meeting on Rethinking the Role of National Development Banks, New York, 1 2 December.

Van der Zwan, N. (2014). "State of the art: making sense of financialization". *Socio-Economic Review* 12, 99–129.

Van der Zwan, N. (2019). "The new political economy of financialization". *Socio-Economic Review* 17(2), 453–59.

Van Treeck, T. (2009). "The political economy debate on 'financialization' – a macroeconomic perspective". *Review of International Political Economy* 16, 907–44.

Van Treeck, T. (2014). "Did inequality cause the US financial crisis?" *Journal of Economic Surveys* 28(3), 421–48.

Van Treeck, T. & S. Sturn (2012). "Income inequality as a cause of the Great Recession? A survey of current debates". ILO Conditions of Work and Employment Series No. 39.

Vaughan, L. & G. Finch (2017). *The Fix: How Bankers Lied, Cheated and Colluded to Rig the World's Most Important Number*. New York: Wiley.

Vercelli, A. (2013). "Financialisation in a long-run perspective: an evolutionary approach". *International Journal of Political Economy* 42(4).

Vercelli, A. (2016). *Crisis and Sustainability: The Delusion of Free Markets*. London: Palgrave Macmillan.

Wade, R. (2008). "Financial regime change?" *New Left Review* 53, 5–21.

Westcott, M. & J. Murray (2017). "Financialisation and inequality in Australia". *Economic and Labour Relations Review* 28(4), 519–37.

Whalen, C. (2012). "Money manager capitalism". In J. Toporowski & J. Michell (eds), *Handbook of Critical Issues in Finance*, 257–61. Cheltenham: Elgar.

Williamson, J. (2004). "The strange history of the Washington Consensus". *Journal of Post Keynesian Economics* 27(2), 195–206.

Williamson, J. (ed.) (1990). *Latin American Adjustment: How Much Has It Happened*. Washington, DC: Institute for International Economics.

Williamson, O. (1964). *The Economics of Discretionary Behavior: Managerial Objectives in a Theory of the Firm*. Englewood Cliffs, NJ: Prentice Hall.

World Bank (1989). *World Development Report*. Oxford: Oxford University Press.

World Bank (1994). *Averting the Old-Age Crisis: Policies to Protect the Old and Promote Growth.* New York: Oxford University Press.

World Inequality Lab (2019). *World Inequality Report 2018.*

World Inequality Lab (2021). *World Inequality Report 2022.*

Zallewski, D. & C. Whalen (2010). "Financialization and income inequality: a post Keynesian institutionist analysis". *Journal of Economic Issues* 44(3), 757–77.

Zingales, L. (2015). "Does finance benefit society?" *Journal of Finance* 70(4), 1327–63.

Zorn, D. (2004). "Here a chief, there a chief: the rise of the CFO in the American firm". *American Sociological Review* 69, 345–64.

INDEX